READING COMPREHENSION IN POLISH AND ENGLISH

Monika Kusiak

READING COMPREHENSION IN POLISH AND ENGLISH

EVIDENCE FROM AN INTROSPECTIVE STUDY

Jagiellonian University Press

This volume has been published thanks to the financial support of the Jagiellonian University – the Institute of English Studies at the Faculty of Philology

REVIEWERS
dr hab. Danuta Gabryś-Barker, prof. UŚ
dr hab. Mirosław Pawlak, prof. UAM

COVER DESIGN
Agnieszka Winciorek

First edition, Kraków 2013

ISBN 978-83-233-3513-9

WYDAWNICTWO UNIWERSYTETU JAGIELLOŃSKIEGO

www.wuj.pl

Jagiellonian University Press
Michałowskiego 9/2, 31-126 Kraków
Phone: +48 12-631-18-81, +48 12-631-18-82, fax: +48 12-631-18-83
Sales: phone: +48 12-631-01-97, fax: +48 12-631-01-98
Mobile: +48 506-006-674, e-mail: sprzedaz@wuj.pl
Bank account: PEKAO SA, nr 80 1240 4722 1111 0000 4856 3325

TABLE OF CONTENTS

ACKNOWLEDGEMENTS

I would like to express my thanks and appreciation to those who have helped me in the production of this work. I would like to thank Professor Anna Niżegorodcew for her continuous encouragement and support. I feel particularly indebted for her faith in my abilities. I am also grateful to Professor Ewa Willim, Head of the Institute of English Studies, Jagiellonian University for her sound advice in the process of publishing this book.

I owe special thanks to Professor Danuta Gabryś-Barker and Professor Mirosław Pawlak, whose invaluable comments on the completed manuscript have helped me to prepare the final version of it.

My acknowledgements are also due to my colleagues at the Institute of English Studies, Jagiellonian University for their interest in my research. My special thanks go to Anna Kosiarz-Stolarska. I also need to express appreciation to the students who agreed to participate in the think-aloud study described in this book. I am thankful for their time and comments.

Last, but not least, my sincere thanks go to my family and close friends for their tolerance and emotional support that I have experienced in the process of writing this book.

INTRODUCTION

This book is about reading. It is useful to realize that reading has been widely studied and has held the interest of various disciplines, such as philosophy, psychology, education, artificial intelligences and linguistics (see Kusiak 2010b). Treated as an ability without which learners cannot develop their language competence, it has always been at the centre of first language and foreign language education. Within the field of applied linguistics, reading research is a little more than one hundred years old. The psycholinguistic perspective focuses on the cognitive processes of the reader during the reception of texts; whereas the socio-cultural view examines the social factors of text production and reception. Literary theories provide interesting insights into the role of author, text and reader in text interpretation; while linguistics enhances understanding of how language and discourse can be perceived. Over the years, the study of reading has focussed on both first (L1) and foreign/second language (FL/L2) reading. Initially in FL/L2 studies L1 constructs and research paradigms were applied; however, slowly it has become clear that FL/L2 reading should be treated as a separate language phenomenon. Cross-linguistic studies, which investigate the role of L1 and FL/L2 in FL/L2 reading and the nature of transfer between the languages, are quite recent.

In this work, reading is discussed and researched within a psycholinguistic orientation. The main aim of the book is to explore reading in English in the foreign/second language context as a cross-linguistic phenomenon and to present the results of an empirical study which investigated reading in Polish as the L1 and English as the FL of Polish learners of English. The book consists of three parts. Part One presents the theoretical background to the empirical project, which is described in Part Three. The first part consists of five chapters, which look at the most essential components of reading competence. First, it addresses the question whether FL/L2 reading is a language problem or a reading problem (Chapter One). Then, the following are discussed: lower-level language processing related to phonology, word recognition, vocabulary knowledge and sentence processing (Chapter Two); higher-level language processing, which focuses on discourse level and text structure knowledge (Chapter Three) as well as language-independent factors, i.e., background knowledge, metalinguistic knowledge and metacognition (Chapter Four). In relation to each component, the most important theoretical perspectives and research agendas are delineated. This is accompanied by a review of studies on L1 and FL/L2 reading and further a survey of contrastive studies which investigate a given component in different languages as well as an overview of research into cross-linguistic influences on FL/L2 reading comprehension. The first part of the book also explains the concepts and theoretical perspectives on which I drew in the think-aloud study presented in the book. Special focus is placed on expository text comprehension models.

Part Two narrows down the discussion to think-aloud research. First, in Chapter One the theoretical underpinnings of the think-aloud methodology are discussed with special attention devoted to the use of this method in reading research. General methodological guidelines directed to researchers of think-aloud studies are discussed. The other three chapters present reviews of selected think-aloud studies: in Chapter Two – the studies conducted within the L1 context, in Chapter Three – research exploring FL/L2 learners and in Chapter Four – cross-linguistic studies, most of which investigate the reading competence of bilingual readers. The discussion examines various aspects of reading comprehension, such as strategies used by readers, interpretation problems and test-taking strategies. The issue of transfer between L1 and FL/L2 is addressed too.

Part Three presents and discusses the results of a think-aloud study conducted among Polish adult learners of English as a foreign language. The project aimed to explore how the subjects, proficient readers of Polish (L1) and advanced readers of English (FL), read expository texts in their native language and a foreign language (English). This general aim, which arose from my teaching experience and research interests, took on a more specific form and resulted in six studies (called "stages" in this book), each focussing on a different aspect of reading. Thus, Stage 1 (Chapter Two) investigates the strategies applied in L1 and FL, Stage 2 (Chapter Three) looks at the problems the students experienced in reading and the solutions they applied, Stage 3 (Chapter Four) is an analysis of how the students constructed their representations of the texts, Stage 4 (Chapter Five) explores the subjects' idiosyncratic patterns of developing comprehension, Stage 5 (Chapter Six) evaluates how well the students understood the texts, and Stage 6 (Chapter Seven), which presents the results of interviews with the students, continues to investigate the learners' individual reading styles in Polish and English and the differences between how the subjects read in Polish and in English. The last chapter in Part Three concludes the discussion; it presents implications for further research and elucidates the usefulness of think-aloud protocols in foreign language instruction.

Part I ESSENTIAL COMPONENTS OF READING – A CROSS-LINGUISTIC APPROACH

In this part of the book, reading is referred to as reading competence or ability and the two terms are used interchangeably, as it is often the case in the literature discussing reading. It is assumed, as in many theoretical perspectives (Koda 2005), that reading comprehension involves an interaction of information derived from text and pre-existing reader knowledge.

Reading is discussed within a psycholinguistic orientation and the componential view of reading. A psycholinguistic perspective conceptualizes reading as a set of mental operations during which the reader creates his/her own representation of a text. The componential view of reading, in contrast to a unitary perspective, "dissects reading into its components" (Koda 2007: 1), allowing researchers to explore constituent components of the reading comprehension process. In theory and empirical research, two levels of cognitive processing are usually distinguished: "lower" – focusing on letter identification, word recognition and syntactic parsing; and "higher" – involving discourse processing and knowledge about text characteristics which enable the reader to construct his/her representation of the text. Components included in both levels are addressed in this book. Chapter Two explores lower-level aspects of reading: phonological, word-related components and sentence processing. Chapter Three discusses higher-level processes, i.e., the impact of discourse processing on reading as well as the relationship between text structure and comprehension.

The discussions conducted in the subsequent chapters draw on the assumption that FL/L2 reading involves two languages. As explains Koda (2007: 1):

> The dual involvement implies continual interaction between the two languages as well as incessant adjustments in accommodating the disparate demands each language imposes. For this reason, L2 reading is crosslinguistic and, thus, inherently more complex than L1 reading.

In contrast to the earlier universal perspective, which sees reading procedures as universal across languages (Goodman 1971), the cross-linguistic view claims that reading involves language-specific processes. The assumption that dual-language involvement is a characteristic of FL/L2 reading has stimulated cross-linguistic analyses, which explore the impact of L1 and FL/L2 factors on FL/L2 reading. Cross-linguistic studies have focussed on text-information processes that are thought to differ across languages, such as those related to decoding, morphology, parsing and discourse. The universal framework, on the other hand, has concentrated on exploring conceptual processing and strategic manipulation, e.g., the role of background knowledge, metacognition and metalinguistic knowledge – aspects of reading regarded as language-independent. In this book, Chapters Two and Three discuss reading components that are believed to be language-specific.

Chapter Four concentrates on a universal character of background knowledge, metacognition and metalingistic knowledge – aspects of reading which are believed not to vary from language to language. In relation to each reading component, regardless of whether it is considered language-specific or universal, studies conducted in both monolingual and bilingual contexts are presented. This is done to explore the role of each component in L1 and FL/L2 reading.

The next issue addressed in this part is a possibility of transfer between readers' L1 and FL/L2. In the subsequent chapters, the question whether FL/L2 readers transfer the reading components from L1 to FL/L2 is discussed.

1. FL/L2 reading – a language problem or a reading problem?

The discussion begins with a presentation of two conflicting hypotheses about FL/L2 reading: the Linguistic Threshold Hypothesis (Clarke 1980; Yorio 1971) and the Linguistic Interdependence Hypothesis (Cummins 1979a, 1986, 1991). The short circuit hypothesis, recently referred to as the Linguistic Threshold Hypothesis (LTH), claims that in order to read in FL/L2, a learner must reach a certain level of FL/L2 linguistic ability. The Common Underlying Proficiency (CUP) Hypothesis, recently referred to as the Linguistic Interdependence Hypothesis, states that FL/L2 reading performance largely depends on L1 reading abilities. Let us focus on the two hypotheses and the research evidence supporting their presumptions.

1.1. The Linguistic Threshold Hypothesis

FL/L2 proficiency plays a considerable role in FL/L2 reading. The **Linguistic Threshold Hypothesis** claims that in order to read in FL/L2, the learner must reach a certain level of target language linguistic ability. The results of reading studies, e.g., Devine (1993) and Kusiak (2000), indicate that there is an interdependence between FL/L2 language proficiency and FL/L2 reading abilities.

The Linguistic Threshold Hypothesis also concerns the question as to whether limited proficiency in FL/L2 restricts readers in using very specific types of textual information, such as the discourse constraints of a text. Cziko's (1978) studies indicated that the reading performance of advanced English proficiency French students resembled that of native English speakers; they were more sensitive to syntactic, semantic and discourse constraints in a text and applied more nontextual information. Low language proficiency readers, on the other hand, based their reading on bottom-up strategies, e.g., sensitivity to the graphic information of a text. On the basis of these results, Cziko suggested that FL reader strategies are related to the level of FL competence.

Alderson (1984) suggested the modification of the Linguistic Threshold Hypothesis. He assumed that inefficient FL/L2 reading is due to L1 reading strategies not being activated in FL/L2 reading because of poor FL/L2 knowledge. Clarke's (1993) study indicated that there is some transfer of skills but the language of the text "short circuits" the good reading ability, reverting the reader to poor reading strategies.

Researchers have attempted to answer the question: What is the linguistic threshold? Cummins (1979b, cited in Devine 1993) claims that the threshold cannot be defined in absolute terms. It will depend on the kind of reading task and the reader's level of available and relevant background knowledge. Laufer and Sim (1985) attempted to express the qualities of the linguistic threshold in a numerical manner. In their study, they used the reading section of the Cambridge First Certificate of English and their own reading strategy examination. They concluded that the linguistic threshold necessary to read English for Academic Purposes successfully corresponds to a 65%–70% score on the Cambridge FCE test. The FL/L2 threshold was characterised by the researchers as knowledge of vocabulary, subject matter, discourse markers and syntactic structure, in decreasing order of importance.

1.2. The Linguistic Interdependence Hypothesis

The **Linguistic Interdependence Hypothesis** states that FL/L2 reading depends upon the reading abilities in one's L1 rather than upon the learner's level of FL/L2 competence. Coady (1979) asserts that FL/L2 reading is a reading problem, not a language problem. Therefore, difficulties in FL/L2 reading would be due to lack of the "old" L1 reading skills or failure in transferring L1 reading skills into FL/L2 reading.

Cowan (1976, cited in Alderson 1984) posited a parallel processing theory of reading, which claims that the strategies readers use are language-specific. Reading difficulties in a FL/L2 result from the reader's predictions about the syntactic clues which are related to the strategies used in reading in a native language. Cowan gives an example of English readers reading German, who being used to subject-verb-object order will be confused by German sentences with object-verb-subject order. Alderson (1984: 11) concludes that the "corollary of the parallel processing theory is that the knowledge of the foreign language will affect the development of the foreign language strategies: the less of the foreign language you know, the more likely you are to read as in your first language." The issue of cross-linguistic variations in sentence processing is discussed in Section 2.4. below.

Similarly, Grabe and Stoller (2002) consider a level of L1 reading abilities crucial. They claim that

> students who are weak in L1 literacy abilities cannot be expected to transfer many supporting resources to L2 reading contexts. The types of abilities that students use in their L1 reading represent the upper limit of what can be expected for linguistic transfer, strategic practices, problem-solving experiences, task completion skills and metacognitive awareness of reading processes (Grabe and Stoller 2002: 56).

1.3. Consolidating the Linguistic Threshold and the Linguistic Interdependence Hypotheses

Bernhardt and Kamil (1995) reviewed the studies investigating the contribution of L1 reading and FL/L2 proficiency to FL/L2 reading, and observed considerable consistency in the amount of variance accounted for by L1 reading (from 20% upwards) and FL/L2 proficiency (from 30% upwards), with FL/L2 proficiency consistently a more powerful predictor. They pointed out that most studies leave 50% of the variance in FL/L2 reading ability unexplained.

Reading studies conducted at the end of the 20th century indicate that both first language reading ability and foreign/second language proficiency have significant effects on foreign/second language reading ability, e.g., Bossers (1992, cited in Alderson 2001), Carrell (1991). An interesting connection between the level of FL/L2 knowledge and FL/L2 reading was observed by Bossers, who found that FL/L2 knowledge (especially vocabulary knowledge) was strongly related to FL/L2 reading comprehension at a lower level of FL/L2 proficiency. The researcher found that only "at relatively advanced levels of L2 proficiency did first-language reading ability prove to be the sole predictor of second-language reading" (Bossers 1992, cited in Alderson 2001: 39). Similarly, Block (1986) observed that proficient FL/L2 readers performed similarly to proficient L1 readers; less proficient FL/L2 readers performed similarly to less proficient L1 readers. Block (1986: 336) concluded that "strategic resources, thus, seem more important than specific linguistic knowledge for these readers."

In a recent study, van Gelderen *et al.* (2007) contributed considerably to the results discussed above. In a longitudinal study, the researchers investigated the effects of metacognitive knowledge, language knowledge and processing skills on L1 (Dutch) and FL (English) reading comprehension. The researchers looked at the development of 13-year-old adolescents over a period of two years (from grade 8 to grade 10). The findings indicated high and growing correlations between L1 and FL reading comprehension. L1 and FL reading comprehension proved to be highly related to each other at the beginning of grade 8; this relationship became even stronger in the following two years. The results indicated that the interconnection between L1 and L2 reading comprehension would rise to 70% of the explained variance by L1 reading comprehension alone, much higher than the other studies, e.g., those quoted above, suggest. The researchers discuss the implications of their study in relation to the Linguistic Threshold and the Linguistic Interdependence Hypotheses. The finding that L1 reading comprehension seemed to bear many similarities to FL reading comprehension, even in grade 8, did not support the threshold hypothesis. It was clear that at the beginning of the study the learners did not present a high level of FL competence – a language threshold assumed to enable FL learners to transfer strategies from L1 reading. The results showed that good L1 readers were also good FL readers, which was not due to very advanced FL competence. The researchers underline the fact that the interconnection between L1 and FL reading comprehension increased in the following two years, which shows that FL reading comprehension becomes even more similar to L1 reading comprehension "subsuming more and more the skills that are also involved in L1 reading comprehension" (van Gelderen *et al.* 2007: 487). The investigators concluded that their study seems to support a cross-language transfer of reading skills.

To sum up, it seems that most research points to a more significant impact of FL/L2 competence than L1 reading on FL/L2 reading. However, the most recent studies suggest the possibility of an inter-language transfer of reading strategies. More research is needed into the contribution of FL/L2 competence and L1 reading to FL/L2 reading, preferably in relation to other factors, such as background knowledge.

2. Lower-level language processing – word and sentence level

Difficulties in FL/L2 reading may also be caused by transfer effects from language processing differences. Linguistic differences between learners' L1 and FL/L2 influence word recognition, fluency and reading comprehension. Numerous studies, e.g., Just and Carpenter (1987) or Rayner and Pollatsek (1989), have shown that FL/L2 reading may be influenced by learners' L1 orthographic, syntactic and discourse knowledge. In this chapter, we focus on lower-level language processing, defined here as components functioning at word and sentence level.

At the beginning of the chapter, it is important to explain the terms "word recognition" and "decoding," which are often used interchangeably. In this discussion, following Koda (2005), the term "word recognition" refers to a process that consists of two components: decoding, which involves extracting phonological information from words, and semantic access, which entails obtaining words' meanings. Below, the interplay between the two components in L1 and FL/L2 will be discussed.

2.1. Phonological processing

2.1.1. The importance of phonological decoding in L1 reading

Research points to the significant role that this component plays in L1 reading. It seems that phonological decoding facilitates information storage in working memory. Research, e.g., Gough (1975), indicates that changing print into its phonological form enables effective access to oral vocabulary, which is stored in phonological forms. Phonological decoding was found fundamental in both alphabetic languages, e.g., English and non-alphabetic ones, such as Chinese and Japanese (e.g., Perfetti and Zhang 1995). In research which compared the role of phonological competence and visual encoding in retaining visually presented material (e.g., Zhang and Simon 1985), phonological transformation was found a more facilitative factor. As regards reading, it was observed that competence in pronouncing printed words is a reliable predictor of early reading success (e.g., Share and Stanovich 1995). The importance of phonological processing in word reading was confirmed in a series of studies conducted by Breznitz and Berman (2003). Investigation of the rate reading of young and adult readers of English as L1 showed the difference between the two groups. Among the young readers word reading rate related to phonological processing at the phoneme level; while among the adult readers word reading rate related to phonological processing at the word level. However, across all the subjects word reading rate was found to relate more to auditory-phonological processing than to visual-orthographic processing.

2.1.2. Phonological processing in different orthographic systems

Writing systems can be divided into two categories: shallow and deep orthographies (Koda 2005). What distinguishes the two types of orthography is orthographic depth, which refers to the degree of regularity in symbol-sound correspondences. In **shallow orthographies**, such as Spanish, Serbo-Croatian and Polish, the symbol-sound correspondences are very regular. Readers follow a phonologically regular system with a highly consistent set of grapheme-to-phoneme correspondences. **Deep orthographies**, such as English, have a phonologically deep system; "while governed by phonemic constraints" they tend "to preserve morphological information at the expense of phonological transparency" (Koda 2005: 36). A good example of this tendency is the past tense morpheme "-ed," which can be pronounced in three different ways, as in "looked," "visited" and "played." While violating one-to-one symbol-sound correspondences, it reflects its underlying morphological information.

The **Orthographic Depth Hypothesis**, proposed by Katz and Frost (1992), may serve as a summary of the above discussion concerning different ways of decoding. The hypothesis claims that phonological decoding in reading depends on letter-sound correspondences. In shallow, sound-based orthographies (e.g.,

Polish), phonological decoding involves letter-by-letter, letter-to-sound translation, i.e., by a direct analysis of phonetic elements. By contrast, in deep, meaning-based orthographies, phonological decoding (obtaining lexical sounds) takes place only after a word has been identified, e.g., by means of memory search or associations. In other words, in shallow orthographies, reading is facilitated by rule-based, thus predictable, procedures; whereas in deep orthographies, it means retrieving particular words from lexical memory. The hypothesis was confirmed by Frost, Katz and Bentin (1987) in their experiments involving Hebrew (deepest), English (deep) and Serbo-Croatian (shallow) writing systems.

2.1.3. Phonological processes in reading English as L1 and Polish as L1

As regards the English language, it is useful to discuss an interesting division suggested by Baron and Strawson (1976, cited in Schmitt and McCarthy 2000), who divide readers in English into two groups which they call "Chinese" and "Phonecian." The Chinese group uses a logographic approach and, relying on lexical decoding, recognizes words as whole units. Such readers are good at lexical reading and transforming symbols into words (e.g., transforming *$2* into "two dollars"), but poor at orthographic processing. The Phonecian readers use orthographic processing, which involves following "sound-to-spelling" rules, a strategy useful for a language with regular orthography, but not helpful in reading words that do not follow the expected "sound-to-spelling" rules. The researchers claim that reading English, which is an orthographically irregular language, involes employing a system combining both strategies, which will enable readers to read both regular and irregular words. Research (e.g., Bradley and Bryant 1979, cited in Sochacka 2004: 90) showed that English children use logographic strategies when they begin to read and alphabetic strategies when they begin to write. An interesting observation is that because of the deep phonological system of English, letter-to-sound strategies do not allow beginner readers to understand irregular words.

The study described below allows us to understand the differences between a phonological stage in reading in Polish and that in English. Sochacka (2004) wanted to observe the development of reading in L1 Polish children and compare it with the stages suggested in Frith's (1985) model of reading development, which often serves as a universal model to characterize the development of reading in various languages. The model suggests three stages: logographic, alphabetic and orthographic. The **logographic** stage involves recognising words in print by looking for features of the words that are somehow "salient," e.g., the last letter of the word. Once recognised, the word is connected with the visual semantic system and then with the verbal semantic system, which in consequence leads to sounding out the word. At the **alphabetic** stage, the reader begins to decode a word by sounding it out to him/herself. His/her phonological awareness (see Note 1) enables him/her to map letters to sounds. Letter-to-sound reading helps the child to "attack" unknown and artificial words. At the last **orthographic** stage, the child can recognise words by using the features of orthography of his/her language. There is no need to convert graphemes into phonemes. Due to a development of morphosyntactic awareness, the reader is able to recognise clusters of letters and, without sounding out letters, to read words. At this stage, the reader becomes more competent and can select phonological or logographic strategies depending on the situation. Frith (1985) argues that the reader can enter the last orthographic stage only after successful completion of the first two stages.

The most important conclusion Sochacka (2004) drew from her study was that Frith's model does not reflect the development of Polish children's reading. It was the alphabetic strategy, i.e., decoding words letter by letter, that prevailed throughout the two-year study. However, over time the children developed a holistic approach to words; by synthesising all letters in words, they learned to read the whole words. The development proceeded from the phonological strategy to the lexical one. When applying the holistic strategy, the children did not rely only on visual semantic mechanisms, as suggested by Frith's logographic stage. The readers connected letters with sounds, which is the ability they had acquired at the earlier stage. The lexical strategy, i.e., connecting letters with sounds, helped the children to memorise words as a combination of elements. In other words, they drew on both their visual abilities and phonological awareness.

2.1.4. Cross-linguistic variations: The influence of L1 orthographic background on FL/L2 reading

Comparative research underlines the role of L1 print-processing experience in FL/L2 reading, suggesting that readers bring to FL/L2 reading a set of language skill processes specific to their L1. Below, a selection of such studies is presented.

The research into young learners' reading points to transfer between two languages. In the study of Chinese bilingual kindergarden learners, Chang and Watson (1988) found out that the children transferred what they knew about reading in English to their Chinese. When investigating Turkish children learning Dutch as L2, Verhoeven (1994) observed transfer between the two languages in both directions.

The studies into adults' reading bring similar results. Koda (1989) investigated FL learners of Japanese with a logographic and alphabetic L1 background, focussing on the effect of L1–L2 orthographic distance on word recognition and text comprehension. The logographic group outperformed the alphabetic group at all word recognition tasks; all word recognition results correlated positively with reading comprehension scores. The longitudinal observation confirmed a difference in performance between the two groups and over time this gap increased. Interestingly, research suggests that L1 reading skills may have a facilitative or debilitative impact on reading in FL. Suarez and Meara (1989) observed that their Spanish subjects applied a phonological "sound-to-spelling" system when reading irregular words in English, the approach appropriate to Spanish but inappropriate to

English. On the other hand, Koda (1988) found that Japanese readers' performance, unlike that of the Arabic and Spanish subjects, was similar to that of the English-speaking readers and that this similarity seemed to help Japanese readers in reading in English.

In a contrastive study, Kurcz and Polkowska (1990) investigated how Polish and American students processed texts written in their native language in a reading aloud task. The subjects read three parts of the text; after each part they stopped to summarise what they had read. Several sentences were distorted in the text at the orthographic, lexical, syntactic and semantic levels. The results revealed significant differences between the two groups. The Polish readers focussed more on word endings; whereas the American readers concentrated on sentence integration, "gathering information across a broader span of words" (Kurcz and Polkowska 1990: 202). The findings confirmed the researchers' hypothesis that the reader's native language influences the reading process, which may be due to differences between the languages at the orthographic level.

To sum up, it seems that comparative studies of FL/L2 reading clearly point to the undeniable long lasting influence of the L1 orthographic background on FL/L2 reading. Differences between the orthographies of the two languages require from the reader adjusting his/her processing skills to the demands of the new writing system. This explains why Polish learners may experience difficulty in approaching English words; they would process English words in the way they do it in their native language, i.e., using a phonological "sound-to-spelling" strategy.

2.2. Word recognition

2.2.1. The role of phonological mediation in word recognition

The focus of this section is the semantic aspect of word recognition and its role in reading. Several conceptualisations of phonological mediation in relation to L1 and FL/L2 reading are discussed.

The question as to whether recognition of the printed word is mediated by some version of its spoken equivalent (often named "inner speech" or "subvocalisation") has given rise to a number of hypotheses and stimulated various studies. In the **phonological recoding hypothesis**, first offered by Rubenstein, Lewis, and Rubenstein (1971), phonemes are viewed as abstract, hypothetical entities; therefore, it denies the existence of any form of speech or subvocalisation. The hypothesis claims that word recognition is preceded by the conversion of letters into phonemes and a search in the mental lexicon for an entry which matches this phonological form. The hypothesis has inspired numerous studies; however, their findings fail to support its predictions concerning the presence of phonological mediation in the process of word recognition. For example, clinical studies of brain-damaged patients (Saffran and Marin 1977) indicated that patients who had lost an ability to recognize the spelling-sound correspondences (presumed by the phonological recoding hypothesis) and therefore unable to decode pseudowords, can still correctly recognize many words. The findings undoubtedly show that there must be a different route to the mental lexicon than phonological receding, reconfirming the assumption that there must be a dual access to the internal lexicon: one direct and the other involving phonological receding (Coltheart *et al.* 1979; McCusker, Hillinger and Bias 1981; Meyer, Schvaneveldt and Ruddy 1974). The two routes are assumed to operate in parallel, with word frequency being an important factor influencing the speed of the direct route. This approach seems to explain why even skilled readers phonologically recede unfamiliar words; it also accounts for the absence of phonological mediation in reading familiar words.

Let us now focus on the presence of **phonological mediation** in silent reading, often named as subvocalization or "silent speech." Research (e.g., Dooley and George 1988; Edfeldt 1960; Kleiman 1975; Swanson 1984) implies that an amount of phonological recoding depends on the level of the reader's proficiency and the difficulty of texts. Good readers are less likely to subvocalize and easy texts "provoke" less "silent speech." Subvocalisation improves the comprehension and retention of complex material, which requires a heavier load on memory, e.g., in the case of comprehension questions.

Interesting implications concerning sounding out words in reading have been suggested by cognitive psychologists. In their experimental studies of memory, Baddeley, Eldridge and Lewis (1981) showed that suppressing **subvocalisation** does not affect the speed of reading and understanding the gist of the text. However, it makes readers less sensitive to errors in text, such as wrong word order. The researchers (Baddeley, Eldridge and Lewis 1981: 1, abstract) concluded that "subvocalisation allows the creation of a supplementary articulatory code which is produced and utilised in parallel with other aspects of reading. Such a code seems particularly suitable for monitoring order information." In further research, Baddeley (1999) focused on what he calls the articulatory or phonological loop, i.e., a process of rehearsal, usually via subvocal speech and its main function – maintaining the memory trace.

The exploration of the conception of a **phonological loop** confirmed the assumption put forward by earlier studies that subvocalisation can facilitate reading comprehension. Baddley (1999: 53) says:

> You probably use it [subvocalisation] when reading difficult prose – a legal document, for example – where accurate understanding is essential, but I suspect that you do not subvocalise very much when reading a novel. You might well argue that, although you do not subvocalise, you still think you hear a voice when you read; I suspect that this "voice" is based on another system, an auditory imagery system, related to but different from the articulatory loop.

The role of "an auditory imagery system" was further discussed by Smith (1994: 160), who explains that sounding out specific words, for example in reading poetry, does not so much contribute to a literal comprehension as "establish a different – a complementary or alternative-kind of mood or meaning." This assumption is shared by Eysenck and Keane (1995: 315), who conclude that apart from reducing the memory load in comprehension, inner speech "may provide the prosodic structure (e.g., rhythm, intonation, stress) that is lacking in written text but present in spoken language." Similarly, Ridgway (2009) assumes that subvocalisation can be important in monitoring more affective and interpersonal aspects of language, especially where the text resembles speech, e.g., in reading poetry and drama.

Subvocalisation has also been the subject of discussions in relation to reading in a foreign/second language. It is assumed that FL/L2 readers are less familiar with the phonology or prosody of the language than native language readers. In fact, many FL/L2 readers, if interviewed about this phenomenon, would be aware of some form of subvocalising in their FL/L2 reading (as demonstrated in the study described in this book; see Part Three). More laborious subvocalisation taking place in learners' minds in reading in the FL than in their native language was observed by Ridgway (2009). The main reason can be the weaker linguistic competence of FL/L2 readers, which makes reading in FL/L2 more demanding for short-term memory (Birch 2002). Automatic word recognition in FL/L2 reading is considered important in FL/L2 reading (e.g., Eskey 1993). Thus, developing a phonological store of words that can be automatically recognized in a written text is a factor that will undoubtedly contribute to more fluent reading.

2.2.2. Word recognition in the rauding theory

The role of word recognition in reading was also explored by Carver (1977) in his **rauding theory**. This model of reading is interesting because of the theoretical assumptions and practical implications it offers for both L1 and FL/L2 reading instruction. A detailed discussion of the rauding theory is offered in Kusiak (2011). In this book, only the most important aspects of this model are presented. Special attention is given to advanced FL/L2 readers.

In his investigation, Carver (1977) focuses on the similarity between reading comprehension and listening comprehension (the word "rauding" is a combination of two words: "reading" and "auding"). An ability to recognize words quickly and efficiently is considered to play the key role in the process of reading. Reading is conceptualised as a competence that encompasses five reading "gears:" scanning, skimming, general reading (called by Carver rauding), study reading and memorizing. At various levels of comprehension information is retained to a different extent. **Rauding reading**, also called normal reading, involves "comprehending each consecutively encountered complete thought in a passage, ... comprehending about 64% or more of the thoughts in a passage" (Carver 2000: 405). Carver (2000) hypothesizes that an advanced reader would be at the raudamaticity point, which means that he/she has raudamatized all of his/her audamatized words. In other words, an experienced reader is able to decode automatically and understand quickly words that he/she knows when spoken and which he/she is able to pronounce when presented in print. Drawing on his theory, Carver designed a model containing precise mathematical equations, which has been applied in both L1 (e.g., Rupley 1996) and FL/L2 reading research (e.g., Asano and Sudo 2006; Hirai 1999; Lee 2006). All the studies confirmed the assumptions of the Carver model, indicating that similar processes underpin reading and listening in both L1 and FL/L2.

As regards teaching implications in both L1 and FL/L2 reading, the rauding theory suggests creating opportunities which would help learners to recognise and develop their individual rauding rate. Raudamaticity training concerning vocabulary is recommended, also by means of computer technology. Readers are advised to develop their sight vocabulary (i.e., words recognized in print) by extensive reading for pleasure. Manuals and textbooks promoting quick improvement in reading rate are considered as "dangerous" materials that can frustrate readers and be detrimental to the development of their comprehension skills (McLay 2007).

2.3. Vocabulary knowledge

2.3.1. The importance of vocabulary knowledge in L1 and FL/L2 reading

A major factor differentiating beginner L1 and FL/L2 readers is their linguistic repertoire. Vocabulary knowledge serves as the foundation for acquiring and developing reading. Before beginning to read, native English readers have already acquired the vocabulary knowledge of approximately 6,000 words (estimates for a six-year-old reader), which undoubtedly constitutes an important linguistic resource base for beginning reading (Grabe and Stoller 2002). Learning to read in L1 involves connecting an already existing oral vocabulary with its visual forms. FL/L2 readers, by contrast, begin to read at the same time that they learn to use the language orally. They lack a repertoire of words that they have learnt in oral contexts and which can be matched with the words they encounter in texts.

Vocabulary knowledge (see Note 2) is important in reading comprehension; in order to comprehend a text, one needs to understand individual words. Two conflicting hypotheses have been discussed in relation to vocabulary knowledge and reading comprehension: instrumental and knowledge (Anderson and Freebody 1983). The **instrumental postion** assumes a direct causal link between vocabulary and reading comprehension – knowing more words means better comprehension. The **knowledge hypothesis** assumes an indirect correlational relation between the two constructs, with the reader's background knowledge as a link between vocabulary knowledge and reading comprehension.

Studies have attempted to estimate learners' vocabulary knowledge necessary in comprehending texts. Drawing on a common belief that developing FL/L2 vocabulary at the beginning of FL/L2 learning is crucial, Laufer (1997) and Nation

(2001) concluded that beginner FL learners should learn approximately 2,000 high-frequency words. The researchers estimate that this number of words accounts for approximately 80% of the words in most texts and acquiring them will facilitate reading. Hu and Nation (2000) explored the relationship between readers' vocabulary knowledge and reading comprehension. They examined EFL college students and found out that adequate unassisted comprehension requires 98% text-word coverage (the proportion of known word tokens in a text). Similar results were obtained by Carver (1994, 2000), who estimated 99% coverage for pleasure reading among native English readers.

As regards the role of background knowledge, it is assumed that the learner activates his/her knowledge of the world when reading a text (Anderson and Pearson 1984). Background knowledge provides the reader with conceptual scaffolding, which guides the reader in comprehending a text. Reading comprehension is a result of the integration between the reader's prior knowledge and the information derived from the text. This reasoning gave rise to a claim that the reader's knowledge of a given topic is a better predictor of text comprehension than any other factor (Johnson 1981). A more detailed discussion of the role of background knowledge in reading comprehension is provided in Section 4.1. in this part.

2.3.2. Cross-linguistic studies

Cross-linguistic studies have looked at factors that contribute to understanding vocabulary in FL/L2 reading. It is assumed that while reading in a FL/L2 learners can draw on considerable conceptual knowledge as well as a wide repertoire of L1 words acquired during their L1 education and real-life experiences. Both factors facilitate understanding words in FL/L2 text comprehension. Koda (2005: 59) assumes that "[k]nown L1 equivalents ... can be used to link unrecognised L2 lexical labels to existing conceptual insights. Paired word associations – through bilingual dictionaries, text glossaries, and similar aids – frequently afford L2 readers almost instant access to their stored knowledge base." In this view, L1 is considered a factor that mediates between FL/L2 learners' word and conceptual knowledge.

Bilingual research has attempted to investigate what links L1 and FL/L2 lexicons: interlanguage word associations involving L1 words (as the word-association model posits) or conceptual knowledge, which does not activate L1 word knowledge (as the concept-mediation model presupposes). Picture naming and word translation tasks (e.g., Kroll and Curley 1988) revealed that beginning learners were much better in translation than in picture naming. The researchers concluded that L1 plays a mediating role in FL/L2 lexical processing until a sufficient FL/L2 competence is achieved. In another interesting study, Kroll and Sholl (1992) looked at efficiency in forward (from L1 to FL/L2) and backward (from FL/L2 to L1) translation. The research indicated superior performance in backward translation, which the authors of the study attributed to the stronger links between L1 vocabulary and conceptual knowledge. Consolidating these results, Kroll and Stewart (1994) proposed a hybrid model, which is a combination of the concept mediation and word-association models. The model claims that the role of L1 vocabulary and conceptual knowledge change over time. It assumes that both L1 and FL/L2 words are linked to concepts but initially the linkages are stronger for L1 than for FL/L2. Over time the connection strength between FL/L2 vocabulary and concepts increases, enabling FL/L2 learners to understand FL/L2 words without referring to their L1.

In more recent studies, models of an interactive character have been proposed. For example, Dijkstra and van Heuven (1998) suggested the **bilingual interactive activation** (BIA) **model**, which assumes the integration of the bilingual's lexicon across languages. The model claims that "lexical information in both languages is activated whenever the input shares features – visual, phonological, and semantic – with lexical alternatives in each of the languages involved" (Koda 2005: 65). Experimental research (e.g., Dijkstra, van Jaarsveld and Ten Brinke 1998) has supported the model, confirming the assumption that both languages are activated during FL/L2 lexical processing.

Contrastive studies highlight yet another factor that characterises the vocabulary-comprehension relationship – namely cross-cultural variations in word meanings. Research conducted by Wierzbicka (1995, 2001) shows that emotions and the linguistic means through which emotions are expressed differ across languages and cultures. For example, in her study of "przykro," one of the most important Polish emotion words, Wierzbicka (2001) concludes that "[t]he situation conceptualised by a Polish speaker in terms of *przykro* would be likely to be conceptualised in English in a different way." The researcher explains that the Polish concept of "przykro" "focuses on painful effects of a perceived lack of expected interpersonal 'good feelings,'" adding that this category has no exact equivalent in English. As regards reading, it seems that research into how different languages conceptualise emotions points to an important factor in FL/L2 text comprehension. I think it would be useful to draw on the results of the above described study and observe the comprehension of L1 and FL/L2 texts containing words that evoke "similar" emotions. In such studies, asking readers to talk about how they understand texts could facilitate the comparison.

2.4. Sentence processing

2.4.1. Factors influencing sentence processing

Sentence processing is another component essential to reading comprehension. There are a number of factors that can influence, i.e., inhibit or facilitate, sentence processing. One of them is **sentence length**. The correlation between syntactic complexity and sentence length seems obvious; however, the assumed relation between sentence length and reading difficulty has raised doubts among reading researchers. Irwin and Pulver (1984), and Pearson (1975) indicated a preference of native English readers for syntactically complex sentences rather than loose simple sentences. Davison, Wilson and Hermon (1985) as well as R. C. Anderson and Davison (1986) showed that sentence length and complexity have little effect on comprehension. R. C. Anderson and Davison (1986: 51) claim that:

> [t]he presence of long sentences and complex words in a text in some way reflects or is correlated with complexities of subject matter, but need not directly cause a text to be difficult. While these factors may impede comprehension for some readers who have difficulty segmenting words and parsing sentences or who have limited working memory capacity, these very same factors also provide the reader with explicit information about the composition of a word or the relations between sentences.

Instead of calculating the length of text sentences (Note 3), Berman (1984) suggests estimating text "**heaviness**" and "**transparency**." Berman explains that "heaviness" "is not a straightforward function of linear *length*" (Berman 1984: 142). It concerns "the amount and depth of information which the reader must store in memory in moving from one constituent to the next, and how hard the transition becomes as a result." Nominalisation is an example of a factor contributing to text "heaviness." By violating the basic NVN (noun, verb, noun) structure, it may make understanding an English text more difficult for FL/L2 readers. As examples of factors that make English texts less transparent, i.e., opaque, Berman points to lack of relative pronouns in English relative clauses, nominal "one" or verbal "do" as grammatical substitutes for repeated lexical material. Berman warns, however, that both cohesive devices and grammatical/lexical substitution are not universal across languages. For example, in Hebrew and Arabic lexical/grammatical repetition are common rhetorical devices. This seems an important conclusion for FL/L2 educators.

To investigate the role of syntax in L2/FL reading, Berman (1984) conducted a series of studies. In her introspective study with EFL Israeli college students, Berman asked students to explain what they had not understood in the text they were assigned to read. The study aimed to find out whether the text the students considered difficult seemed difficult because of its language or concepts. The results of the study showed that many sources of problems were caused by syntactic, rather than lexical or conceptual factors. The researcher concluded that problems in processing FL sentences may be due to the learners' mother tongue. Berman (1984: 141) also stresses the role of SVO ordering, claiming that "FL readers' comprehension is liable to be impaired by shifts in SVO ordering; for where the typical expectations of the reader, certainly in a foreign language, are violated, his fluency may be disrupted and hence comprehension hindered."

2.4.2. Sentence processing in the competition model of language acquisition

In research exploring principles governing syntactic parsing, apart from introspective methods (as the one applied by Berman 1984), sentence processing models proved useful. The **competition model** of language acquisition (Bates and

MacWhinney 1982), developed in the functionalist approach, has inspired many studies. The model views language processing as a series of competitions between lexical items, phonological forms, and syntactic patterns. Language is viewed as a set of correspondences between linguistic forms and their functions. The acquisition of processing competence involves internalisation of such form-function correspondences and is constrained by form-function relationships. A lexical item is understood as a direct mapping between the formal and functional levels of processing. When more than one mapping is possible, the final choice is determined by the strength of available cues. Syntactic parsing, thus, is viewed as a process of competition among alternative mappings; the choice of the final alternative depends on the strength of the cues supporting these alternatives.

The competition model addresses the question as to whether parsing processing is language-specific or universal across languages. This has given rise to a number of experimental contrastive studies which attempt to predict and account for differences in form-function mappings during sentence processing in typologically diverse languages. Working within the competition model, Bates and associates (1982) assume that syntactic parsing depends on the form-function mapping pattern specific for a particular language. The researchers compared the strength of syntactic (i.e., word order) and semantic (i.e., animacy) cues in governing thematic interpretation among native speakers of two contrasting languages: rigidly ordered English and loosely ordered Italian. The subjects' task was to listen to a series of word strings and state which word was the subject of the sentence. The results of the study confirmed the researchers' expectations that English subjects relied more heavily on syntactic cues, whereas for Italian speakers semantic information was more important. Recently, the Competition Model has been used as a starting point for constructing a Unified Model (MacWhinney 2008), which would account for both L1 and FL/L2 learning. It is assumed that "rather than attempting to build two separate models of L1 and L2 learning, it makes more sense to consider the shape of a Unified Model in which the mechanisms of L1 learning are seen as a subset of the mechanisms of L2 learning" (MacWhinney 2008: 342).

2.4.3. Cross-linguistic variations in sentence processing

Studies on FL/L2 sentence processing look at the transfer of syntactic processing. For example, McDonald's (1987) study, also conducted within the framework of the competition model, investigated Dutch learners of English and American learners of Dutch across three different proficiency levels. The task involved listening to sentences in a thematic-role task. The finding indicated that the subjects demonstrated reliance on the cues typical of their L1s, i.e., word order for English and case inflections for Dutch. Interestingly, the learners changed their sensitivity as their proficiency rose, gradually adapting their mapping procedures to FL patterns. Similar conclusions were drawn by Kilborn and Ito (1989) in the study involving adult FL learners of Japanese and English. The results implied a gradual change from L1 to FL cue usage. The studies showed, as MacWhinney (2008: 351) concludes, that "[t]he process begins with L2 cue weight settings that are close to those for L1. Over time, these settings change in the direction of the native speakers' settings for L2." It is worth pointing out that the Competition Model also suggests some amount of transfer from FL/L2 back to L1. Studies into sentence processing, e.g., Dussias (2001, cited in MacWhinney 2008) showed the evidence for such effects.

It is worth discussing competition model studies showing that cross-linguistic transfer is not a simple bidirectional process and may depend on the languages involved, as shown by Gass (1987) and Sasaki (1991). Replicating the Gass study, Sasaki observed that while American learners of Japanese resembled native Japanese readers' performance, Japanese learners of English depended on their L1-based syntactic cues. Sasaki (1991: 61, cited in Koda 2005: 114) concluded that "transfer takes place only from a less syntax-centered language to one that is more so."

An important research question concerning sentence processing is whether L1 syntactic influence on the FL/L2 is temporary or persistent. Lardiere (1998a, 1998b, 2000) observed a L1 Chinese learner with a long immersion in English. She observed that the subject had problems with supplying past tense and third-person singular "-s" on main verbs. Lardiere explained that Chinese lacks these linguistic features, i.e., verbs do not inflect for tense or subject-verb agreement. The researcher attributed the learner's failure to both language universals and L1 learning. She concluded that: "Tense and agreement features may be present in the inventory of syntactic features in the language faculty at birth, but, if they are not selected during L1 acquisition, they become inaccessible at some point during a person's maturation." Lardiere says that her study yields similar results to Brown (2000), who also reports FL/L2 learners' persistent failures to acquire certain phonemes which are not present in their L1.

Another possible factor influencing the transferability of syntactic elements is psychotypology, the notion developed by Kellerman (1983). It is the learner perception of the distance between the L1 and the FL/L2, which changes as the reader learns more of the target language. Kellerman's (1983) and Gass's (1983) studies seem to confirm this assumption.

In summation, the research on cross-linguistic variations in sentence processing presented here points to the significant role of L1 especially in early stages of FL/L2 development. It is important to note that there are also other factors influencing FL/L2 syntactic mechanisms, such as universal principles or FL/L2 knowledge. An interplay among all the above-mentioned factors needs further attention.

Notes

1. Phonologic or phonological awareness is defined as the ability to manipulate mentally the sounds that make up words (Torgesen *et al.* 2007). Many researchers (e.g., Harrison 1996) agree that phonological awareness seems

to be related to familiarity with rhymes, which in turn goes with the ability to read and spell words (Bryant *et al.* 1989). As regards reading in Polish as L1, the impact of the ability to manipulate sounds on early reading was observed by Krasowicz-Kupis (1999). A necessity to explore the role of early development of FL (English) on phonological awareness in L1 (Polish) was raised by Kusiak (2011).

2. Vocabulary knowledge, often named the learner's mental lexicon, has been considered an important aspect of multilingual competence (Singleton 1999). A comprehensive definition of a mental lexicon has been provided by Gabryś-Barker (2005: 39), who suggests that "it should be seen more as a conceptual system than a pure inventory of entries, a system which is composed of concepts and their linguistic realisations both phonological and orthographic, and with strong emphasis on lexical processing."
3. It is useful to note that Berman's approach to text difficulty is an utterance-based approach, not a sentence-based approach. As Alderson and Urquhart (1984: 157) emphasise, drawing on Lyons (1968) distinction, both constructs proposed by Berman are features of utterances. This means that the researcher is interested in how readers process texts composed of utterances, not linguistic sentences.

3. Higher-level language processing – discourse level and text structure knowledge

3.1. Discourse processing

Text comprehension does not entail only understanding isolated words and sentences. Rather, it is an attempt to comprehend the author's communicative intention expressed in the text. A number of models focus on text comprehension aiming to find principles governing this process. Below, several models and a selection of studies inspired by the models are presented.

3.1.1. The Kintsch model

The Kintsch model (1974) views comprehending a text as developing the representation of the text in memory in the form of a network of interrelated propositions. The key notions of the model – propositions are defined as "ideas that can be expressed in words, not the words themselves" (McNamara, Miller and Bransford 1991: 342), "units of meaning roughly corresponding to phrases or

clauses" (Louwerse and Graesser 2006: 426). It is useful to note that during their studies Kintsch and Keenan (1973) observed very high correlations between reading times and the numbers of propositions, not the numbers of words in sentences.

The Kintsch model from 1974 evolved into the next conceptualisation of discourse processing – the Kintsch and van Dijk model (1978), which led to the rapid development of discourse comprehension research. According to this model, processing the text is done automatically in cycles due to limited memory capacity. Comprehension operates at two different semantic levels: the **micro** level, referring to the local discourse of the text, and the **macro** level, referring to the more global discourse of the text. The two processes: local (microprocessing involving the construction of a locally coherent propositional network) and global (macroprocessing, i.e., organising micropropositions in a hierarchical and coherent order) lead to two levels of discourse organisation: the microstructure and the macrostructure. The macrorules of deletion, generalisation and construction work on the microstucture to obtain the macrostucture. While reading a text, the reader develops the **microstructure** (by applying local coherence relations, e.g., referential, temporal, causal) and gradually constructs the **macrostructure** – a global coherence network. At the highest level of comprehension, micropropositions are transformed into one macroproposition, which might be, for example, a title of the text. In fact, Kintsch and van Dijk (1978) demonstrated this effect in the study of recall after reading. They showed that after 30 days the only material that was recalled was the summary-type information, i.e., information represented as macroproposition(s) in the model.

3.1.2. Mental models

With time the theory of reading based on propositions underwent criticism. Researchers seemed to realise that "propositional representations are often more representative of the structure of the text than they are of the structure of memory for the text" (McNamara, Miller and Bransford 1991: 492). Mental model theories, drawing on the theoretical premises of propositional models and schema models, offered a more general approach viewing reading as a process of building and maintaining comprehension of the situations described in a text (McNamara, Miller and Bransford 1991). According to these theories (Johnson-Laird 1983; van Dijk and Kintsch 1983), "readers not only process a text at a propositional level, but also construct a **mental model** that is analogous in structure to the events, situations or layouts described by the text" (McNamara, Miller and Bransford 1991: 493). A mental model built by the reader in the process of reading consists of "mental tokens arranged in a structure that depicts the situations described by a text" (McNamara, Miller and Bransford 1991: 494).

Mental models enrich the view of text representation suggested by the earlier models. Text representation is not based entirely on the text. The reader's knowledge and the strategies he/she applies are also taken into account. Let us look at two mental models: the van Dijk and Kintsch (1983) model and the construction-integration model developed by Kintsch (1988, 1998). According to the first model, text information is represented in memory at three levels: surface form, propositional textbase and situation model. The **surface form** refers to the representation of the exact wording and syntax; the **propositional textbase** corresponds to a multileveled, locally coherent propositional network of semantic text information; and the third level, the **situation model**, depicts real-life situations presented in the text, as perceived by the reader, i.e., the reader's interpretations of the text. The construction-integration model, which extended the earlier models developed by Kintsch and van Dijk (1978), views the development of text representation as two phases. In the constructive phase, the reader builds an approximate mental model drawing on the text and his/her background knowledge. In the integration phase, redundant information is abandoned and the tentative model undergoes the process of stabilisation, resulting in a well-structured mental representation. Both models inspired research into L1 and FL/L2 reading. Their main advantage is that they drew researchers' attention to the role of the reader in constructing different levels of understanding the text. As Louwerse and Graesser (2006: 427) comment: "The situation model can, for instance, explain individual differences in interpretations of texts, differences in the meaning of translations, and the fallibility and flexibility of memory." The models can also facilitate investigating the role of different linguistic and non-linguistic factors in reading and relate them to different types of mental representations of the text generated by readers. Below, a selection of research inspired by the two models is presented.

3.1.3. Studies on L1 and FL/L2 discourse comprehension

Mental model theories are supported by several studies of the mental processes that occur during reading. For example, Garnham (1981) demonstrated evidence that readers choose whether to focus on propositional or mental models processing. When the subjects were not warned about a memory test following the reading, they seemed to process the texts as mental models. They had difficulty recalling exact sentences and distinguishing between the sentences that had been present in the text and the sentences that had not been present. Their recall seemed to reflect a mental representation of the text, rather than the propositional one. Similar results were obtained by Tardieu, Ehrlich and Gyselinck (1992).

Studies comparing mental representations of text between L1 and FL/L2 readers brought illuminating results. Jenkin *et al.* (1993) found that readers were able to form propositional relations and develop mental models in their L1; however, in their L2 only propositional networks were developed. The researchers concluded that the content information is represented differently in text memory during L1 and L2 processing.

3.2. Coherence development

3.2.1. Coherence in the psychological perspective

Coherence (see Note 1) building is an important aspect of developing the propositional textbase. In this section, coherence is discussed within the psychological view on coherence, which emphasises the role of the reader in developing text representation (see Note 2). According to the psychological view (Sanford 2006: 585): "A text is coherent to the extent that is it intelligible, that there are no aspects of the text that do not relate to the message, and that there is no sense that things are missing from the text." The psycholinguistic approach emphasises the role of two factors that contribute to coherence development: the text itself and the reader. The text offers cues that help the reader to develop a coherent mental representation of the text; the reader attempts to understand what the writer of the text tries to convey following the text cues and drawing on his/her background knowledge.

Cohesive devices are one type of text cues guiding the reader in his/her attempts to make connections between different parts of the text. The most popular categories quoted in the literature are the ones proposed by Halliday and Hasan (1976), who identify referential, ellipsis, substitution, lexical and conjunctive devices. Psychological studies show that the presence of some connectives facilitates comprehension. For example, Sanford (2006) gives an example of the role of connectives in reading short stories. Readers spend less time reading the last sentence of a short story when this sentence contains an explicit connective than when it does not. The researcher also claims that the presence of causal connectives makes the mental representation more stable and clauses linked by causal connectives are better remembered.

3.2.2. Contrastive studies

Research on FL/L2 discourse comprehension examines how relational cues are represented in the text memory of L1 and FL/L2 readers. Horiba, van den Broek and Fletcher (1993) compared how L1 and FL English readers use text-structure information, e.g., causal chain status and story-grammar categories during the comprehension of narrative texts (see Chapter 3, Section 3.4.1.2. in this part for a discussion of story grammars and their role in cross-linguistic research). The analysis of recall protocols revealed that relational cues were incorporated into the text representations of both L1 and FL readers. However, there was a qualitative difference between the two groups. L1 readers demonstrated greater sensitivity to global coherence markers. FL readers, in contrast, paid more attention to local coherence information. In addition, FL readers relied extensively on their knowledge of coherence markers while inferring the meaning of unknown words. The results of the study corroborate Jenkin *et al.*'s findings (1993, presented above), implying that L1 and L2 text representations differ qualitatively.

Similar conclusions were drawn by Geva (1992), who investigated ESL adult learners' ability to process relational information expressed by conjunctions at intrasentential, intersentential and discourse levels. The results suggest that the understanding of logical relationships at intrasentential and intersentential levels is an important skill but in itself does not guarantee successful coherence building at a higher discourse level. This conclusion emphasises L2 readers' poorer capacity to read at a global level. It also points to L2 students' ability to develop with increased L2 proficiency an understanding of logical relationships at discourse level.

Cross-linguistic research seems to imply that discourse processing in FL/L2 reading is influenced by L1. Koda (2005) suggests a number of factors affecting the process of FL/L2 coherence building: some of a facilitative, others of a debilitative nature. One of the factors is L1 literacy experience. She claims that certain aspects of the coherence awareness acquired in L1, such as an ability to distinguish thematic from peripheral information, are not language specific and will undoubtedly facilitate FL/L2 coherence building. Another important factor is the difference between text-coherence building in L1 and FL/L2. The two processes can be governed by different factors. Explicit coherence markers, e.g., conjunctions and enumerators, may play a different function in L1 and FL/L2 processing. Koda explains that, unlike other words, coherence markers may be more firmly established in learners' lexical memory and therefore more accessible in the process of reading. As a result, coherence markers may compensate for learners' limited lexical knowledge. For example, the reader may have difficulty understanding new words in the sentence, but knowing the causal implication of "because" can facilitate his/her comprehension.

In essence, coherence development seems to be a crucial component in text comprehension. Researchers point to both the universal and language-specific aspects of coherence. Contrastive studies show qualitative differences between how L1 and FL/L2 readers develop text coherence: L1 readers are more sensitive to local coherence markers, whereas FL/L2 readers pay more attention to global coherence markers. More research is needed to investigate coherence building in FL/L2 reading and its relationships with other aspects of discourse processing.

3.3. Establishing coherence through inferencing

While text linguistics focuses on the connections between different parts of the text, the psychological approach is concerned with how the text gives rise to a coherent mental representation of the text. Constructing a mental model from the schematic knowledge and situations described in a text may also involve making inferences about the situations described in a text. An extensive body of research, e.g., Keenan *et al.* 1990; McKoon and Ratcliff 1981, 1986; Whitney and Kellas 1984, among others, investigates the nature of inferences. "Everywhere in discourse, readers are called upon to make inferences; without them, there would be no coherence"

(Sanford 2006: 587). Inferring is assumed to play an important role in almost all aspects of language comprehension (R. C. Anderson 1978; Pearson and Johnson 1978). The role of inferences in text comprehension is discussed below.

3.3.1. Elaborative and bridging inferences

The main distinction made by researchers is between inferences that are necessary for coherence and inferences that are not. If the reader wants to establish coherence between the present piece of text and the preceding one, he draws a **bridging inference**. Bridging inferences are generally assumed to be made only when necessary. Inferring causal and anaphoric connections are regarded as necessary inferences (Sanford 1990). Readers can draw forward **elaborative inferences**, which, in contrast to necessary bridging inferences, aim to embellish the textual information (see Note 3).

Researchers investigate the role of necessary backwards-bridging inferences and forwards-elaborative optional inferences in the reader's construction of text representation. It is generally agreed that bridging inferences are made on the basis of information stated explicitly in the text and serve to support the cohesion and consequently coherence of the reader's textbase. In contrast, elaborative inferences "go beyond what is actually required to connect the explicitly stated ideas in a text" (McKoon and Ratcliff 1990: 409). They contribute to the reader's development of a mental model of the situation described in the text, adding information in order to complete and integrate the reader's representation of the text.

3.3.2. Studies on coherence building in L1 and FL/L2 reading

Inference ability has been investigated in relation to readers' levels of comprehension. McNamara and Magliano (2009: 64) assume that "the readers' levels of comprehension [are] reflected by readers' ability to answer certain types of questions." Text-based questions, which reflect comprehension of idea units (propositions), measure readers' textbase level of comprehension. In contrast, questions that require inference generation assess readers' situation model level. If the reader can answer both types of questions, it means that he/she has constructed both levels of understanding: a coherent textbase and a situation model. This assumption has encouraged researchers to construct strategy training and explore its effectiveness. McNamara *et al.* (2006), who trained L1 middle-school American students reading science texts, observed that the effectiveness of the training depended on learners' strategy knowledge. The low-strategy knowledge learners improved their ability to construct the textbase comprehension; whereas the high-strategy knowledge learners improved their ability to build the situation model comprehension.

Applying concurrent think-aloud protocols, Horiba (1996) observed how L1 and FL learners at two proficiency levels read two texts of varied causal coherence. The results showed that L1 readers relied more heavily on higher-level processing, such as generating inferences. They treated high- and low-coherence texts differently, generating more elaborations for low-coherence texts. Additionally, it was L1 readers who generated backward inferences according to the text's causal structure. In contrast, FL readers read differently. They paid more attention to lower-level processing and did not distinguish between high- and low-coherence texts. More advanced readers generated both backward and forward inferences during reading; less advanced readers, in contrast, did not.

In another study, Horiba (2000) investigated the inference generation of native and non-native readers of Japanese who, performing two tasks (reading freely and reading for coherence), read two types of text (essays and narration). The findings showed that L1 and FL readers process texts differently. Native readers generated more backward inferences when reading essays and more elaborative inferences when reading stories. Non-native readers generated more elaborative inferences when reading essays. As regards reading tasks, non-native readers did not distinguish between reading for coherence and reading freely.

Although inference research is burgeoning, little has been done to unveil FL/L2 inferencing. Shimizu's (2005) investigated the inference generation processes of Japanese EFL learners in reading expository texts as well as the effect of reading questions on inference processes. The main findings pointed to a relationship between readers' FL proficiency and their inferencing. More advanced students generated more inferences that facilitated text coherence than lower FL proficiency learners. The author (Shimizu 2005: 79) concluded that learners of higher FL proficiency "are able to construct a more coherent situation model than lower L2 proficiency learners." As regards reading comprehension questions, the results pointed to questions as factors that can significantly activate inference generation processes and help "learners identify propositional meanings of certain parts of a text" (Shimizu 2005: iii).

To summarise, the studies discussed above picture inference generation as a complex process, revealing the importance of both text- and reader-related factors. They underline the influence of text coherence on inferencing – low-coherence texts require more elaborations. Inferencing depends on the type of text (i.e., an essay or a story) as well as the reading task (i.e., reading freely or reading for coherence). Native readers' inferencing differs from that of non-native readers – FL/L2 readers generate different types of inferences, did not distinguish between high- and low-coherence texts and rely more on lower-level processing. There is another reader-related factor widely considered as crucial in inference generation – background knowledge. The relation between background knowledge and inference building will be discussed in detail below (in Chapter 4, Section 4.1.2. in this part).

3.4. Text structure and comprehension

Knowledge of discourse organization of text is an important aspect of text processing. Knowledge of rhetorical patterns in which information is presented in the text, called formal (textual) schema (Carrell 2006), has been found to be a facilitative factor in FL/L2 reading. As Pearson and Fielding (1991: 832) explain:

> Any sort of systematic attention to clues that reveal how authors attempt to relate ideas to one another or any sort of systematic attempt to impose structure upon a text, especially in some sort of visual representation of the relationships among key ideas, facilitates comprehension as well as both short term and long term memory of the text.

This quotation reflects theoretical and research attempts to understand the effect of text structure on comprehension and recall. Before discussing cross-linguistic variations concerning this aspect of reading, let us analyse the concept of text structure and then look at several approaches which aim to identify typical structural organisations in narrative and expository texts.

It is difficult to define text structure (Roller 1990). On the one hand, the text structure resides in the text; it "specifies the interrelationships among items of information which compose the text, as well as indicating the subordination and coordination of this information" (Meyer 1986: 117). On the other hand, the text structure is part of the reader's knowledge which the reader uses while reading a text to construct his/her representation of the structure of the text. It seems that text structure lies between reader and text. Both theory and research explore all the three understandings of the text structure, i.e., the text structure lying in the text, in the reader and the interaction between the two. Several procedures have been developed to identify the text structure of various text types and to explore factors influencing the interaction of text and reader. Two types of text attracted linguists' attention: narrative and expository. It is interesting to note that research on narrative text has been interested in the role of knowledge; research on expository text, by contrast, has been focused on the role of text structure (Voss and Bisanz 1985).

3.4.1. Narrative texts

Narrative discourse is considered easier to comprehend and recall than other types of text. Research (e.g., Scollon and Scollon 1981) shows that even preschool children do not experience much difficulty understanding event sequences in stories and folktales. Much research has investigated the role of knowledge of story structure in recalling and summarising simple stories (e.g., Kintsch and van Dijk 1975; Rumelhart 1977; Thorndyke 1977). Researchers concluded that with practice readers develop a schema that incorporates knowledge about the prototypical sequences of story events. Mandler (1978) and Mandler and De Forest (1979) found that readers tend to recall stories in prototypical order regardless of how stories are presented or how subjects are requested to recall them. The most commonly used approaches that characterise the individual's knowledge of story structure are story grammar and causal-network approaches.

3.4.1.1. Story grammar

Based on structural linguistics, story grammars, e.g., Mandler's grammar (1987), contain elements concerning the following structural properties of stories: characters, a conflict in which characters are involved, a goal sought, a plot describing how the characters attempt to achieve the goal and the outcome specifying whether the goal was achieved. Story grammars represent a narrative text as a sequence of elements stored as a tree; nodes of the tree may be individual elements or episodes, which are higher-level text structures. Comprehending a text entails processing it according to the structural hierarchy of explicit text statements. Story grammars predict that superordinate information in this hierarchy is more prominently represented in text memory that subordinate information. Discourse processing studies demonstrate the definite influence of node-category salience on story recall across cultures and ages (e.g., Mandler 1984). Studies show that direct training in story grammar, involving teaching learners to recognise the elements of narrative texts, can improve reading comprehension and the recall of stories. These results concern both reading in English as a first language (e.g., Morrow 1985; Short and Ryan 1984) and reading in English as a foreign language (e.g., Amer 1992). Amer (1992: 716) concluded that story grammar and guided-reading questions encouraged Egyptian students "to abstract the episodic sequence and the metastructure of the story. In other words, students developed a mental representation of the story, i.e., a story schema." Success in applying story grammar in FL reading instruction raises the question about the universality of story grammar. For example, Matsuyama (1983) argues that the story grammar approach is not suitable to describe the structure of Japanese folktales, which are usually less goal-oriented and plot-focused than traditional Western stories.

3.4.1.2. Causal network models

Another approach widely used in narrative-comprehension research is a causal network model. Critics of story grammars, e.g., Graesser, Golding and Long (1991), argue that story grammar fails to account for important aspects of discourse comprehension, such as elaboration or inferences. They do not provide sufficient explanation of what causes events to happen. These limitations seem to be overcome by causal network models, e.g., the one proposed by Trabasso and van den Broek (1985). Causal relatedness model specialists claim that text comprehension requires constructing links among text sentences, which are often causal, especially in narrative texts. The models were evaluated by numerous studies of the readers' processing of causal relations in narrative texts (e.g., Trabasso and van den Broek 1985). The studies measured reading times, story recall scores, and importance ratings in the readers' summaries. They provide evidence that causal connections do underlie the construction of the memory representation of a text. Other empirical studies imply that readers recall statements containing multiple causal connections better than those with fewer connections: statements with more connections were included more frequently in text summaries (e.g., Fletcher and Bloom 1988).

As regards cross-linguistic research, Zwann and Brown (1996) applied Trabasso and Magliano's (1996) think-aloud methodology to investigate the causal inferences of students learning French. They compared the number of causal inferences drawn during L1 reading by skilled and less skilled readers with the number of causal inferences made in L2 reading. They observed that although the better readers developed a strong textbase, neither group was able to construct a strong situation model. The investigators concluded that regardless of skill, it may be difficult for FL/L2 learners to move beyond the textbase level. These findings corroborate the results of Jenkin *et al.* (1993) concerning L2 students' difficulty in developing a situation model in their representation of the text.

3.4.2. Expository texts – focus on the text structure

In contrast to narrative texts, which appeal to readers' shared knowledge of the world, expository texts aim to inform readers and induce insights on a given topic. As Black (1985: 249) explains:

> Expository texts are the meat and potatoes of the textual world, because expository texts are the ones that convey new information and explain new topics to people. In contrast, stories and other narrative texts mostly describe new variations on well-learned informational themes. Although such variations on familiar themes can be enjoyable, they are necessarily the dessert that comes after the main course provided by expository texts. Thus, the recent increase in the amount of research devoted to investigating expository text means that after years of enjoying story desserts, text researchers are now seeking a more balanced diet.

Two models widely used in research are the Kintsch system (already discussed in this chapter in Section 3.1.1.) and Meyer's system. Here, only the latter approach is presented.

3.4.2.1. Meyer's system

In Meyer's (1975) system, as in the Kintsch model, representation of text structure is organised hierarchically. Meyer's top-level structure corresponds to Kintsch's macrostructure. The information from the text is represented in a tree structure called the **content structure**. Relationships among sentences, paragraphs and longer pieces of text are specified by rhetorical relationships. Meyer (1975) suggests five top-level relationships:

- An **antecedent/consequent** or **covariance** rhetorical relationship shows a causal relationship between topics.
- A **comparison** relationship points out differences and similarities between two or more topics.
- A **collection** relationship shows how ideas or events are related together into a group on the basis of some commonality, such as a sequence of events organised by time order.
- A **description** relationship gives more information about a topic by presenting attributes, specifics, explanations, or settings.
- A **response** relationship includes the remark and reply, question and answer, problem and solution formats (Meyer 1986: 114–116).

Meyer (1986: 117) claims that "a text structure provides an organisational structure which can be used during reading for understanding information and judging its importance." In a series of empirical studies, Meyer and her associates confirmed the importance of text structure in reading prose. They observed better recall and retention of the macropropositions located high in text structure (Meyer 1971, 1975). The findings indicated that recall depends on the type and structure of relationship among ideas in prose; the same relationship when located at the low levels in the content structure has little effect on recall (Meyer 1975). Furthermore, it turned out that training students in identifying and using top-level structures in prose facilitates recall from text (Meyer, Brandt and Bluth 1980).

3.4.2.2. Contrastive studies

Meyer's system has been used in FL/L2 text comprehension research. Carrell (1984) examined how college EFL learners with different L1 backgrounds read and recall four types of expository texts – problem-solution, comparison, causation and collection. She was interested in the effect of rhetorical-structure knowledge on students' recall. The research indicated a greater number of text ideas in the recall protocols of students who drew on the rhetorical organisation of the text while recalling the passage. Additionally, the study pointed to differences in the effect of the four rhetorical structures on the recall performance depending on the students' L1. Spanish learners retained more information from the comparison, problem-solution and causation texts than from the collection. Arabic-speaking learners performed best on comparison and worst on causation. Asian students (Korean and Chinese) recalled twice as much information from the problem-solution and causation texts than from the collection. The results indicate the differential effects of text type on text memory among FL/L2 readers with diverse L1 backgrounds.

Stanley (1984) examined the differences and similarities in the way native and non-native speakers of English read complete texts representing the problem-solution discourse structure (as defined by Hoey 1983). She aimed to see whether the subjects of her study were able to recognise and utilise the underlying discourse structure of English texts. The non-native readers were a Nigerian student, a Malaysian student who spoke Chinese as L1 and two Arabic-speaking Algerians. Students read texts and four summaries of the texts: a model one (reflecting the complete structure of the texts), two distorted summaries (one without a "problem" component and one without a "solution") and a random summary (produced by summarising every third sentence of the original text). The subjects' task was to read the texts and their summaries, and rank the summaries in order of preference. Then they also were asked to explain their choices. The results showed that both native and non-native subjects were able to identify the summaries which most reflected the problem-solution structure of the original texts and those that reflected this structure least. Although the ranking of the native speakers was very similar to that of the non-native speakers, the native group was more consistent in their choice of the best and worst summaries. This implies that both groups of readers could recognise the problem-solution structure of the texts. The analysis of the reasons the readers gave for their choice of the order of summaries showed differences between the native and non-native informants. The native speakers commented on readability, the "flow" of the summaries and their content. The non-native readers commented on the structure of the summaries. The researchers concluded that for native speakers reading is an acquired, subconscious skill, which enables them to process the text in terms of understanding content and style. For FL/L2 readers, by contrast, reading is rather a language activity than a means of communicating ideas.

Sharp (2002) examined how Hong Kong Chinese ESL school learners read four rhetorically different English texts: description, listing, cause-effect and problem-solution. Cloze tests indicated significant differences between the four texts. The most loosely organised text, i.e., the description, turned out to be the easiest and the cause-effect text – the most difficult. The researcher concluded that the rhetorically different texts affect reading comprehension. She ascribed the results of the study to Chinese-English interference, particularly to Chinese students' difficulties in comprehending cohesive devices, such as "because," "as," "so;" the phenomenon observed by Young (1982) and Hu, Brown and Brown (1982). Further, she assumed that the cause-effect text contains counterfactual statements, which according to Bloom (1981) and Kaplan (1987) are difficult for Chinese speakers. Similar results underlying differences in recalling different text patterns were obtained in a more recent study by Zhang (2008), who observed Chinese EFL college students.

In short, the research discussed in this section emphasises the importance of text structure knowledge in text comprehension. The awareness of text structure facilitates understanding in both L1 and FL/L2 reading. The studies indicate that native and non-native readers process the same text structure differently. Koda (2005: 173) explains that one of the factors responsible for the difference in approaching texts is L1/L2 rhetorical distance, which allows one to estimate "the extent to which L1 text-structure schema facilitates L2 discourse processing." Cross-linguistic variations in written discourse structure are discussed below in this chapter in Section 3.5., which addresses the issue of contrastive rhetoric.

3.4.3. Expository texts – focus on the reader's comprehension

Although both approaches, i.e., the Kintsch model and Meyer's system, discuss the connection of text structure with text memory, they do not really account for how readers comprehend expository texts. More recent models, e.g., the one by Gernsbacher (1990), focus on the construction of comprehension. They intend to account for mental representations of text as well as describe and explain the processes that are involved in this construction. The Gernsbacher model is described below. Since I find it a very promising theoretical perspective for both L1 and FL/L2 research, the model is discussed in detail and relevant empirical studies are presented.

3.4.3.1. The Gernsbacher model

The Gernsbacher model, called the **Structure Building Framework** (SBF), suggests that the goal of comprehension is to build coherent mental representations, called by Gernsbacher – structure. Three operations are involved in structure construction: foundation laying, structural mapping and substructure progressing. The **foundation** of mental representation is laid when the reader, on encountering new ideas, activates relevant information in the long-term memory. The **structure** is developed through combining incoming information with previously processed ideas, i.e., mapping on incoming information. However, if the incoming information is not coherent with the established structure, the reader begins to build a new structure again, moving to initiate a new **substructure**. In most cases, the reader constructs several substructures while developing the representation of the text.

The research of Gernsbacher and her colleagues provides support for the assumption that comprehension, regardless of the mode of perception, is a general cognitive skill. Reading and listening comprehension as well as picture-story comprehension and comprehension of silent filmed stories are underpinned by the same cognitive amodal mechanisms. Comprehension ability is not a linguistic skill (Gernsbacher, Varner and Faust 1990); rather, it is independent of a linguistic skill although developed at the same time as L1. In this section, only reading comprehension explored within the Gernsbacher model is discussed.

The Structure Building Framework emphasises the activity of memory. The building blocks of mental structures are memory nodes, which are activated by incoming stimuli. Their initial activation forms the foundation of mental structures. Incoming information is mapped on a developing structure. If the information stimuli are coherent with the previous material, similar nodes are activated and the construction of the main structure proceeds. If, however, the incoming information is not coherent with the old material, different memory nodes are activated, forming the foundation for a new substructure. Memory nodes, when activated, send processing signals, which can either **enhance** or **suppress** their nodes activation.

The Structure Building Framework provides an explanation for numerous comprehension phenomena. The process of foundation laying explains why readers spend more time on reading the first word of a sentence (e.g., Aaronson and Ferres 1983) and the first sentence of a paragraph (e.g., Haberlaudt 1984). This indicates that readers tend to consider the first segments, i.e., words, sentences, even pictures, crucial for understanding larger units of text, such as sentences and paragraphs. The first segments serve as material to lay foundations for mental representations of larger pieces of text. Since the process of laying a foundation entails cognitive effort, readers slow down.

Gernsbacher, Hargreaves and Beeman (1989) went on to explain why the first clause of a multiclause sentence is most accessible shortly after readers have read the whole sentence. The investigators claim that according to the Structure Building Framework each clause of a multiclause sentence is represented as a substructure. However, the substructure representing the first clause serves as the foundation for the whole sentence-level structure, which explains why it becomes most accessible.

The next process, i.e., the process of structural mapping, explains why sentences that are referentially coherent (i.e., refer to previously mentioned concepts) are read faster than less referentially coherent sentences (e.g., Haviland and H. Clark 1974). The process of mapping also explains why certain sentences are read faster, for example, sentences that are temporally coherent, i.e., maintain a previously established time frame (A. Anderson, Garrod and Sanford 1983) and sentences that are locationally coherent, i.e., maintain a previously established location or point of view (Black, Turner and Bower 1979). The process of mapping explains why sentences with the definite article "the" are read faster than the sentences that contain indefinite articles (Gernsbacher and Robertson 1994, cited in Gernsbacher 1996). The process of shifting from one substructure to initiate another explains why words and sentences that change the topic, point of view, location or temporal setting consume more time to comprehend than sentences that do not signal such changes (A. Anderson, Garrod and Sanford 1983). Further, the process of shifting explains why readers remember stories in episodes; each episode is represented in a separate substructure (Beeman and Gernsbacher 1994).

The mechanisms of **suppression** and **enhancement** account for the role of anaphora devices in the improvement of the mental accessibility of their referents (i.e., the concepts to which they refer). Gernsbacher (1989) explains that the mechanism of enhancement activates referents after an anaphoric device is read. Other concepts to which anaphoric devices do not refer are not enhanced to the same extent. The mechanism of enhancement explains the role of cataphoric devices in the construction of text representation. The presence of cataphoric devices improves their concepts' privileged position in the reader's mental representation. Finally, the mechanisms of suppression and enhancement explain why readers better remember the surface forms of abstract sentences than the thematic information of concrete sentences (Begg and Paivio 1969). Gernsbacher (1996) claims that usually thematic content is repeatedly introduced and thus it is enhanced. Surface information, in contrast, is changing and as a result gets suppressed. However, if in abstract and unrelated sentences the thematic information is not developed (and enhanced), surface information is more noticeable and therefore enhanced and remembered.

It is interesting to look at how this approach accounts for differences and similarities between good and poor readers. The studies showed that poor readers have less efficient suppression mechanisms. Less successful readers are less able to reject the contextually inappropriate meanings of ambiguous words or the incorrect forms of homophones (Gernsbacher and Faust 1991). Gernsbacher and Robertson (1995) also explain why more skilled readers are better at understanding riddles and puns. They analysed understanding of the following pun: "Two men walk into a bar, and a third man ducks." Understanding this play on words means moving beyond the "appropriate" meaning of "bar." "It is as though the ability to ignore the contextually less predictable meaning of *bar* (as an obstruction that men might walk into) hinges on the ability to ignore the contextually more predictable meaning of *bar* (as a place men are considerably more likely to walk into)" (Gernsbacher and Robertson 1995: 169). The study that the linguists conducted confirmed their assumption that less skilled readers are slower in accepting inappropriate meanings because of problems with rejecting appropriate meanings. To sum up, research indicates that skilled reading involves efficient suppression mechanisms – even the suppression of appropriate information.

The Structure Building Framework has inspired cross-linguistic research. Walter (2004) investigated the question whether the transfer of reading comprehension skills from L1 to FL/L2 is associated with the development of mental structure-building skill (as defined by Gernsbacher 1990) and FL/L2 verbal working memory. The researcher examined two groups of EFL French readers at lower-intermediate and upper-intermediate level. To measure subjects' skill in developing mental structures, a co-reference resolution technique, which tests readers' ability to recall earlier information from the text, was designed. The findings showed that the more advanced group comprehended L1 and FL texts similarly well. The less advanced readers comprehended well in L1 but experienced difficulty understanding FL texts. The resolution test showed that the upper-intermediate group was equally good in both L1 and FL situations, while the lower-intermediate students performed worse in their FL. Walter (2004) concluded that only the upper-intermediate readers managed to transfer from L1 to FL the ability to develop logical representations of texts and this skill correlated with the development of FL/L2 working memory.

In her next study, Walter (2007) investigated EFL French readers' ability to distinguish between main-point and subsidiary-point anomalies in reading French and FL stories. Again two levels of FL proficiency were examined: lower-intermediate and upper-intermediate. Drawing on Gernsbacher's approach, the researcher assumed that the subjects would be better at detecting main-point than subsidiary-point anomalies. She also wanted to find out whether the subjects would demonstrate similar anomaly-detection skills in their L1 and FL. The results showed that both groups performed equally well on L1 tasks, confirming thereby the hypothesis based on the SBF that "competent structure building allows adolescents and young people reliably to differentiate between main and subsidiary points in their L1" (Walter 2007: 29). As regards reading FL texts, both groups detected main-point anomalies better than subsidiary-point anomalies. Both groups performed worse in their FL than in their L1, with the FL lower-intermediate students performing worse than the FL higher-intermediate group. When looking for an explanation of these findings, the researcher excluded a poor understanding of the sentences and the conceptual difficulty of the texts as the main reasons behind the results. Instead, Walter (2007: 29) concluded that "the results are consistent with the hypothesis that lower-intermediate learners, when reading texts in their L2, are unable to access the structure building skill that they deploy well in identical circumstances in their L1."

The emphasise that the SBF put on the role of memory in text processing has inspired Frey (2010) to conduct a computer-based response-time experiment. She compared the suppression mechanisms in native (English) and fluent non-native (Estonian) reading. The aim was to study the time-course of processing contextually inappropriate meanings of homonyms and the suppression of these meanings. The results showed delayed suppression in FL as compared to L1 and no difference in response speed in L1 and FL. Assuming that the two groups of subjects demonstrated the same level of suppression efficiency in their L1, Frey (2010) concluded that "the mechanism responsible for inhibiting irrelevant meanings shares resources with some other processes that are less efficient in the L2." The study encouraged the researcher to continue research to look more closely at processes leading to the L1–FL differences.

In summary, Gernsbacher's mental model appears to be a very promising approach. As a theory, it is broad in scope – accounting for listening, reading and understanding of pictures. It is "expansive" (see Sadoski and Paivio 2007 for their evaluation of reading theories) as it promotes research into various aspects of comprehension. As regards text comprehension, it offers an explanation of comprehending not only sentences but a number of elements that are crucial in understanding sentences, such as articles and anaphora devices. It attempts to explain the role of coherence in comprehension; it accounts for how readers understand riddles and puns. Extensive L1 studies confirmed the assumptions of the SBF. More recent cross-linguistic research indicates clear differences between L1 and FL/L2 reading – low language proficiency readers seem unable to transfer their L1 structure building ability, thus demonstrating weaker abilities in their FL/L2 reading. Cross-linguistic studies within the SBF are still rare. More research is needed to operationalise the main concepts of the theory in the bilingual context. There is one more important implication that the SBF offers – namely, a didactic one. If we accept that both L1 and FL/L2 comprehension are "governed" by the same general cognitive ability, FL/L2 teachers face new challenges which can encourage them to reconsider the role of their learners' L1 reading skills in FL/L2 pedagogy.

3.4.3.2. Britton's grammar of exposition

The model proposed by Britton (1994) is an approach that views reading an expository text as a dynamic mental process in which the text structure and the reader's background knowledge intertwine. Since Britton's grammar has been used in the study described in this book, below I present a detailed description of the model.

Working within the structure-building framework suggested by Gernsbacher (1990), Britton (1994: 641) claims that "[e]xpository texts are intended to build a structure in the readers' mind." The author of an expository text guides the reader by providing: (a) the instructions that will enable the reader to construct the correct structure of the text; and (b) the building materials, i.e., the concepts and propositions that the reader can use to develop the intended structure. The reader's role is: (a) to recognize and execute text instructions; (b) to add any structure building instructions not provided by the author; (c) to use the concepts and propositions provided by the text; (d) recall and draw on any prior knowledge necessary to build the structure; and (e) to add any building material not provided by the author. Britton (1994: 644) suggests that "the mental structures that readers derive from a text often will be incomplete or incorrect, when compared to the structure intended by the author."

To signal a development of ideas in the text, the author of an expository text makes certain moves. Britton (1994: 646) claims that "[a] large part of the responsibility for making the author's moves evident is carried by a standard grammar of exposition." The grammar of exposition offers the writer a set of rules to build his/

her exposition. The role of the reader is to parse the text, i.e., to identify relations between units of exposition. The **grammar of exposition** is similar to sentence and story grammars in that it is often signalled in the text by linguistic elements that guide the reader in his/her organization of the representation of the text.

The basic expository move is to develop the topic of the discourse, to expand it and enlarge on it. This move occurs at all levels of exposition. It occurs at the topmost injunction of exposition, where the idea to be expanded on is the overall subject of the text often expressed in the title; Britton calls this move an **expand**. It also occurs at the middle levels, where the topic to be enlarged on is the subject of a section of the text, as expressed, e.g., in a heading, and at the lowest levels, where the to-be-enlarged-on node is the newly introduced information from the previous sentence. Britton calls the last two types of moves an **enlarge-on**. An enlarge-on is the most common, important and complex move.

Britton distinguishes three other moves: a move-on, a unitise and a stop. A **move-on** often follows an enlarge-on. It instructs the reader to stop the enlarging-on of any particular topic and start a move to the next topic. In the text, this move is signalled by conventional phrases like "moving on to," "our next topic is," "turning to," and so on. This move can be also signalled by means of, what Britton calls, mixed linguistic physical signals; it can be indicated by the period at the end of each sentence, by the end of the paragraph at the paragraph level and by a new heading at the section level. There are a few forms which a move-on can have. The most popular is a **move-down**, which is the default form of a move-on. It occurs when further enlarging-on is intended. The new node is intended to be linked to the currently active node, i.e., an immediately preceding node. This move is usually unmarked. Other forms of a move-on are a move-across, a move-up and a move-out. A **move-across** introduces a new node that is not related to the most recently active one, but to one that is immediately superordinate to it. A **move-up** makes reference to nodes that are superordinate to ones that are superordinate to the last active one. These moves can be marked by phrases such as "Let us now look at X which has been introduced earlier." **A move-out** refers the reader not to the node introduced previously, but either to the reader's background knowledge that is to be activated, or new information that the writer is about to introduce.

The **unitise** operator signals the movement toward unity. It is very important in comprehending expository discourse. It reduces the contents of active memory after it has been filled up by the enlargement-on of the current topic. It helps the reader to cope with the limitations of active memory capacity, combined with the necessity to continue reading. Another role of the unitise move is to direct the reader in deciding on the hierarchy of the structures of the representation of the text. The unitise mechanism is used to summarise a section of the text, to construct macropropositions (cf. Kintsch and van Dijk 1978) and to extract a conclusion. The operation of a unitise can be induced by phrases left by the writer such as "in summary," "the point is." The last move, a **stop,** brings the discourse to an end. (For an example of how to analyse a text by means of Britton's grammar model, see Appendix 1 and 2).

Britton (1994) compares the nature of the processing instructions embedded in expository text to the linguistic notions of speech acts. All of them include both the information concerning the subject developed by the text as well as instructions about actions that the reader should perform to insert this information properly into his/her mental representation. However, it is worth emphasizing that the structure-building injunctions are very rarely expressed directly. Most often they are indirect or absent. The most direct instructions are phrases that do not contain information about the topic of the text, but information that instructs the reader about what he/she should do with the information about the text. Examples of such phrases are "for example," "in summary," "the second point is." Another way that can help the reader to construct the structures intended by the writer is the use of various paralinguistic devices, such as the layout of the text, as well as mixed linguistic physical signals like punctuation, paragraph indentation, headings and their position, size of font, colour, and so on. Britton makes a very interesting comment, useful for reading research, also with regard to the think-aloud study described in this book, which draws on his theory about understanding expository text. He claims that purely linguistic structure building signals often serve simultaneously two functions: they carry text information and instruct the reader what actions he/she should take. Out of these two roles, only the first one is easily accessible to introspection. The latter one, i.e., processing the linguistic signals which guide the reader in constructing structures from the content information, has become part of the reader's procedural knowledge. The reader performs it automatically and that is why it does not appear in introspection.

Britton discusses the reasons why the writer can produce a text that fails to guide the reader, which he calls them "the pathologies of expository text." Britton (1994: 661) claims that "one underlying explanation for these widespread failures of expository text is certain illusions which are characteristic of the subject matter experts who write expository text." Authors, who in most cases are experts in the subject matter of their texts, begin to produce texts with a mental structure for the subject matter area that tends to be highly structured and well developed. Their knowledge is also highly proceduralised and automatic, and therefore opaque even to experts themselves. The result is that their text can be too dense for non-expert readers; the rate at which the expert develops his/her exposition may be too fast for the novice to follow, lacking the propositions and links that the non-expert would need. In terms of a grammar of exposition, the expert-writer tends to move on too fast, i.e., introduce new information too quickly, without overlap clues and unitise instructions, which would make the text more understandable.

These observations inspired linguists to examine the comprehensibility of textbooks (which are examples of exposition texts) and correlate it with reading comprehension. Research has indicated that instructions provided by writers may not be sufficient for readers to build the intended mental structure. Britton and Gülgöz (1991) used the Kintsch and van Dijk model (1978) to improve the instructional text and prepared the modified version that apparently reflected the author's intentions better than the author's original text. In a study examining the reading comprehension of 170 undergraduates, they observed a significant increase in the students' free recall of the improved version when compared with that of the original text.

3.4.3.3. Inducing insights by exposition

As has been said before, expository texts build a structure in the readers' minds. Their aim is "to induce specific insights about the text's subject matter in the reader" (Britton 1994: 664). Drawing on Kintsch's (1988) computational model, Britton explains the process of comprehending expository texts in terms of a connectionist theory. Insights are defined as the new understandings the reader develops in the process of reading the text; they take the form of new arrangements of ideas (nodes) and links among these nodes. Insights are set off by **insight-propositions**, i.e., propositions that provide the occasion for new understandings to occur. The writer uses a number of strategies so that appropriate nodes and relations are activated in the reader's mental representation of the text. The following techniques are used by the writer to prepare the reader to encounter insight-propositions and introduce changes in his/her mental structure:

- at the text level, **using expository moves** (expand, enlarge-on, unitise and move-on) and **providing the overlap clues**, between-sentence syntactic rules, the given-new clues and explicit signal words and phrases.
- at the proposition level, **shaping the word meanings** of terms that are later to appear in the insight-propositions, e.g., by emphasizing certain aspects of word meanings by phrases like "the most important aspect of X is" or adding new "meanings" (subnodes) to the main term (the main node), e.g., by means of phrases like "X inevitably leads to Y." The result of this procedure may be that the meaning of a critical term will be changed dramatically from its original meaning. Britton gives an example of political discourse, in which terms are "wrapped" in other terms and consequently enriched in a positive or negative direction.
- **activating ideas** necessary to induce the insight-proposition, e.g., (a) by emphasizing them linguistically by means of phrases such as "the most important thing in this chapter is," (b) by repeating in the text terms corresponding to ideas. Britton (1994: 672) says that "the text can play a major role in setting the levels of excitatory activation of ideas by directly or indirectly controlling the strength, recency, and frequency of their activation."
- **inhibiting ideas** (the process opposite to activation) by means of inhibitory links to the ideas activated before, e.g., by setting a negative bias on them such as presenting statements of negative criticism about the ideas.

Drawing on the principles of a connectionist approach, Britton explains that reading an expository text resembles operating on a large network of nodes and links – some derived from the text, and some from the reader's prior knowledge. Each node has an activation value, which can be presented as its "brightness;" more active nodes are brighter in the network. Nodes are connected with other nodes; some of the connections are excitatory and others are inhibitory. The instructions in the text "tell the reader what nodes to place at which location in the structure, what biases to assign to them, what excitatory and inhibitory links to establish between them and other nodes, and what weights to assign to each link" (Britton 1994: 673).

It is important to emphasise the role of the reader's background knowledge and sustained reflection in this process. A reader with the relevant knowledge about the subject of the text has this knowledge automatised, which means that the activation of relevant mental structures is done at a high speed. Successful spread of insights can be also facilitated when the reader stops reading and reflects on the fragment of text he has read before. Sustained reflection will not result in a "Eureka experience," but rather in the slow development of understanding.

To sum up, an expository text is in code. The writer directs the reader in his/her comprehension, i.e., in the construction of mental structures that the author intends. The reader, drawing on the information provided in the text and his/her background knowledge as well as following the signals left in the text, develops his/her understanding of the text. Unfortunately, text clues may be unclear, the reader may not know much about the subject of the text or, for some reasons, he/she may decide not to use the instructions left in the text. The result may be an incomplete or incorrect representation of the text.

Britton's grammar model has a number of advantages. In contrast to the earlier models, e.g., Meyer's system or the Kintsch model, it elucidates dynamic relationships between text structure properties and the reader's background knowledge. What is particularly interesting is that it focuses on both the writer and the reader, explaining the communication between them. It describes the strategies that the writer applies to communicate his/her ideas as well as factors that influence the reader's construction of text representation. In L1 and FL/L2 reading pedagogy, the model has contributed to the discussions on the simplification and authenticity of written texts (such as that by Davies 1984, cited in Alderson 1984). Additionally, it lends itself to being a research tool that can be used to analyse and compare texts (see Appendix 1 and 2 for an example of this kind of analysis). I believe the model can be also very useful in teaching, particularly advanced FL learners. It can encourage students to approach texts in a strategic way and to search for clues left by the writer. As regards writing, it can show learners how to plan their texts and how to leave clues for the reader of their texts. There is a need for more research into the usefulness of the model in teaching FL students of various levels of language competence.

3.5. Contrastive rhetoric

Drawing on the Whorfian hypothesis of linguistic relativity, contrastive rhetoric claims (Kaplan 1997: 18) that "the logic expressed through the organization of written text is culture specific; that is, it posits that speakers of two languages will organize the same reality in different ways." Research within contrastive rhetoric offers valuable information concerning differences between L1 and FL/L2 writing and reading practices. Since different languages provide writers with different resources to organize texts, FL/L2 writers are not aware of this phenomenon and, as numerous studies (some of which are discussed below) show, produce FL/L2 texts which may strike native writers as incoherent and incomprehensible. Additionally, contrastive rhetoric accounts for FL/L2 readers' difficulties in understanding L2 texts. Text organisation (apart from, e.g., vocabulary and grammar) can be another factor responsible for FL/L2 reading problems.

3.5.1. Pioneering studies

In his pioneering study, Kaplan (1966) analysed how EFL/ESL students of diverse L1 backgrounds organized paragraphs in their essays. Five types of paragraph development for five groups of students were identified (see Figure 1.1.). The Anglo-European expository essays follow a linear development, i.e., a topic sentence is supported by other sentences; in Semitic languages an essay consists of a series of parallel coordinate clauses; in Oriental languages arguments are presented in an indirect way with the main point given at the end; essays written in Romance languages and Russian contain digressions from the main point, which would be seen unacceptable for an English writer.

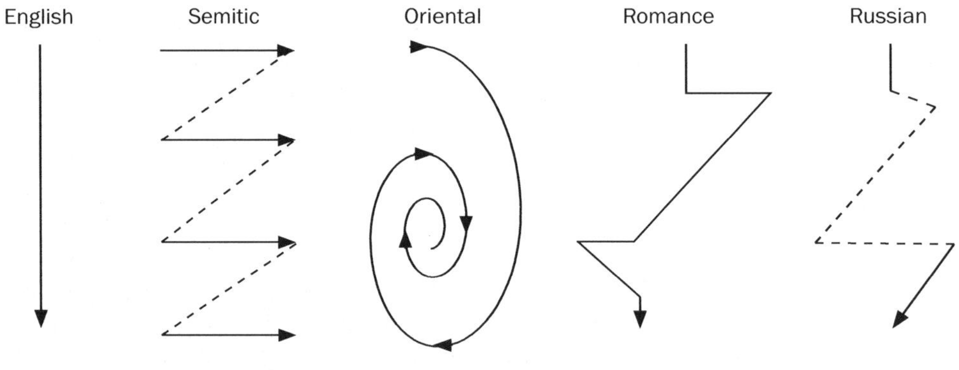

Figure I.1. Five types of paragraph development of second language writers (from Kaplan 1966: 15, doi: 10.1111/j.1467-1770.1966.tb00804.x).

Although Kaplan's conclusions were criticized (e.g., Matalene 1985), they stimulated a series of contrastive investigations into the impact of learners' native language and culture on FL/L2 reading and writing practices.

3.5.2. European languages

In this chapter, several European languages investigated in the field of contrastive rhetoric are presented. The discussion concerns German, Finnish, Spanish, Czech, Ukrainian and Polish. (See Kusiak 2010b, for a discussion of studies of Chinese, Arabic and Japanese).

Clyne (1987) compared the organization of academic papers produced by English and German linguists and sociologists. The results indicated that German writers appeared to produce more digression and discontinuity in argument; in contrast, English writers favoured a linear development of arguments. The analysis of newspapers showed that English papers had "advance organizers," which classified the organization of the paper for the reader. In contrast, German papers usually lacked such devices. The researcher attributed the differences between German and English texts to the different attitudes of writers towards the role of the text and the reader. He believed that English writers pay more attention to the form of their texts (thus making their texts readable), while for German writers content is more important than form.

Markkanen, Steffensen and Crismore (1993) examined persuasive essays produced by Finnish and American college students. They compared the metadiscoursal markers used in the texts, which reflected how the two groups of writers interact with the reader by organizing the content and expressing their opinions and attitudes. A number of differences were found. Finns seemed to use fewer selective demonstrative references, which made the text less accessible to the reader. Another feature of Finnish texts was relatively little metalanguage for organizing the text and guiding the reader, and the relatively late introduction of the main concepts. Another difference concerns the use of hedging. Crismore, Markkanen and Steffensen (1993: 63, cited in Connor 1996: 48) concluded that "Finnish students considered hedging the propositional content and expressing their attitudes about it more important than the US students. ... [By contrast] the US students considered expressing certainty and attributing ideas to sources more important than the Finnish students." In summary, the research shows that Finnish texts can be called reader-responsible, i.e., they suggest things rather than express them explicitly.

The researchers provided an explanation for these differences. As regards the difference in the use of metadiscoursal features, Crismore and associates (1993, cited in Connor 1996) point to socio-cultural reasons. The more frequent use of hedges by Finns and their reservation to express their feelings was explained by their long history of living next to two powerful countries, Sweden and Russia. Thus, frequent use of certainty markers by Americans was considered to stand for power and freedom; Finnish preference for hedges – caution. The Finnish academic style was also attributed to the nature of the training Finnish students received at school: in their L1 writing classes students are taught to write for the intelligent and patient reader.

The Spanish style was characterized as "loose coordination" (Reid 1988). Spanish L1 writers use long sentences, which makes their style elaborate. A L1–L2 transfer was observed, which means that Spanish learners tend to imitate their L1 writing style when producing English texts (Reppen and Grabe 1993).

Czech writing was found reader-responsible (Čmejrková 1994). The analysis of Czech and English academic articles indicated that Czech texts lack abstracts and clear divisions of the content. An elaborate style and a tendency to delay the purpose of the text make texts difficult for the reader. Čmejrková claims that Czech academic writing was influenced by the German style, which resulted in adding to Czech syntax a large number of nominalisations and agentless passives.

Yakhontova (2002) analysed cultural variation in conference abstracts written by Ukrainian, Russian and English academics in the field of applied linguistics. She observed that the English native texts and Ukrainian/Russian abstracts differed significantly in both their cognitive organization and their language. The most visible difference was that the English writers emphasised the originality of their research and attempted to interest, even intrigue the reader. Ukrainian and Russian academics, on the other hand, described their research and produced much more impersonal texts of a neutral, objectivised character. The analysis of linguistic features revealed differences in the use of the pronoun "we" in the texts. The English writers used inclusive "we" to refer the reader to shared knowledge; the Slavic authors used exclusive authorial "we" to present their views and to introduce and summarise their papers, a technique which seemed to compensate for the lack of textual organizers.

The researcher attributes the differences between the texts to social and ideological factors within the two academic contexts. The competitive nature of Western society, also present in the world of academic professionals, and the collaborative, communal character of Ukrainian academic life (a remnant of the post-communist times) account for the "selling" promotional function of English texts and the "telling" informative formal style of the Ukrainian abstracts. Another explanation suggested by the researcher is that the aforementioned differences seem to stem from certain intellectual traditions, which have an undeniable influence on the style of writing represented by the two groups. Yakhontova refers to Galtung (1985), who claims that due to historical circumstances Eastern Europe experienced the influence of the so-called Teutonic (German) intellectual style. Within this tradition, the main aim of the writer is to present knowledge to the reader by intellectualizing and emphasizing the content of texts, which may require certain intellectual efforts on the part of the audience. In contrast, the Anglo-Saxon tradition emphasizes communicating ideas to the audience by organizing the content in a comprehensible "reader-friendly" manner. Yakhontova concludes that the abstracts analysed in her study reflect these two different traditions. English texts are reader-oriented; they organise the content in a clear straightforward way and use metadiscourse that directs the reader in following the text. Slavic abstracts, on the other hand, avoid textual organizers that could facilitate an interaction with the reader and seem to impress the reader by extensive theorizing.

3.5.3. The Polish language

As regards Polish, the majority of studies have focused on sentence-level features, without analyzing textual aspects. They were the product of the Polish-English Contrastive Project and appeared in the publications edited by Fisiak (1984, 1990). Researchers whose studies go beyond the sentence implications are Duszak (1994, 1997), Golebiowski (1998, 2005) and Salski (2005, 2012).

Duszak (1994) investigated Polish and English research papers. She found that expressions in English texts were more direct, assertive and positive. Polish texts contained indirect, affective and tentative statements; Polish researchers adopted defensive positions as if anticipating criticism or questions. Polish researchers delayed presentations of their intentions; whereas English writers revealed their goals early in their papers.

Golebiowski (1998) investigated the rhetorical framework of research papers. She looked at papers produced by Polish scholars in English and Polish, as well as papers written by English and American writers. She found a major cultural difference between Anglo-American and Polish intellectual styles. Golebiowski (1998: 85) attributes this difference to the Polish tradition, in which "evidence of the possession of knowledge is considered far superior to the form in which it is conveyed." Polish authors of English texts did not seem to obey rigorously the conventions typical of a scientific article accepted within the Anglo-American writing tradition. This feature was reflected particularly in the poor organization of content into article sections. Instead, they seem to help the reader in his/her understanding of the topic through a very extensive presentation of background information.

Similar results were obtained in Golebiowski's (2005) next study. The researcher analysed three sociology articles: one written by native speakers of English within an English-speaking academic discourse community, another produced by a native speaker of Polish for an English discourse community, and one by a native Polish speaker for a Polish-speaking audience. The findings showed that the native English writers were "particularly conscious of assisting their readers in their textual journey" (Golebiowski 2005: 67). They used facilitative metadiscourse, e.g., advance organizers and other organizational devices that help to establish dialogue with the audience. On the contrary, the text written by a Polish author for the Polish audience resembled a monologue. The writer used almost no metalanguage organizing discourse, such as advance organizers; moreover an implicit structure of the texts, e.g., through considerable hedging, placed high demands on the reader's understanding. To sum up, in Polish texts writers are more concerned with demonstrating their knowledge rather than facilitating the reader's comprehension. Golebiowski concludes that Polish academic writing follows the Teutonic style – and thus resembles the rhetorics of German (Clyne 1994) and Czech (Čmejrková 1994) written discourse. The same conclusion concerning the impact of intellectual tradition on Russian and Ukrainian writing styles was drawn by Yakhontova (2002), whose research has been described earlier.

Salski (2005) did not focus on academic genres. Instead, he analysed thematic development in twenty descriptive essays written in English by American freshman students, and in twenty descriptive essays written in Polish by Polish EFL students. The results showed that the paragraphs from the Polish essays proved to be shorter, which was demonstrated by a smaller number of sentences and shorter sentences. Further, significant differences were found between the theme-rheme relationships in native English and Polish EFL texts. Native English writers showed a preference for parallel progression, which involves repeating the theme (topic) of the previous sentence as the topic of the next sentence. In contrast, texts written by Polish EFL students were lower on parallel progression and much higher on sequential progression (where the comment of one sentence becomes the topic of the next one). Consequently, the Polish paragraphs were characterized by a significantly higher ratio of topics per clause than the English paragraphs. Salski (2005) concludes that variation in topical structure is one of the reasons why native English readers may find texts written by Poles difficult to follow.

In another study, Salski (2012) explored the autobiographical essay writing in an attempt to see whether extensive digression characterizes Polish EFL writing. He analysed essays written by Poles in English as a foreign language, texts produced by American students in English as a native language and essays written by Poles in Polish as a native language. The analysis of the texts showed that the autobiographical essays written by Poles in English as a foreign language were indeed more digressive than similar texts written by American students in English as a native language. However, hardly any significant difference was found between the ratio of digressiveness in the texts written in Polish as a native language and those by American native language English writers. Additionally, the study revealed that the essays produced by Polish EFL students had the greatest number of digressive relations. On the other hand, the texts written by both native language groups demonstrated considerably less variation. On the basis of these results, the researcher concluded that digression is not an inherent feature of Polish writing. It seems to be natural both in English and Polish texts. As regards the highest level of digressiveness of the EFL texts produced by Polish EFL writers, Salski (2012: 149) explains that it is not necessarily a result of the transfer of native language writing skills. He adds that: "Instead, it should be seen as a developmental phenomenon, specific to EFL texts. It may then also result from little awareness of audience expectations on the one hand, and lack of confidence in language use on the other."

3.5.4. Summary

All the above studies seem to indicate that speakers of different languages organise written texts in different ways. Writers apply different strategies, which influence the way readers comprehend their texts. They differ in how they help their readers to understand the content of their texts. Some languages, writer-responsible, express their message in a direct way (e.g., English); others, reader-responsible, expect their readers to infer what they intend to say (e.g., Finnish). Some writers organise their texts in an inductive way, placing the main idea at the end of paragraphs (e.g., Japanese, the language not discussed here); others prefer the deductive style and state the main idea at the beginning (e.g., English). These differences can be explained by a number of factors, such as different linguistic resources available in particular languages, historical and political factors (as reflected in the use of hedges in Finnish) and intellectual traditions, as explained in Galtung's (1985) distinction between the "Saxonic" style in academic writing, characteristic of English, and the "Teutonic" style, identified in German, Polish, Czech and Russian. Another important factor that is likely to influence FL/L2 writing is L1 training background. It is important to note that most of the studies described above (e.g., Golebiowski 2005; Yakhontova 2002) suggest that there is a transfer between L1 and FL/L2, which means that learners tend to produce FL/L2 texts according to their L1 rhetoric strategies. This conclusion was not confirmed by Salski (2012), whose study sheds new light on the nature of FL/L2 writing and the role of L1.

3.5.5. Implications for FL/L2 reading

It seems that contrastive rhetoric theory and research can contribute to our discussion about reading in FL/L2. By way of repetition, contrastive rhetoric holds that speakers of two different languages and cultures "will organise the same reality in different ways" (Kaplan 1997: 32). This suggests that learners may experience difficulty also in constructing meaning from FL/L2 texts, whose unfamiliar rhetorical structures may make their reading difficult. Research confirms this assumption. Hinds (1987) investigated how Japanese-speaking and English-speaking readers evaluated the Japanese version of a newspaper article, translated from the English-language version for unity, focus and coherence. The results showed that the Japanese readers preferred the Japanese-language version. In a similar study, Kubota (1992) examined how the Japanese students evaluated Japanese and English styles. The results indicated that not all students preferred the Japanese text. The researcher found that half of the students described the Japanese text as "indirect, ambiguous, roundabout, illogical, digressive, ... [with] the main idea at the end, and ... a long introductory remark and long, complex sentences; English is direct, clear, logical, ... [with] the main idea stated at the beginning and ... unity in the paragraph and little digression" (Kubota 1992, cited in Connor 1996: 44). In another study, examining writing patterns in Korean, Eggington (1987) found that the nonlinear development of text typical of Korean rhetoric was not preferred by Koreans who had gained education at American colleges. The results of Kubota and Eggington suggest that training (also in the form of a conscious comparison of one's L1 style with another one) may have an impact on readers' awareness and perception concerning rhetorical structures of text.

Contrastive rhetoric, recently called intercultural rhetoric (Connor 2004), has begun to stress the importance of the social factors which influence the production of texts. The socio-cultural approach, with its recent emphasis on the social context, changes a definition of text and the culture of writing and reading, extending the role of the FL/L2 reader. For an extensive discussion concerning culturally based approaches to reading and their implementations in teaching, see, e.g., McCormick (1994).

To sum up, contrastive rhetoric points to the following factors related to FL/L2 texts that may influence FL/L2 reading comprehension: expectations about how the ideas are organised in the text, i.e., in an inductive or deductive way; assumptions about explicit guidance of reader interpretation; the reader's expectations about the amount of information in the text as well as the way texts express interpersonal relations with the reader, e.g., the use of "I," "you" and "we" pronouns (Grabe and Stoller 2002).

Notes

1. Coherence and cohesion of text are important issues in the field of reading because of their theoretical insights and pedagogical implications. According to Halliday and Hasan (1976), cohesion refers to semantic relations within text, to the devices by means of which such relations are established in text. Halliday and Hasan refer to cohesion as occurring outside the individual sentences, and to syntax as occurring within a sentence. However, many researchers (e.g., Lubelska 1991; Steffensen 1988; Williams 1983) use the term "cohesion" for both intrasentential and intersentential semantic relations.
2. The relation between cohesion and coherence of text has been the object of theoretical discussions. Halliday and Hasan (1976) assume that coherence is created by cohesion. Steffensen (1988: 140) elaborates this assumption in the following way: "Cohesion is a system of analysis that describes the coherence of text as a function of semantic relations realized in surface-level features." However, a number of researchers do not accept the assumption that coherence is created by cohesion. They argue that this premise ignores the contribution of the reader by placing too much focus on the text itself. For example, Morgan and Sellner (1980) claim that it is the reverse, i.e., coherence affects cohesion. The same opinion is expressed by Steffensen (1988: 141): "cohesion is the result of a coherent rendering of content." This view is confirmed by the advocates of the interactive perspective of reading, e.g., Carrell (1982), who stresses the impact of the reader in reconstructing text meaning. The role of the reader and the text itself is also emphasised in the psychological approach.
3. Some researchers, however, question this argument. For example, Sanford (1990) points to examples which suggest that background inferences making can be incomplete and some kind of forward inferential processing takes place. Similarly, Lorch and O'Brien (1995) claim that forward inferences are generated frequently and one of their aim is to make reading enjoyable.

4. Language-independent factors

4.1. Background knowledge

According to the principles of the universal perspective on reading, conceptual processing is one of the reading components that do not vary from language to language. Thus, within this view background knowledge is considered universal in reading across all languages. As regards reading comprehension, background knowledge is viewed as an important factor influencing "all aspects of text-information processing" (Koda 2005: 135). Its role in the reading process has been emphasised in schema theory models, e.g., those by Minsky (1977), Schank and Abelson (1977), and Adams and Collins (1979). A fundamental assumption in those theoretical perspectives is that successful comprehension requires from the reader reconstruction of the text meaning with the aid of the knowledge that he/she brings to the text. Schemata seem to serve three functions in reading comprehension (Anderson, Reynolds, Schallert and Goetz 1977). First, schemata provide the material for filling the gaps in one's comprehension. They allow the reader to construct a coherent interpretation through inferencing. Next, schemata control the reader in his/her comprehension of an ambiguous message. Third, schemata permit meta-comprehension; by developing a correspondence between ideas suggested by schemata and those given in the text the reader monitors the process of his/her understanding and becomes aware whether he/she has understood the text. Research has looked at the role of several types of background knowledge: conceptual, domain and cultural. The most salient studies that explored the role of each type of background knowledge are discussed below.

4.1.1. Conceptual knowledge

Conceptual knowledge refers to what the reader knows about the topic of the text. Ample research indicates that conceptual knowledge is a powerful factor in FL/L2 reading comprehension. Carrell (1984, 1987) shows that L2 readers understand and remember more of the text if they are familiar with the topic of the text. Ulijn and Kempen (1976: 504) emphasise the importance of concept words in the text as "salient carriers of conceptual information in the text," arguing that the reader's conceptual knowledge can compensate for the lack of knowledge about linguistic contrasts between L1 and FL/L2.

4.1.2. Domain knowledge

Similarly, domain knowledge, i.e., specialised content knowledge, is reported to be a significant factor in both L1 and FL/L2 reading comprehension. Erickson and Molloy (1983) examined college students – native and non-native English speakers. They found that engineering students performed better than non-engineering students in reading both general and specific engineering texts. This finding was true for both native and non-native English speakers. Also Alderson and Urquhart (1985) provide evidence that domain knowledge can surpass the limited L2 competence of college students.

Studies have focused on how domain knowledge interacts with other variables. McNamara *et al.* (1996), drawing on the principles of the construction-integration model (Kintsch 1988), examined the role of domain knowledge and text coherence in learning from text. Readers who know little about the domain of the text were expected to benefit from a coherent text; those with extensive domain knowledge – benefit from a minimally coherent text. The researchers assumed that understanding the text at a deeper level involves more inferencing to integrate information explicitly stated in the text with the store of knowledge concerning the domain of the text. A text representation constructed in this way is organized according to the reader's understanding of the domain knowledge as a whole and is thereby linked to his/her long-term memory. Not only does it allow the reader to reproduce the text but to extrapolate from the text and use it in a more critical way as well. The experiments confirmed the researchers' assumption concerning the relation between coherence of the text and the reader's domain knowledge in learning from a text. Less coherent texts required of the readers more active inferencing, thus facilitating learning from a text. However, this condition was effective only for those readers who had sufficient domain knowledge related to the text. These results were confirmed in a more recent study by Gasparinatou, Tsaganou and Gridoriadou (2007). Readers with low knowledge about the domain of Computer Networks benefited more from a coherent text; while those who knew more about this specialized topic benefited more from a minimally coherent text. Gasparinatou, Tsaganou and Gridoriadou (2007: 153) explained that "the text with coherence gaps [forced] the high-knowledge readers to engage in active processing, leading to a better situation model of the text information."

4.1.3. Cultural knowledge

Also readers' L1 cultural knowledge has proved important in FL/L2 reading comprehension. Johnson (1981) observed the impact of L1 cultural knowledge on L2 reading. The study conducted among Iranian ESL readers suggests that cultural background knowledge has a greater effect on reading comprehension than the semantic and syntactic complexity of texts. In another study, conducted by Kang (1992), Korean graduate students were asked to think aloud when reading a culturally unfamiliar text. Here also the results demonstrated the importance of readers' cultural familiarity. The subjects, when inferring the meaning of unknown vocabulary, drew extensively on their L1 cultural schema.

The role of cultural knowledge has been investigated in a number of cross-cultural studies. Steffensen, Joag-dev and R. C. Anderson (1979) examined the interaction between the readers' text knowledge and their cultural knowledge. The study investigated how readers from the USA and India comprehended letters about an Indian wedding and an American wedding. The results pointed to the readers' background knowledge as an important factor in reading comprehension. When reading the native text, the subjects recalled more of the native story and produced more elaborations of text information. In a similar study, Steffensen (1986) examined whether readers who share the cultural knowledge with the writer of the text approach the text equipped with appropriate schemata. The researcher assumed that an absence of the schemata might hinder reading comprehension at the level of inference. The findings of the study showed that readers' background knowledge facilitated the processing of textual cohesion, which led to more effective construction of text representation. In a more recent study, Keshavarz, Atai, and Ahmadi (2007) examined the role of cultural knowledge in Iranian students' reading comprehension. The learners read two English texts: one about an Islamic religious leader and the other about a non-Islamic religious figure. A significant correlation between familiarity with the text content and reading comprehension scores was found. Similar conclusions results were drawn by Sasaki (2000), who investigated students' test performance when reading texts containing culturally familiar and culturally unfamiliar items.

Cross-cultural research has drawn researchers' attention to the impact of affective factors in reading. Steffensen, Goetz and Cheng (1999) looked at text-induced imagery and emotional reactions among Mandarin-speaking learners of English. The subjects read a Chinese text about a trip to China and an English text about a trip to the USA. More imagery and stronger emotions were observed in the group reading the L1 text. The researchers advanced the question as to whether poorer imagery in reading the L2 text was due to insufficient linguistic knowledge or cultural unfamiliarity.

4.1.4. The relationship between background knowledge and FL proficiency

Another issue widely explored in FL research is the relation between background knowledge and the level of FL proficiency. Hudson (1982) investigated the effect of different pre-reading exercises (aiming to activate learners' schemata) on the reading performance of beginner, intermediate and advanced students. Beginner and intermediate students seemed to benefit from pre-reading activities; however, no significant effects were observed in the case of advanced students.

In another study which investigated the thresholds of the background knowledge in FL reading, Ridgway (1995) concluded that the effect of background knowledge depends on the level of FL knowledge. Background knowledge is a significant factor at the intermediate level, but not at the upper-intermediate and advanced level. At the intermediate level, background knowledge is used to compensate for language problems, and the effect of background knowledge is detectable in empirical research. Numerous studies, e.g., Clapham (1996), Zhang (2001) and Liu *et al.* (2009), report similar findings. In the study of high-proficiency and low-proficiency students, Zhang (2001) observed that the more advanced learners reported the use of background knowledge in reading less frequently than the less advanced students. Clapham (1996) and Liu *et al.* (2009) investigated the impact of background knowledge on reading test performance. Both studies indicated the impact of the learners' language proficiency level on their use of subject knowledge in reading. Both confirmed the finding of the previous studies: it is at the intermediate level that the influence of background knowledge is most detactable.

The studies discussed above suggest that there is an important interaction between background knowledge and FL proficiency. At the low proficiency level, insufficient FL knowledge limits the facilitative impact of background knowledge and top-down processing in general. At the higher levels, advanced FL knowledge compensates for the lack of background knowledge, which becomes less important. As Bernhardt (1991: 170) puts it, "[a]s a reader's linguistic knowledge grows, it begins to override knowledge-driven inferencing." It seems that a more significant role of language competence explains why EFL teachers can understand texts on subjects at which they are not experts and why, unlike native readers, "non-native readers show virtually no significant effect of background knowledge" (Carrell 1983: 183).

4.1.5. Teaching implications

The studies discussed above show that background knowledge plays a significant role in both L1 and FL/L2 text comprehension. The research investigating FL/L2 reading consistently indicates that background knowledge influences text-information processing, interacting with other factors, such as FL/L2 proficiency, the coherence of the text, and the affective involvement of the reader.

The studies offer important implications for FL/L2 teachers. It seems that the teacher should consider the role of background knowledge, both its debilitating and facilitating effects, on reading. In teaching beginning and intermediate learners, using pre-reading activities is recommended. This can provide learners with necessary knowledge about the topic of a text, thus facilitate reading comprehension. Using texts on topics of a particular interest to the learners can compensate for the linguistic complexity of the text and facilitate potentially difficult reading. As regards teaching more advanced learners, the concept of background knowledge should be extended, as suggested by R. Clark (1995) in her idea of critical reading. Background knowledge in this case would involve also being aware of the ideological nature of reading, i.e., of the social process of production and interpretation of texts. In reading, the learner should draw on his/her general knowledge of the world, knowledge of other texts that the particular text brings in as well as his/her world view, i.e., ideology. The reader should be aware of his/her own beliefs, standpoints, and cultural values activated during reading as well as his/her positioning, i.e., the way the writer attempts to influence the reader. Critical reading courses have been successfully incorporated into teaching FL reading skills, e.g., by Wallace (2005), Kusiak and Bandura (2007), or Skopinskaja (2009).

4.2. Metalinguistic knowledge

4.2.1. Definition of the term

Metalinguistic knowledge is defined in many different ways. According to Bialystok (2001), the term "metalinguistic" has been used as a qualifier for three entities: knowledge, ability and awareness. Although these terms are often used interchangeably, Bialystok suggests differentiating between them. Bialystok (2001: 124) claims that "metalinguistic knowledge is the explicit representation of abstract aspects of linguistic structure that becomes accessible through knowledge of a particular language." In other words, it is knowledge of universal linguistic principles which becomes explicit during language acquisition. Bialystok emphasises the fact that **metalinguistic knowledge** is different from linguistic knowledge related to a particular language. The content of metalinguistic knowledge is broader and has a more general character.

To understand the concept of **metalinguistic ability**, let us look at the conceptualisation suggested by van Lier (1999). Drawing on the examples described by Polanyi (1958), van Lier emphasises the role of attention in language learning. He claims that in successful communication only limited attention to the language is sufficient. However, when communication breaks down, either due to comprehension or production problems, the attention of participants to the language involved in this communication rises. Participants look at the linguistic resources they use as if from the outside, not for what they mean but in order to control and manipulate them. Van Lier calls these repair attempts "construction work." "The function of metalinguistic abilities, whether of an intuitive or explicit kind, is to assist in such construction work" (van Lier 1999: 75). In other words, metalinguistic abilities are experiences (similar to metacognitive experiences involving regulation of cognition; cf. Chapter 4, Section 4.3.1., in this part) that may occur, e.g., during communication problems and which may facilitate language users' attempts to solve these problems. The example of a communication breakdown indicates a link between a linguistic and a metalinguistic domain. It illustrates well the meaning of Bialystok's (2001: 127) words: "Metalinguistic ability must be continuous with linguistic ability; it cannot be isolated from it and operate according to independent principles of development and use."

To define **metalinguistic awareness**, it is useful to refer to Cazden's (1976, cited in van Lier 1999) distinction between transparent and opaque language use. In transparent language use, the focus is on meaning; in opaque language use, language becomes an object of observation and analysis. Cazden was one of the first to define metalinguistic awareness. She defines it as follows: "The ability to make language forms opaque and attend to them in and for themselves, is a special kind of language performance" (Cazden 1974: 29, cited in Bialystok 2001: 121). Van Lier (1999) suggests a similar definition; he views metalinguistic awareness as a result of the ability to see language as something that can be controlled and manipulated (which is possible when language use becomes opaque). From what Cazden and van Lier suggest, it may be concluded that with the rise of metalinguistic awareness language becomes opaque and language users become conscious of language forms, their meaning and use. This happens when, e.g., they encounter failures in communication and exercise metalinguistic abilities.

It is useful to refer to two other conceptions of metalinguistic awareness. Mora (2007) claims that metalinguistic awareness involves the ability not only to think about but also to talk about language as an abstract "thing" or process. She also emphasises the ability to analyse language as a characteristic of metalinguistic awareness. Mora (2007) claims that metalinguistic awareness has "various components that reflect the complexities, dimensions and forms of language." This characteristic of metalinguistic awareness has been observed in research which focuses on phonological awareness, morphological awareness, intraword awareness and the components of reading analysed in the earlier sections of this book.

4.2.2. Interrelations among metalinguistic knowledge, metalinguistic awareness and metalinguistic ability

The discussion presented above suggests that metalinguistic knowledge, metalinguistic awareness and metalinguistic ability are somehow interrelated. Below, interrelations among the three concepts are discussed.

Mora (2007) claims that metalinguistic awareness leads to metalinguistic knowledge. Implicit and unarticulated awareness, present in a L1 and developing in a FL/L2, is made explicit through structured experiences, such as the purposeful uses of text and discussions of learners' insights and understandings. This growth of metalinguistic awareness leads to explicit knowledge of language form and function and the ability to articulate this knowledge, i.e., metalinguistic knowledge. We may ask the question: what is the role of metalinguistic ability in this development? I would assume that metalinguistic ability, which as Bialystok claims is parallel to linguistic ability, accompanies the growth of awareness, i.e., the change from implicit awareness to explicit knowledge of the language and the ability to verbalise this knowledge. At the first stages of this change, metalinguistic ability is of a more intuitive character; at the later stages – of a more explicit kind. Mora underlines the role of metalinguistic knowledge in linguistic performance. Raising awareness results in increased self-regulatory control over language production and enhanced use of language in cognitive performance.

The process of developing linguistic control described above underscores the role of metacognition. An ability to regulate one's control is the outcome of the whole "metalinguistic" development leading to improved language performance. This shows that metacognition and metalinguistic phenomena intertwine and both are indispensable in successful FL/L2 learning.

At the end of this discussion, it is useful to note the role of attention in FL/L2 learning, as emphasised in by Schmidt (1994) in his noticing hypothesis. Drawing on his own experiences while learning Portuguese as a FL, the researcher claimed that "more noticing leads to more learning" (Schmidt 1994: 18). This aspect of FL/L2 learning, based on "structuring" learners' linguistic experiences, raising their awareness and consequently enhancing knowledge about language, has been recently considered an important part of FL/L2 education (see e.g., Thornbury 1997 and Pawlak 2003 for discussions on consciousness raising and enhancing FL learners' language awareness).

4.2.3. Metalinguistic phenomena in bilingual learners' reading

Theoreticians and researchers have analysed the nature of the three metalinguistic phenomena in relation to L1 and FL/L2 in bilingual learners. Let us look at how metalinguistic phenomena have been operationalised in cross-linguistic reading research.

Bialystok (2001: 127) discusses metalinguistic knowledge in relation to L1 and L2 acquisition. She writes that

> [s]econd-language learners need not relearn the fundamental principles of language structure because these are already known from the metalinguistic knowledge that grew out of first-language acquisition. To the extent that a learner has metalinguistic knowledge, second-language acquisition is facilitated because a language template is available.

The importance of L1 knowledge was confirmed by Morris (2003) and Butler (2002), whose studies are discussed below.

Morris (2003) investigated correlations between the different forms of linguistic and metalinguistic knowledge and academic performance of TESL (Teaching English as a Second Language) trainees in the Canadian province of Quebec. The initial aim of the research was to identify criteria for TESL candidates. The skill of reading sophisticated texts was considered a component of the academic performance measured in the research. The study looked at the extent to which the metalinguistic knowledge of L2 students, measured by a grammatical explanation task involving correcting English sentences, correlated with the academic results the students achieved. Linguistic knowledge was measured by means of the expressive vocabulary used by the subjects in academic writing in their L1 (French) and L2 (English). The results showed that both L1 vocabulary and L2 vocabulary knowledge correlated to a significant degree with academic success, with L1 vocabulary indicating stronger correlation with academic performance. Also metalinguistic knowledge correlated significantly with academic performance. The bilingual students who demonstrated better L1 vocabulary achieved higher grades than those who were less literate in their L1 – even when the L1 of those students was English, which was the language of instruction on TESL courses. However, the comparison of the predictive strength of all the three factors pointed to metalinguistic knowledge as the only significant predictor of academic performance. Morris (2003: 121) concluded that "findings indicate that metalinguistic knowledge, or skills directly related to metalinguistic knowledge, could correlate more strongly with academic performance ... than pure linguistic knowledge."

Butler (2002) investigated the metalinguistic knowledge of Japanese students employed in reading gapped texts and selecting English articles. She was interested whether students' hypotheses on English articles depend on their level of language proficiency. Butler (2002: 451) refers to metalinguistic knowledge as to "linguistic knowledge accessible at the conscious level with regard to the use of articles." In the context of her study, it means the students' mental representation of the English articles that the students were asked to fill in and about which they were interviewed. Butler also looked at the students' metalinguistic strategies, which after Bialystok (2001) we may be called metalinguistic ability. Butler defined these strategies as techniques that the students applied to execute their metalinguistic knowledge concerning English articles. The results showed that the learners' explicit knowledge of the English article system depends on their language proficiency. Lower proficiency learners were influenced by pedagogic rules they thought had been given by their teacher and textbooks; higher proficiency students were more sensitive to contextual clues. The findings also revealed the influence of L1 (Japanese) on the students' choice of English articles.

Whyatt (2007) looked at the use of metalinguistic knowledge in the process of translation as reflected in metalinguistic comments reported by Polish EFL students. After Paradis (2004), she hypothesised that metalinguistic knowledge is used by translators as an expression of some internal control mechanism. Her study confirmed her prediction. The students made metalinguistic comments while working on a specific problem, thereby attempting to tap into their implicit linguistic knowledge. The students' metalinguistic comments indicated that the students had made use of their metalinguistic knowledge. Additionally, the comments signalled the students' growing linguistic awareness and control over both L1 and FL linguistic systems. Drawing on the definitions of the metalinguistic phenomena presented above, it can be suggested that along with metalinguistic knowledge Whyatt investigated metalinguistic awareness (an ability to see language as something that can be controlled) and metalinguistic ability (demonstrated as the students' experiences during translation problems). The results of the study point to the close relationship of metalinguistic knowledge with metacognition, especially metacognitive knowledge concerning the task the students performed (called task knowledge) and regulation of cognition (see Chapter 4, Section 4.3.1. in this part). The study also underscores the close link between metalinguistic and linguistic knowledge, confirming thereby Bialystok's (2001) assumption, which has been discussed above.

Mora (2001) investigated the transfer of metalinguistic knowledge of Spanish students developing reading in English. She analysed in detail the alphabetic principles of Spanish (L1) orthography that Spanish learners transfer to their FL, i.e., English. The researcher found that bilingual students had applied Spanish spellings to English words and had used Spanish approximations for English phonemes that do not exist in Spanish. Mora concludes that metalinguistic transfer involves transfer of phonemic awareness and phonological processes, knowledge of phoneme-grapheme relationships and recognition of syntactic features.

4.2.4. Summary

The studies described above looked at various aspects of metalinguistic phenomena involved in different types of reading. Butler (2002) investigated the role of metalinguistic awareness related to lower-level components of reading. The nature of Japanese learners' metalinguistic knowledge was viewed as students' mental representation of the English article system during the completion of gapped texts. Whyatt (2007) examined the use of metalinguistic knowledge as reflected in metalinguistic comments during translation from English (FL) into Polish (L1) and from Polish into English. Mora (2001) looked at the transfer of the metalinguistic knowledge of Spanish students developing reading in English (FL) as demonstrated in phonemic awareness, phonological processes and syntactic knowledge. Morris (2003) explored the correlations between linguistic knowledge (represented as L1 vocabulary and L2 vocabulary knowledge), metalinguistic knowledge (measured by means of a grammar explanation task) and the academic performance of French TESL trainees (which was measured by the skill of reading sophisticated texts).

On the basis of the findings of the studies discussed above, the following can be suggested about metalinguistic knowledge in relation to reading in FL/L2:

- Metalinguistic knowledge related to lower-level reading skills, such as phonological and syntactic skills, can be transferred between L1 and FL (Mora 2007).
- The nature of metalinguistic knowledge depends on students' level of FL proficiency (Butler 2002).
- Metalinguistic knowledge can be a more important predictor of students' academic success than linguistic knowledge (Morris 2003).
- Metalinguistic knowledge becomes explicit when readers encounter comprehension problems and during their "construction work" look at the language resources involved in their reading tasks as objects (Whyatt 2007). This seems to provide evidence for van Lier's (1999) assumption about the role of metalinguistic abilities in learners' endeavours to solve communication breakdowns.
- Metalinguistic and linguistic phenomena intertwine with each other (Whyatt 2007), which confirms Bialystok's (2001) argument that metalinguistic ability interacts with linguistic ability.

To summarise, the studies demonstrate the complex nature of metalinguistic knowledge, which seems to be related to various aspects of language, such as phonological and syntactic. As regards reading, the studies indicate the "omnipresent" character of metalinguistic knowledge in text-information processing. Metalinguistic knowledge plays an important role in FL/L2 learners' reading, interacting with students' linguistic knowledge and metacognition. More cross-linguistic research is needed to explore the interplay of this component with other reading aspects.

4.3. Metacognition

4.3.1. Various conceptions of metacognition

Metacognition has attracted interest in the field of cognitive development. Developmental psychology and information-processing cognitive psychology have turned out to be the most influential perpsectives, structuring the definition of metacognition and stimulating ample research. In this discussion, I focus on Flavell, who, in my opinion, offers the most comprehensive conceptualisation of metacognition.

Flavell, the author of numerous studies in the field of educational psychology (1978, cited in Baker and Brown 1984: 353), defined metacognition as "knowledge that takes as its object or regulates any aspect of any cognitive endeavor." This definition encompasses two aspects of metacognition: knowledge about cognition and regulation of cognition. **Knowledge about cognition**, as explained by Baker and Brown (1984: 353), is "a person's knowledge about his or her own cognitive resources and the compatibility between the person as a learner and the learning situation." **Regulation of cognition** involves self-regulatory strategies used by the learner when performing a task, such as checking the result of any learning action, planning one's next step, monitoring the effectiveness of any attempted action, and testing, revising and evaluating one's learning strategies (Flavell 1978).

In 1981 Flavell extended his view of metacognition. Within the concept of metacognition, he distinguishes **metacognitive knowledge**, which he defines as the knowledge we possess about ourselves, the tasks we are to perform and the strategies we apply; in the literature it is usually called **person, task** and **strategy knowledge**. Let us look at how this complexity of metacognition is investigated in relation to reading.

4.3.2. Metacognition of L1 readers

The concept of metacognition has contributed to the studies which investigate the knowledge and strategies of effective and less skilled readers. Research, e.g., Brown (1980, cited in Baker and Brown 1984: 356), indicated that competent successful readers show the ability both to realise that their comprehension has failed and to decide what strategic actions they should apply to overcome reading difficulties. The awareness of miscomprehending as a factor distinguishing between successful and less successful reader has been identified by, e.g., Garner and Reis (1981) and Markman (1975). Markman presented elementary school children with meaningless passages and asked them to judge the comprehensibility of the texts. Having observed that even six-grade children had difficulty recognising inconsistency, the researcher assumed that this tolerance for one's miscomprehension could be due to readers' conceptions about the reading process. Numerous experimental and interview studies (e.g., Canney and Winograd 1979; Chan and Law 2003; Myers and Paris 1978) showed that younger and poorer readers have limited awareness of the necessity to make sense of text, i.e., they focus on reading as a decoding process rather than a search for meaning. Studies into adults' reading (e.g., Baker and R. I. Anderson 1982) showed that adult readers evaluate and monitor their comprehension during reading. They also apply various strategies when they encounter problems. Baker and Brown (1984) suppose that these self-regulation processes are characteristic of mature effective readers and it is what children should acquire to become successful readers.

Another skill distinguishing successful readers from less successful ones is the ability of assessing the correctness of one's reading comprehension answers. Readers who evaluate their answers as correct when they are indeed correct or if they indicate their answers as incorrect when they are wrong are considered good reading comprehension monitors. In contrast, poor comprehension monitors are more likely to misjudge the correctness of their answers. Forrest and Waller (1979) observed this phenomenon while investigating confidence in children's comprehension skills. The next difference lies in the ability to talk about one's process of reading. In an introspective study, Strang and Rogers (1965) found that good readers tried to describe how they read and poor readers seemed unaware of their processes of reading. Similar results were obtained by Smith (1967): his less effective readers were found less able to report the actions they took in their reading.

To sum up, the results of the studies described above outline differences in metacognitive knowledge and strategy use between effective and less effective readers. Better readers are more aware of their comprehending process, e.g., they realise that their comprehension has failed and are able to recognise inconsistency in the text. More skilled readers are able to evaluate and monitor their comprehension; they also use effective strategies to overcome reading problems. The ability to report the steps taken during reading is another factor that distinguishes between successful and less successful readers.

4.3.3. Metacognition of FL/L2 readers

A number of studies (e.g., Barnett 1988; Block 1986; Carrell 1989; Devine 1988; Haastrup 1987; Hosenfeld 1977; Kusiak 2001; Zhang 2001) have investigated the metacognitive knowledge and strategies applied by successful and unsuccessful second/foreign language readers. Several of them are discussed below.

Devine (1988) examined readers' internalised models of the reading process and how these models affect reading behaviour, i.e., the influence of readers' task knowledge on their strategy use. A model of reading was defined as a set of assumptions about reading that a reader brings to reading and draws upon during reading. The study started with interviewing learners in order to uncover their general attitudes to reading and their conceptions about what makes effective reading. The results of the interviews allowed the researcher to identify three models of reading: sound-, word-, and meaning-centred. A significant correspondence was found between the type of reading model the learners held and the kind of information the learners focused on during an oral reading task; for example, sound-centred readers focused on the graphic information of a text. Also a relationship between the reading models of the learners and the success in reading comprehension was found. The learners who in the interviews expressed an opinion that good reading means good pronunciation of the words (sound-centred readers) usually demonstrated poor understanding of the text. On the other hand, those who held the view that effective reading means understanding the author's message (meaning-centred readers) turned out good or excellent at recalling and understanding the text.

Hosenfeld (1977), in an exploratory study based on introspective think-aloud data, produced the computer "reading maps" of the examined readers, thereby investigating readers' strategy use. The researcher observed that more successful readers are more likely to remember the meaning of the text they read, they read in broad phrases, skip unimportant words and use the context to guess the meaning of important ones; they also hold positive self-concepts as readers. In contrast, unsuccessful readers lose the meaning of the words as soon as they decode them, read in short phrases, seldom skip unimportant words because they treat all words as equally important for the broader text meaning, and have negative self-concepts as readers.

Kusiak (2001) examined intermediate Polish learners of EFL and found significant differences between the good and poor readers. She concluded that although both groups liked reading to the same extent, the good readers perceived themselves as better readers and considered reading as less difficult. Another difference concerned the evaluation of reading strategies: the good readers valued as less effective bottom-up strategies, which involved understanding the meaning of every word in the text, the ability to pronounce every word in the text and looking up every word in a dictionary. Moreover, the analysis of self-evaluation questionnaires showed that the good readers had more effective self-evaluation skills.

Zhang (2001) compared the knowledge of reading strategy use in two groups of Chinese learners at different levels of English. The results of a guided interview indicated that the subjects' knowledge of strategy use varied across EFL proficiency levels. In comparison with the low proficiency students, the more advanced learners demonstrated greater awareness of the strategies they use in reading and a more frequent use of monitoring strategies. They also valued cooperating with the text as a solution to their reading comprehension problems. Additionally, they reported a more frequent use of inferencing as a strategy to guess meaning from the context. The less advanced students, on the other hand, preferred using dictionaries.

Summing up, the findings of FL/L2 research are reminiscent of L1 reading studies. Both indicate that more skilled readers are more consistent and effective in monitoring their reading. They also demonstrate more effective self-evaluation skills. FL/L2 research, like L1 studies, emphasises the importance of readers' perceptions of reading and of themselves as readers and explains the relationship between these perceptions and readers' performance. Not surprisingly, in comparison with L1 studies, the results of FL/L2 studies provide more information concerning the role of readers' language competence in reading. Better FL/L2 readers focus on higher-level skills, such as reading for meaning rather than bottom-up skills, e.g., pronouncing words.

4.3.4. Metacognition in the Bernhardt constructivist reading model

Bernhardt's (1991) model is one of the best known interactive models of reading in FL/L2. It views reading as the process of building a representation of the text by the reader on the basis of text and non-text information. Bernhardt used her constructivist model of reading in the analysis of the recall protocol data from the studies of Allen *et al.* (1988), Bernhardt and Berkemeyer (1988), and Berkemeyer (1989). The results of these studies provide interesting information about the nature of metacognition and its role in FL/L2 reading. The aim of her analysis was to follow the learners' reading problems and to find their origin. The results revealed that reading problems can be differentially linked to FL/L2 literacy development. Certain kinds of errors may be characteristic of certain stages of reading development.

In the early stages of development, word recognition and phonemic/graphemic feature errors are very common. As proficiency develops, the error rate decreases almost to 0. The development of syntax errors resembles a normal-curve shape. They increase up to a medium point, which may be explained by a greater growth of the language proficiency. Syntax errors decrease later, as language and reading proficiency improve. Errors due to background knowledge and intratextual perceptions decrease with the development of proficiency. However, the error rate is never as high as that of word recognition and phono-graphemic errors in the initial stages of development, and never as low as the one in the later stages. Bernhadt's analysis provides interesting insights into the role of metacognition. Metacognition seems to be present in all the stages of language proficiency of her subjects. Interestingly, the term "error rate" does not apply here, as the factor either appears in the examined readers' recalls or not. Therefore, Bernhardt decides to treat metacognition as an individual learner characteristic.

The results show the interaction of the reader's text-driven knowledge and conceptually-driven knowledge. With the development of proficiency, the reader begins to depend more on the language itself than on the speculations about what the language may mean. Metacognition "accompanies" readers, regardless of their language proficiency level.

4.3.5. Cross-linguistic studies

The previous sections indicate that metacognition is an important element of reading in both L1 and FL/L2. In this discussion, let us look at the relationship between metacognition in L1 and that in FL/L2 in FL/L2 reading.

The role of metacognition in L1 and FL reading was highlighted in the study conducted by Schoonen, Hulstijn and Bossers (1998). The researchers investigated to what extent vocabulary knowledge and metacognitive knowledge account for L1 and FL reading comprehension. The study emphasised the role of both factors. While vocabulary demonstrated a greater influence on FL reading than on L1 reading, especially at lower levels, it was metacognitive knowledge that was an important factor in both L1 and FL reading (although making a bigger contribution to reading at a higher level of language competence). Since the results indicated that metacognition is responsible for the variance that L1 and FL reading comprehension had in common, the investigators concluded that metacognition is a language independent factor. Similar conclusion was drawn by Bernhardt (1991), whose model of reading has been discussed above.

The interaction with other linguistic factors has been investigated by van Gelderen *et al.* (2004), who examined the influence of metacognitive knowledge, vocabulary knowledge, grammar knowledge and processing efficiency on L1 (Dutch) and FL (English) reading comprehension. Metacognitive knowledge was measured by means of a questionnaire consisting of statements concerning L1 and L2 reading, writing as well as text characteristics. The results indicated that metacognitive knowledge was the most powerful predictor of both L1 and FL reading comprehension.

The study was replicated by van Gelderen *et al.* (2007), who over a period of two years investigated the effect of the same components, i.e., metacognitive knowledge, language knowledge and processing skills, on L1 (Dutch) and FL (English) reading comprehension. A significant influence of metacognitive knowledge on L1 and FL reading throughout the two years of study was observed. The findings of this study allowed the investigators to enrich their conclusions concerning metacognition drawn from the earlier study (van Gelderen *et al.* 2004). The finding that metacognitive knowledge continues to influence also L1 reading comprehension points to a more general developmental influence of metacognitive knowledge on reading comprehension in any language. It seems that metacognitive knowledge does not depend only on L1 reading experiences but is a result of other intellectual practices, such as writing and general learning at school and outside school. Also experiences connected with FL/L2 reading can contribute to a development of metacognitive knowledge about reading strategies and text characteristics. Van Gelderen *et al.* (2007: 8) suggest that metacognitive knowledge can be regarded as "a separate component contributing to both L1 and L2 reading development rather than a carrier of cross-language transfer of L1 reading strategies." This confirms Bernhardt's (1991) conclusion about the continuous influence of metacognition on FL/L2 reading development. It is in line with Grabe and Stoller's (2002) opinion that raising learners' awareness of reading in their L1 may enhance their awareness of reading in FL/L2.

Let us discuss a more recent study which looked at the role of readers' perceptions in relation to L1 and FL reading (according to Flavell 1981, also a component of metacognitive knowledge). Yamashita (2004) investigated the relationship between L1 (Japanese) and FL (English) reading attitudes, and the relationship between learners' L1 and FL reading attitudes and their FL proficiency. The researcher viewed reading attitudes as consisting of two components: cognitive (personal, evaluative beliefs) and affective (feelings and emotions). While analysing the results of learners' responses to the questionnaire, four reading attitude variables were identified: Value (related to various values that learners ascribed to reading), Self-perception (which reflected how students saw themselves as readers), Comfort (reflecting learners' positive and negative feelings) and Anxiety (related to the feeling of anxiety that readers experience while reading).

The findings showed correlations between the same L1 and FL reading attitude variables, which implies similarities between L1 and FL reading attitudes. Drawing on the Linguistic Threshold Hypothesis (see Chapter 1, Section 1.1. in this part), Yamashita (2004) assumed that this correlational relationship may be interpreted as an indication of the transfer of reading attitudes from L1 to FL reading. Further analysis suggested that there are different degrees of transferability among the four attitude variables. The values that the learners attach to reading turned out to be the most likely aspect of students' metacognitive knowledge to be transferred and shared in both languages. Additionally, the findings showed that: (1) the learners were more anxious in reading in L1 than FL; (2) the subjects felt more comfortable while reading in L1 than FL; and (3) self-perception as a reader was more positive in L1 than in FL. As regards the relationship between L1 and FL reading attitudes, and FL proficiency, the research indicated that FL proficiency did not have a strong effect on reading attitudes, implying thereby that the Linguistic Threshold Hypothesis does not apply to the transfer of reading attitudes. To sum up, this study strengthens the importance of L1 reading. It suggests that there is transfer between L1 reading and FL reading in the affective domain and that this transfer does not depend on FL proficiency. The results indicated that what students think (e.g., values) is more likely to transfer from L1 reading to FL reading than what learners feel (e.g., anxiety or comfort).

All in all, the cross-linguistic research reviewed above points to the important role of metacognition in reading comprehension, demonstrating it as "an oversight mechanism regulating cognitive resources during comprehension" (Koda 2005: 12). The relationship between L1 reading and FL/L2 reading elucidates the interaction of metacognition with other linguistic factors, such as vocabulary and general language competence. Metacognitive knowledge has turned out to be a crucial factor in both L1 and FL/L2 reading comprehension. Most of the studies imply that metacognition is a language independent factor, continuously influencing FL/L2 reading development. Interestingly, metacognitive knowledge has been found to be the best predictor of both L1 and FL/L2 reading comprehension. As regards transfer between the two languages, the studies point to the complex nature of this phenomenon, suggesting a possibility of transfer between L1 and FL/L2, also in the affective domain.

4.3.6. Effects of metacognitive training

Research into the role of metacognition in reading has given rise to numerous investigations concerning the effectiveness of metacognitive training. Before a selection of studies is presented, a short discussion of the differences between L1 and FL reading in respect to metacognition is provided.

It seems that metacognition may play a different role in L1 and FL/L2 reading. As has been already explained, learners approach and process L1 texts equipped with a tacit knowledge of their native language. However, due to direct language instruction their knowledge of FL/L2 is more explicit. With the recent stress in FL methodology on learner reflection in learning, it may happen that students develop greater metacognitive awareness of how they learn a FL and what makes their learning successful. This would mean that FL learners may be more aware of how they learn a FL than how they use (and learn) their mother tongue. Grabe and Stoller (2002) suggest that teachers take advantage of the metacognitive abilities students developed in learning a FL/L2 to increase their awareness of L1 reading. The researchers claim that it may be more beneficial to increase learners' awareness and practice of the strategies that are most useful for students in L1 reading than to practice in FL/L2 situations strategies that students have never used before. I think that this way of reasoning underlines the importance of L1 reading in FL/L2 reading development and suggests a transfer of L1 reading strategies into FL/L2 reading (cf. Chapter 1, Section 1.2. in this part for a discussion of the importance of L1 reading in FL/L2 reading).

Studies into FL/L2 reading instruction provide evidence that metacognitive instruction can bring promising results. Even a short four-day training period resulted in improved reading performance (as demonstrated by Carrell, Pharis and Liberto 1989). The training proved more helpful for learners of lower language proficiency than for those of a more advanced language competence (Kusiak 2001). The instruction was also successful in sensitising students to the facilitating role of top-down strategies and helped to improve learners' self-evaluation skills (as shown by Kusiak 2001, 2003). There seems to be an interaction between reading in L1 and reading in FL. Having examined reading strategies used in L1 (Turkish) and FL (English) reading, Salataci and Akyel (2002) concluded that reading strategy instruction in FL influenced students' use of reading strategies in Turkish and English, implying that the process of transfer is bi-directional.

All the studies offer clear implications for FL teachers. They emphasise the importance of encouraging FL learners to become researchers of their own reading. They also suggest presenting reading strategies as possibilities rather than prescriptions. This approach can enhance students' metacognitive awareness and expand their repertoire of reading strategies. As regards directions for future research, I believe more studies are needed to investigate the effectiveness of metacognitive training in various teaching contexts and in teaching different age groups. Cross-linguistic research should devote more attention to the issue of the transfer of reading strategies between any two languages.

5. Summary of the findings and implications for future research

The aim of this part has been to explore the conceptualisation of FL/L2 reading within the psycholinguistic cross-linguistic perspective. The review of the literature discusses the studies conducted in both monolingual and bilingual contexts. The principles of the componential view of reading have created an opportunity to conduct a more fine-tuned analysis of the cross-linguistic nature of FL/L2 reading; i.e. to look at L1 and FL/L2 aspects in FL/L2 reading and to examine the differences between L1 and FL/L2 reading. Below, a summary of conclusions is presented in relation to all the reading components characterised in this part. First, the discussion focuses on the role of L1 in FL/L2 reading; then – on the differences between L1 and FL/L2 reading. Finally, the universality of reading competence and a possibility of the transfer of reading skills between languages are addressed. In this discussion, first, the aspects of reading related to vocabulary, syntax and discourse components are discussed; later, the non-structural components (metacognition, background knowledge and metalinguistic knowledge) are presented.

5.1. Vocabulary, syntax and discourse

5.1.1. The role of L1 in FL/L2 reading

Cross-linguistic studies point to the long lasting impact of the L1 orthographic background on FL/L2 phonological processing (e.g., Suarez and Meara 1989). As regards vocabulary knowledge, the studies put forward the question concerning the relationship between FL/L2 vocabulary and conceptual knowledge as well as the importance of L1 in FL/L2 lexical processing. Several models have been suggested, pointing to L1 as a mediating factor between FL/L2 learners' word and conceptual knowledge (Koda 2005), and underlining the role of FL/L2 competence in this interaction (Kroll and Stewart 1994). Also an integration of the bilingual's lexicon across languages has been proposed (Dijkstra and van Heuven 1998), suggesting that both L1 and FL/L2 are activated during FL/L2 lexical processing.

The sentence processing research conducted within the competition model of language has revealed the significant role of L1 (e.g., MacWhinney 2008; McDonald 1987). The studies indicate a gradual change from L1 to FL/L2 cue usage along with an increase in FL/L2 proficiency. Discourse processing studies have emphasised the importance of text structure knowledge in text comprehension. Contrastive rhetoric studies have indicated that unfamiliar rhetorical structures can make FL/L2 reading difficult. Readers seem to approach FL/L2 texts the way they approach their native language texts (e.g., Kubota 1992).

5.1.2. Differences between L1 and FL/L2 reading

Phonological decoding has been found important in both alphabetic and non-alphabetic languages (e.g., Perfetti and Zhang 1995). However, research (e.g., Frost, Katz and Bentin 1987) showed that phonologically regular languages are processed in a different way than phonologically irregular languages, which confirms the Orthographic Depth Hypothesis (Katz and Frost 1992). When the reader's native language is phonologically different from his/her FL/L2, this phenomenon can have a significant impact on his/her FL/L2 reading.

Word recognition studies have investigated the nature of subvocalisation in L1 and FL/L2 reading. More laborious subvocalisation has been found in FL/L2 reading than in L1 reading (Ridgway 2009), which has been explained by FL/L2 readers' less automatic word recognition skills. The investigation of word recognition within the Carver (1977) rauding theory has led to the conclusion that both L1 and FL/L2 reading shares certain similarities with listening, which means that reading and listening are underpinned by similar processes.

As regards vocabulary knowledge, apart from "obvious" quantitative differences between L1 and FL/L2 readers' knowledge, cross-linguistic studies (e.g., Wierzbicka 2001) have highlighted cross-cultural variations in word meanings as still another factor underpinning a dual-language involvement in FL/L2 reading.

The discourse processing studies conducted within mental model theories point to differences in how L1 and FL/L2 readers develop their mental representations of text. For example, Jenkin *et al.* (1993) and Zwann and Brown (1996) imply that L1 readers are able to construct both the propositional textbase and the situation model of the text, whereas FL/L2 readers are able to form only propositional relations. This means that although non-native readers are able to construct a network of ideas on the basis of the text, they lack the skills to develop their subjective interpretations of the text. Similarly, the studies inspired by the Gernsbacher model (e.g., Walter 2007) indicate that FL/L2 readers are unable to "access" the structure building skills which they use in their L1 reading, i.e. skills which enable them to construct a coherent mental representation of the text. Additionally, FL readers show delayed suppression skills, as compared to their L1 (Frey 2010), which means that in reading comprehension they are not able to suppress irrelevant meanings. Text structure is another factor that influences L1 and FL/L2 reading. Contrastive rhetoric studies (e.g., Kaplan 1997) examine differences in how writers organise texts in their native languages. As regards reading, research (e.g., Hinds 1987) has found that readers expect to find in FL/L2 texts rhetorical structures typical of their native language texts.

5.1.3. Interlingual transfer

It is important to emphasise that "oddly, despite its significance, it is only recently that reading skills transfer has attracted serious research attention" (Koda 2005: 14). Two perspectives have influenced reading transfer research: the universal framework and the language-specific view. By way of repetition, the first perspective, claiming that reading comprehension does not vary from language to language, emphasises the role of conceptual processes and reading strategies in reading (e.g., background knowledge and metacognition). It neglects, however, the importance of decoding, morphological analysis, syntactic parsing and discourse processing – cognitive aspects of reading which have become the focus of cross-linguistic studies, conducted within the language-specific perspective. Let us look at what the studies described in this chapter indicate about the universality of reading comprehension and a possibility of transfer.

Phonological processing

As regards phonological processing, the following directions of transfer have been observed: transfer of L1 skills to FL reading (Japanese learners reading EFL texts, as shown by Koda 1989), transfer between two languages in two directions (Turkish children learning Dutch as L2, as observed by Verhoeven 1994) as well as transfer of FL reading skills to L1 reading (Chinese bilingual children reading English, as examined by Chang and Watson 1988). Transfer effects seem to depend on L1–FL/L2 orthographic distance; transfer can facilitate or hinder word recognition and text comprehension (Koda 1988).

Sentence processing

Most sentence level studies have been conducted within the competition model (Bates and MacWhinney 1982). The results indicate heavy reliance on L1 cues, especially at the beginning of FL/L2 development and a gradual change from L1 to FL/L2 syntactic patterns with an increase in FL/L2 proficiency (e.g., Kilborn and Ito 1989). A possibility of transfer from FL/L2 to L1 (e.g., Dussias 2001, cited in MacWhinney 2008) and impact of L1–FL/L2 distance on transfer procedures (e.g., Sasaki 1991) was also observed. Additionally, cross-linguistic research points to the influence of language universal principles (e.g., Lardiere 2000) and learner perception of L1–FL/L2 distance (e.g., Gass 1983).

Discourse processing

Discourse processing research has been conducted within diverse theoretical perspectives, covering numerous issues, such as constructing mental representations of the text, coherence development, inference generation, comprehending different text types. The studies discussed in this chapter offer valuable insights into a possibility of transfer. FL/L2 coherence building seems to be influenced by L1. Both language-specific (e.g., coherence markers in L1 and FL/L2 reading) and universal aspects of coherence awareness (the ability to distinguish thematic from peripheral information) seem to have an impact on FL/L2 coherence development (Koda 2005).

The universal character of reading comprehension has been emphasised by Gernsbacher (1990), whose research sees reading comprehension (as well as listening comprehension and picture-story comprehension) as general cognitive processes, independent of a linguistic skill. This assumption has been confirmed by neurolinguistic studies, e.g., Robertson *et al.* (2000, cited in Gernsbacher and Kaschak 2003). Gernsbacher's Structure Building Framework has given rise to reading comprehension transfer studies, e.g., Walter (2004, 2007). The following words (Walter 2004: 333, 334) may serve as a summary of her findings:

> [A] crucial element in transferring reading comprehension skill from L1 to L2 appears to be the transfer of the structure-building ability; and this transfer appears to be linked to the development of WM [working memory] in L2. ... If successful structure building is accomplished in L1 but not in L2, it is not the ability to build mental structures that is absent; what is lacking is the attainment of some level of L2 ability which acts as a precondition for the structure-building skill to operate.

Walter's opinion is a valuable contribution to the discussion on the nature of reading comprehension transfer and Alderson's (1984) question whether FL/L2 reading is a reading problem or a language problem (see Chapter 1 in this part). In the next study, Walter (2007) has attempted to challenge "the transfer metaphor" and to investigate a notion of access instead. Following Gernsbacher's view on comprehension processes, Walter (2007: 16) explains that

> skill in comprehending texts is not a linguistic skill; rather, it is a general cognitive skill developing at the same time as the L1, but independently from it. It follows that the metaphor of 'transfer' of L1 comprehension skill to the L2 is misleading: what happens is more appropriately characterised as *access*, via L2 text, to the individual's already established, amodal comprehension skill.

Contrastive rhetoric is another research paradigm which accounts for the phenomenon of reading comprehension transfer. Hinds (1987) and Kubota (1992) revealed the influence of L1 rhetorical structures on readers' comprehension of FL/L2 texts. An interesting finding is the impact of FL/L2 training on readers' perception of rhetorical text structure, also that of native language texts (Eggington 1987).

5.2. Metacognition, metalinguistic knowledge and background knowledge

Metacognition seems to play a similar role in both L1 and FL/L2 reading. It functions as "an oversight mechanism regulating cognitive resources during comprehension" (Koda 2005: 12), continuously accompanying readers in their dual-language development. It appears to be a powerful predicator of both L1 and FL/L2 reading comprehension (van Gelderen *et al.* 2004). Studies show that certain aspects of metacognition transfer between the two languages – both in relation to the cognitive domain (i.e., the use of reading strategies), as demonstrated by Salataci and Akyel (2002) and the affective domain, as implied by Yamashita (2004) in her investigation of the readers' attitudes toward reading. Transfer occurs in both directions, i.e., from L1 to FL and from FL to L1.

As regards metalinguistic knowledge, it appears to be an omnipresent factor of reading comprehension, related to phonological and syntactic aspects of language processing. It depends on the level of language proficiency (Butler 2002), which means that lower-proficiency learners demonstrate different metalinguistic knowledge than higher-proficiency students. Interestingly, metalinguistic knowledge was found a better predictor of EFL students' academic success than linguistic knowledge. This finding emphasises the role of metalinguistic knowledge in FL learning at the academic level. Cross-linguistic studies (e.g., Mora 2007) provide convincing evidence that transfer of metalinguistic knowledge between L1 and FL occurs in relation to both phonological and syntactic skills.

Background knowledge plays a facilitative role in both L1 and FL/L2 reading comprehension; in FL/L2 reading it can compensate for limited language competence (Alderson and Urquhart 1985). Cross-linguistic studies show a significant correlation between readers' L1 cultural knowledge and FL/L2 reading (e.g., Keshavarz, Atai and Ahmadi 2007). Background knowledge seems to be linked to the level of FL/L2 proficiency (Liu *et al.* 2009). The impact of background knowledge disappears at more advanced levels and its effect is not detectable in empirical research, which carries important pedagogical implications.

Studies have explored also how metacognition, metalinguistic knowledge and background knowledge interact with other text-related and reader-related factors. Background knowledge seems to interact with readers' FL/L2 language proficiency, text coherence (less coherent texts generate more active inferencing about the text) and the engagement of the reader (reading culturally familiar texts in L1 induces stronger emotions). As for metacognition and metalinguistic knowledge, it seems that both are important internal mechanisms that control other aspects during the process of reading comprehension. In fact, research (e.g., Whyatt 2007) suggests a close relationship between metalingistic knowledge and metacognition.

5.3. Suggestions for future research

Two suggestions which are the results of the discussions conducted in this chapter are presented here: one is a call to develop a unified theory of reading and the other postulates a need for more cross-linguistic studies in a Polish context.

5.3.1. A call for a unified theory of reading

It is crucial to note that although the studies discussed in this chapter have been carried out within a psycholinguistic approach, they have been prompted by different "subsets" (the term used by Fitzgerald 2003 in relation to reading theories) of this theoretical orientation. As the respective sections demonstrate, even the research focussing a single reading component has been influenced by several theoretical perspectives. This situation has both advantages and disadvantages. On the one hand, different conceptualisations and ways of investigation elucidate the complex nature of the examined aspect and illustrate its potential roles in reading, which can undoubtedly enrich our knowledge of the reading process. On the other hand, however, this "enriched" knowledge can introduce elements of confusion in our understanding of the explored components, making comparisons of the research findings and drawing conclusions difficult. Therefore, it comes as no surprise that recently in the literature there have been voices proposing a need for a theory that could encompass all aspects of reading (e.g., Fitzgerald 2003; Sadoski and Paivio 2007).

As an illustration of this call for a unified theory of reading, let us look at two examples: Carver's rauding theory (1990) and Kintsch's Construction-Integration Theory of comprehension (1998, 2004), both discussed earlier. Based on the simple view of reading suggested by Hoover and Gough (1990), Carver's model suggests mathematical equations, which have been applied in both L1 and FL/L2 reading studies to make precise calculations of reading efficiency. Although this approach lends itself to practical applications in teaching and assessment, its statistical character fails to offer sufficient conceptualisations of its main constructs (e.g., reading efficiency), which considerably limits a possibility of dialogue with other theories addressing similar aspects of the reading process.

Kintsch's theory of comprehension, by comparison, does not focus on one aspect of reading. It aims to explain processes responsible for text comprehension and forms of knowledge representation constructed during those processes:

understanding surface structure information (on the basis of lexis and syntax), constructing a cohesive textbase (on the basis of text information) and finally developing the situation model of the text (which reflects the reader's interpretation and evaluation of the text). Although this theory is broad in scope and carefully defines its main constructs, it is restricted to verbal aspects of reading, leaving nonverbal cognitive and affective aspects of reading comprehension unexplained (as pointed out by Sadoski and Paivio 2007).

This short discussion suggests that "reading theory cries for unification to provide an overall architecture within which we can interpret research and envision more" (Sadoski and Paivio 2007: 352). It seems desirable to develop "a grand theory of interconnected webs of theories" (Fitzgerald 2003: 121), which like "an invisible mansion of the mind" (Judson 1980, cited in Sadoski and Paivio 2007: 344) would serve as "a plan that is open to additions and modifications" (Sadoski and Paivio 2007: 345). Such a unified theory will considerably help in directing further cross-linguistic studies and facilitating constructive interactions among researchers.

5.3.2. The need for more cross-linguistic reading research in Poland

Cross-linguistic studies focussing on the relationship between L1 and FL/L2 competence are not frequent in a Polish research context. A selection of studies addressing this issue is briefly presented below.

A number of studies have investigated the nature of a bilingual or trilingual lexicon. By measuring reaction time in prime-target relation tasks, Cieślicka (2000) looked at the role of FL learning strategies in bilingual lexical processing. Arabski (2002) and Gabryś-Barker (2005) explored a trilingual mental lexicon. Arabski examined the strategies used by trilingual students when learning vocabulary. The aim of Gabryś-Barker's extensive project was to investigate how multilingual learners store, process and retrieve vocabulary in their L1, FL/L2 and L3. In one of her think-aloud studies, the researcher observed how multilingual learners translated texts. The results showed the extent of influence of different languages that learners had at their disposal and the way the languages were consciously or unconsciously used. All the above-mentioned studies underline the complexity of multilingualism at the level of vocabulary, implying that at this stage of investigation it was not possible to establish a model of a multilingual mental lexicon. The extent to which learners' L1 lexicon is affected by their FL was also the focus of Latkowska's (2001) study. The researcher suggests that the L2-L1 transfer occurs at both comprehension and metalinguistic level. The findings emphasised the relationship between the level of FL proficiency, the bilingual learner's use and perception of their native language. Latkowska suggests that interlinguistic transfer from L1 to FL is more frequent at the metalinguistic level, which "hints at the possibility that under the influence of the L2, the bilingual changes his/her perception of the mother tongue and, as a result, includes in it elements that belong to the other language" (Latkowska 2001: 157).

Cross-linguistic transfer has also been the subject of Otwinowska-Kasztelanic's (2001, 2007) research. Otwinowska-Kasztelanic (2001) investigated the notion of latent bilingualism (Rusiecki 1980), according to which Polish learners are equipped with a subconscious knowledge of vocabulary which is common to European languages, such as interlingual synonyms. Her experiment (Otwinowska-Kasztelanic 2001) supported the idea that sensitising students to such "universal" vocabulary can facilitate their FL learning. In another experiment, drawing on the assumptions of psychotypology, Otwinowska-Kasztelanic (2007) found that raising students' awareness of the similarities between L1 (Polish) and FL (English) vocabulary encouraged students to use the vocabulary that they already knew subconsciously. The researcher concluded that both studies provided evidence that transfer between L1 and FL took place.

In a questionnaire study conducted among Polish students learning English and German, Tobiasz (2009) observed an impact of the students' knowledge of English (L2) on the process of learning German (L3). This transfer was both positive and negative. Kusiak (2009) investigated how Polish undergraduate students evaluated their Polish (L1) school education and its role in EFL learning. A surprising result was that the students emphasised a facilitative influence of Polish instruction on their EFL learning in relation to developing writing skills (especially editing texts). The study suggests that language training may facilitate interlingual transfer.

As regards research focussing on reading, this aspect of FL/L2 competence has attracted the attention of several Polish researchers. Two examples are given here. Chodkiewicz (2000) investigated the effectiveness of vocabulary learning from the written context and the relationship between incidental vocabulary acquisition and reading comprehension. Her study showed that reading unedited English texts had a significant effect on acquiring new vocabulary. Piasecka (2001) looked at the relationship between readers' background knowledge and their comprehension of EFL texts. The results show differences between how more and less proficient students integrated their background knowledge with text knowledge.

It is important to note that very few studies conducted in Poland explored reading in a contrastive study or investigated cross-linguistic influences on FL/L2 reading comprehension. The examples of this type of research are Kurcz and Polkowska's (1990) project and Whyatt (2007) study; both discussed earlier in this chapter. By repetition, in a contrastive study Kurcz and Polkowska investigated how Polish and American students processed texts written in their native language, which allowed them to conduct a comparative study of reading in Polish as L1 and reading in English as L1 at the lexical and syntactic levels. Whyatt observed how Polish students read during translation, which revealed the interlingual interaction at the level of metalinguistic control. It seems that more research is needed to explore how Polish learners read in their L1 and FL. I believe that special focus should be given to higher-level processes, e.g., to how readers construct their understanding of texts (as suggested by Kurcz and Polkowska's 1990). I hope that the empirical study reported in Part Three will contribute to the findings obtained in the previous studies and will shed more light on this interesting aspect of FL competence.

Part II THINK-ALOUD READING COMPREHENSION STUDIES

1. Think-aloud methodology

1.1. Aspects of reading investigated by think-aloud methodology

It is important to note that in this book the terms "think-aloud protocols," "verbal protocols" and "protocol analysis" are used interchangeably. They both refer to "a methodology for examining thought and action" (Pressley and Afflerbach 1995: 1). The term "verbal reports" and "protocols" refer to data obtained from subjects during think-aloud tasks.

Let us begin with a brief history of think-aloud (TA) research. Asking people to describe what they think is not a new method. James (1890), a famous American psychologist, developed his theories about the mind by asking people to say what they think. Protocol-based research was applied to watch strategies used by experts, e.g., in solving mathematical problems (e.g., Polya 1954, cited in Afflerbach 2000) and in playing chess (e.g., de Groot 1965, cited in Afflerbach 2000). In reading research, protocol analysis began to be used in the first half of the 20th century, e.g., Huey (1908). Despite the criticism of behaviourists and their "schizophrenic" (as Ericsson and Simon 1980: 216 call it) scepticism concerning investigating people's verbalizations, protocol analysis did continue. For example, McCallister (1930) looked at readers' responses to questions and Piekarz (1954) studied readers' responses to texts. The cognitive revolution changed the conceptualization of reading; reading began to be viewed as a cognitive process. Inspired by the studies that investigated human problem solving (e.g., Newell and Simon 1972), researchers began to see reading as strategic problem solving, (e.g., Olshavsky 1976/1977).

Nowadays protocol analysis research is growing rapidly. It has been applied to investigate various aspects of FL processing, such as lexical inferencing (Haastrup 1987), the language of thought in multi-lingual translation tasks (Gabryś-Barker 2005) and an interactional character of individual lexical search in translation (Zimmermann and Schneider 1987). It is important to note that the studies used various types of TA procedures – concurrent think alouds (Gabryś-Barker 2005) and a combination of concurrent think alouds and retrospection (Haastrup 1987). As regards reading, protocol analysis has allowed researchers to explore an array of details concerning reading and reading-related phenomena. It is viewed as an opportunity to investigate not only cognitive, but also affective and social aspects of reading (Afflerbach 2000). Within cognitive psychology, protocol research focuses on observing single reading-related phenomena, such as generalizing inferences (e.g., Collins, Brown and Larkin 1980) or determining main ideas (e.g., Afflerbach 1990). Another body of research focuses on what Earthman (1992, cited in Afflerbach 2000: 167) names "'the concert' of readers orchestrating complex strategies of cognition, knowledge construction, response within acts of reading." Studies focus on acts of reading, as opposed to single aspects of reading within acts of reading. In attempting to describe the totality of the reading task, numerous inquiries investigate more than just cognitive strategies. They look at interdependencies of strategies, stances, goals, reader affect and motivation; in other words – at the impact of contextual factors on strategy use. The objects of observation are such acts of reading as professors and students reading primary source texts in history (Young and Leinhardt 1998, cited in Afflerbach 2000) or physicists reading professional journal articles (Bazerman 1985, cited in Afflerbach 2000). Reading as a cognitive process influenced by contextual variables has also been explored within the literary tradition. For example, reader response critics (Fish 1980; Rosenblatt 1978), who view reading as transaction between reader and text, investigate how readers interact and respond to literary texts.

In this discussion underlying the impact of think-aloud protocols on the conceptualization of reading, it is worth presenting the synthesis of TA reading research prepared by Pressley and Afflerbach (1995). The researchers examined the theoretical principles that underpin think-aloud studies and identified the aspects of reading that think-aloud research investigates. In their conclusion, Pressley and Afflerbach (1995: 2) proposed a model of constructively responsive reading, according to which "reading is *constructively responsive* – that is, good readers are always changing their processing in response to the text they are reading. The result is complex processing." Pressley and Afflerbach (1995: 117) claim that this complex nature of constructive responsive reading subsumes all processes proposed in the main theories of text processing. The processes embrace: reader response and his/her transaction with text, as conceived by Rosenblatt (1938, 1978); monitoring the use of strategies, as described by Baker and Brown (1984); top-down processing, as proposed by the schema theory developed by R.C. Anderson and Pearson (1984) as well as the bottom-down processing, as emphasized by van Dijk and Kintsch (1983); extensive inferencing, as explored by Graesser and Bower (1990); and an awareness that reading is socially embedded, as investigated by Smagorinsky (1998). To sum up, the researchers concluded that the think-aloud methodology lends itself to investigating a variety of reading aspects: cognitive, affective and social.

1.2. Using protocol analysis in theory building and research

Protocol analysis can be used both **inductively**, i.e., as an exploratory methodology and **deductively**, i.e., in order to test hypotheses about reading that spring from initial explorations (Pressley and Afflerbach 1995). Erickson and Simon (1980) and Afflerbach (2000) emphasise the role that protocol analysis plays in the exploration of the very construct it is used to investigate. Protocol analysis may be first used to initiate the construction of theories concerning reading to break ground for new understandings of reading. It can also direct researchers in their attempts to develop existing theories, facilitating their understanding of a variety of factors that constitute reading. Afflerbach (2000) concludes that this symbiosis between the methodology and the aspects of reading it investigates should be the aim of future use of protocol analysis.

In the study described in this book (see Part Three), protocol analysis is applied for exploratory purposes, i.e., to observe readers' behaviours while they read expository texts in English and Polish. The main aim is to investigate how students approach texts and what strategies they use in order to see whether there is any difference between how advanced EFL learners read an English text and a Polish text.

1.3. Theoretical underpinnings of think-aloud methodology

In the article defending verbal reports as data, Ericsson and Simon (1980) propose a processing model for the purpose of interpretation of verbalisations gathered in research. Firstly, they (Ericsson and Simon 1980: 223) hypothesise that human cognition is information processing, i.e., "that a cognitive process can be seen as a sequence of internal states successively transformed by a series of information processes." Secondly, they assume information is stored in several types of memories: several sensory stores of short duration, short-term memory (STM), and long-term memory (LTM). The STM is limited in capacity but people can quickly access it and report its content. The LTM has large capacity; due to the organisation of its content, it is also possible to access it, although access times are slower when compared with the STM. The researchers assume that information recently acquired is stored in the STM and can be accessed, e.g., for producing verbal protocols. However, information stored in the LTM must first be transferred to the STM before it can be reported. The most important conclusion that Ericsson and Simon draw is that people can produce (self-report) the information that is in their short-term memory. "The optimal verbal report of a cognitive process is obtained when subjects verbalise new thoughts as the thoughts first enter attention as part of the subjects' efforts to complete a task" (Ericsson 1988: 298).

The researchers distinguish two types of verbalisations: concurrent and retrospective. If information is verbalised at the time that it is attended to, the procedure is named **concurrent verbalisation**. If the subject verbalises his/her cognitive processes that occurred sometime earlier, he/she retrospects them, i.e., we deal with **retrospective verbalisation**. It is important that the interval between the moment of acquiring the information and the moment of recall should be very brief. The Ericsson and Simon's model predicts that if this interval is short and verbalising occurs immediately after performing the process, some of the heeded information will still be stored in the STM, which will enable the subject to report it. Ericsson (1988) strongly recommends the use of immediate rather than delayed retrospective reports.

Within Ericsson and Simon's (1984, 1993) model, three levels of verbalisation are distinguished. Level 1, also called **talking aloud**, involves verbalisation of the information which is already encoded verbally in the STM. Since verbalisation does not require any additional attention, there are no intermediate processes connected with verbalisation. It may involve, for example, reading aloud words from the text. In level 2, or **thinking aloud**, the contents of the STM is originally stored in a non-verbal form and verbalisation entails transforming the non-linguistic information into a verbal form. In other words, the subject verbalises the information stored in his/her mind in response to the think-aloud task. Level 3 verbalisation includes **introspective reporting** in which subjects need to attend to the verbalisation itself. They may theorise or explain their performance and express their personal responses to the task. Ericsson and Simon claim that information elicited in talk-alouds and think-alouds are direct representations of subjects' internal processes, whereas data elicited in introspective reports is likely to influence subsequent processes and distort accurate reflections of subjects' cognitive processes.

It is interesting to look at the model of verbalisation processes suggested by Cohen and Hosenfeld (1981). The researchers distinguish thinking aloud and self-observation. In **thinking aloud** subjects let their thoughts flow without attempts to observe or explain them. In **self-observation** subjects look at and analyse their performance; they may even transform their verbalisations into a metalanguage of technical terms. Think-aloud data reflect verbalisations made within a few seconds of the thought. Self-observation data can be of two types: **introspective** (when the observation of a mental state happens within a few second of the thougth) and **retrospective** (when the observation is not made at once). Within retrospection two types are distinguished: immediate and delayed.

Although the model proposed by Ericsson and Simon (1984, 1993) and the one suggested by Cohen and Hosenfeld (1981) are similar, certain differences in terminology can be noticed. Both introspective reporting at level 3 (in the Ericsson and Simon model) and self-observation (in the Cohen and Hosenfeld model) involve subjects' analysing their behaviour. In both models, thinking aloud refers to the same type of verbalisation; it means verbalising thoughts while doing a task, without commenting on one's performance.

1.4. Ericsson and Simon's model and text processing

Drawing on the theoretical framework of their model, Ericsson and Simon (1984/1993) attempted to predict how different types of reading are likely to be reported. Ericsson (1988) assumes that normal reading (see Note 1) would involve the integration of information through recognition and retrieval – processes that do not require attention for intermediate thoughts, and thus are not verbalised and made observable. As regards normal reading, Ericsson draws on Just and Carpenter's (1980) studies, which show that reading well-formed texts is a smooth rapid process with occasional pauses and rereadings. Ericsson (1988: 301) concludes that readers do not have to be active comprehenders when they are "guided by the texts".

Ericsson and Simon (1984/1993) claim that the quality of reporting reading texts depends on how difficult the text is. Having compared the verbal reports of easy and difficult texts, Ericsson (1988) observed the lack of verbal reports in the comprehension of easy texts. He concludes (Ericsson 1988: 321) that "the smooth reading of easy texts is the least likely comprehension activity to involve intermediate thought sequences not driven by bottom-up processes of presented text segments." He also observed that readers found it difficult to verbalise the heeded final product of the comprehension (i.e., the meaning) of a phrase or sentence. For well-written texts, while verbalising the content of phrases that they understood, subjects just repeated this phrase. Thinking aloud an easy text is practically the same as reading aloud this text. In other words, it seems that think-aloud and read-aloud instructions will produce almost the same verbalisations. The main reason is that easy reading is fully automatised and subjects, not being conscious of the process, are not able to report it. To support his assumption about reading and reporting easy texts, Ericsson quotes Kintsch (1988), who emphasises the role of bottom-up processes in the comprehension of well-formed texts. "The meaning emerges directly to attention without any intermediate reportable states, and a think-aloud protocol from reading will not contain any information beyond that in the text itself" (Ericsson 1988: 301). Ericsson (1988) also refers to an interesting conception of reading presented by Neisser (1967), who views the reading and comprehension of text as "externally guided thinking" (Neisser 1967: 136, cited in Ericsson 1988: 301). Decoding a text would mean "'reinstating' mental states the writer attempted to communicate" (Ericsson 1988: 301). In the case of ideal understanding, readers should repeat the same phrases as the writer used. This view provides the next explanation as to why it is difficult to paraphrase easy texts. It seems that in reporting the heeded final product of the comprehension of easy texts, readers would be likely to reproduce those texts.

What about the comprehension of more difficult texts, i.e., those ill-formed and more challenging for readers also in terms of content? Reading more difficult texts is a slower, more conscious process and may result in a verbalisation of information that is not explicitly stated in the text. Ericsson and Simon (1993) explain that although conscious processing is not needed for understanding easy texts, more challenging texts require an active conscious processing on the part of the reader. Readers must be more active while integrating information from the text and their own prior knowledge. These steps in reading comprehension correspond to intermediate steps with heeded information and should be verbalised in concurrent reports.

Since many studies have conceptualised reading as a problem-solving strategic process (e.g., Olshavsky 1976/1977), it seems pertinent to quote Ericsson and Simon's (1984/1993) discussion concerning reports of problem-solving tasks. I will focus on two studies. Maier's (1931) retrospective study indicates that subjects who reported discovering the solution as a single step did not remember any hint that had helped them to solve the problem. However, all subjects who reported more than one step in the solution reported the hint. An interesting study was conducted by Durkin (1937), who investigated think-aloud reports of subjects solving block puzzles. The analysis revealed that although subjects only occasionally reported insights into the problem, it was always possible to infer the steps leading to the insightful ideas from the concurrent think-aloud protocols. Durkin concluded that the emergence of "out of the blue" insights is always preceded by either a gradual process or is determined by trial and error. I would argue that both of the studies described above show that although it may happen that subjects do not report insights into problems, the insights can be determined from the concurrent think-aloud data. This emphasises the importance of careful task (text) analysis and subsequent protocol analysis, which allows the inferring of subjects' comprehension processes. This discussion brings us to the next section, in which general specifications concerning the use of protocol analysis are delineated.

1.5. General methodological guidelines for think-aloud research

Every researcher wishing to apply protocol analysis should be aware of a number of factors that may influence his/her study. Afflerbach (2000) and Ericsson and Simon (1987) point to the intricacies of the method and the need to report and describe details concerning the use of the think-aloud methodology. Detailed description of subjects, texts, tasks assigned, transcription and coding procedures makes it possible to better understand the aims and the results of researchers. Careful reporting facilitates the comparison of think-aloud studies across different theoretical paradigms and develops an understanding of the research method. Afflerbach (2000: 171) provides a list of aspects of the verbal reporting and protocol analysis methodology that require detailed description. These aspects are presented Table II.1. below.

Table II.1. Aspects of verbal reporting to be considered in research design and reports

Aspect of Methodology	Representative Concerns
Subjects	Verbal ability Familiarity with the methodology Knowledge of text content and structure Relationship with researcher
Texts	Degree of intactness Difficulty or familiarity Mode of text presentation
Tasks	Influence of verbal reporting task on designated reading task Automatic or non-automatic processing Novelty of task Amount of text availability for previewing or rereading
Directions to subjects	Focus on specific or general reading strategies To read as one "normally reads"
Transcription process	Faithfulness of print to tape Status of nonverbal utterances Treatment of pause time
Selection of protocol excerpts	Representativeness and typicality
Categories used to score think-alouds	Relationship to previous research and theory
Coding of protocol excerpts	Reliability

Source: Afflerbach 2000: 171.

Special attention is required to describe factors that could influence the availability of information to report and reporting itself. To better understand what verbal reports reveal, it is of vital importance to report in detail the characteristics of reader-text interaction. Below, I present general guidelines for those who would like to apply this methodology in their research. The discussion is based mostly on Pressley and Afflerbach (1995), who draw on Ericsson and Simon's *Protocol Analysis: Verbal Reports as Data* from 1984 (revised in 1993), the standard reference on think-aloud methodology.

Of utmost importance is to specify what type of reading we want to investigate. People may read the same text in many different ways. Instructing subjects how to read the text by giving them a specific task, e.g., to summarise the text or to recall the text, will influence the depth and extent of their comprehension. Too open or too vague tasks may lead to a situation which may elicit inferences about processes instead of thinking aloud about the processes (Pressley and Afflerbach 1995).

Think-aloud data should reflect exactly what is being thought about. When instructing subjects to think aloud, it is important to inform them not to make their self-reports more coherent. It is the researcher's task to make inferences about the data and later describe the nature and process of this inferencing. It is worth remembering that incomplete verbalisations can be due to the fact that the self-reports were not concurrent, i.e., they did not reflect the information actually processed in the short-term memory during the task (Pressley and Afflerbach 1995).

Since protocol analysis is better suited to processes that have not been fully automatised (those that are still under conscious control), it is crucial to slow down the process of readers' attending to text. Text may be presented sentence by sentence or subjects may be asked to retrospect their thinking in response to some signal that interrupts their reading process. However, I would argue that while designing a think-aloud procedure, the researcher must consider the real aim of his/her study. Presenting a text sentence by sentence will not allow him/her to gain insight into a "natural" style of reading. In other words, it is necessary to consider the ecological validity of the study we plan to conduct. Ericsson (1988) warns researchers of the potential problems that their subjects may experience while reporting comprehension of texts. In his opinion, reports of continuous reading are of a retrospective character, i.e., subjects verbalise thoughts after having read parts of a text. Directing subjects to read and report sentence by sentence causes readers to produce richer protocols. In contrast to reports of sentence-by-sentence comprehension, verbalisations of comprehension of the whole text, because of more difficult access to the information to be reported, may be rather poor. Concurrent think-aloud protocols can make it difficult to observe and specify the process components of fluent comprehension. Ericsson concludes that to investigate fluent comprehension, the most useful research method would be to measure reading times. To monitor the comprehension of difficult texts, verbal-report methodology seems the most informative. Ericsson (1988: 321) explains that "[t]he verbal reports reveal the content or heeded information of thought sequences during text comprehension."

Prior to the study, subjects should be discouraged from explaining their processing. Ericsson and Simon (1980, 1984/1993) claim that providing an explanation of one's processing requires extra cognitive energy and can affect both concurrent and subsequent processing. Reports should focus on only the intermediate and final products of processing.

Directions given to subjects to think aloud can focus on different aspects of the think-aloud process, influencing thereby the process of verbalisation and the data obtained from subjects. Instructions "fulfil the role of a monitor in performing the tasks" Gabryś-Barker (2009: 28). Directions given to subjects to think aloud can be open ended or they can instruct readers to report a specific type of information that they keep in their working memory. Ericsson and Simon (1984/1993) see the advantages and disadvantages of each possibility. Open ended directions are likely to elicit naturalistic cognition. However, if this is not the aim of the research, leaving directions open ended may encourage subjects to report any and all information that they have in their short-term memory. Although this can provide rich data for theory building, the researcher can obtain information that is not of his/her primary interest. Specifying directions, on the other hand, can lead to bias processing. The awareness of the results of reporting can encourage subjects to overdo the task of attending to a specific type of data. The researchers claim that think-aloud directions should emphasise the importance of providing accurate self-reports. They even recommend making the agreement with subjects to be as accurate and honest as possible.

To facilitate verbalisations without any (or with minimal) reactive influences (see Note 2) on subjects' thinking, Ericsson and Simon (1998) recommend that subjects should be given a warm-up task, e.g., a mental multiplication (24 × 34). This can help students to practice direct expression of thought without monitoring their reports. Although, as numerous studies show, people do not require lengthy training to think aloud, it might be useful to remind subjects to think aloud during think-aloud tasks so that subjects continue to report (Pressley and Afflerbach 1995).

It is important that verbal self-reports be reliably codified. The bulk of think-aloud research has used a variety of a priori categories and induced categories (i.e., those produced on the basis of data provided from the reports). It is useful to remember that there are individual differences in thinking. Investigators should be careful not to generalise differences in thinking, particularly while analysing group data.

Ericsson (1988) emphasises the importance of a task analysis, particularly an analysis of the text used in the study. The researcher should be able to predict what processes participants of the study are likely to verbalise. In this way, he/she can check whether he/she really understands the processing that can occur in a particular task situation. It is vital to understand the specificity of the think-aloud task, the state of subjects' knowledge and skills as well as other factors that can influence the reading performance during reporting.

It may happen that the researcher experiences difficulty eliciting verbalisation from his/her subjects. It is worth considering factors that can make reports incomplete. Clear differences have been found (e.g., Shiffrin and Schneider 1977, cited in Ericsson and Simon 1980) between automatic and controlled processing. Ericsson and Simon (1980) claim that highly overlearned processes operate automatically and subjects are not aware of the intermediate stages of the process since these processes do not leave any trace in the STM. Another reason why subjects may stop verbalising or may start to verbalise incompletely is giving subjects tasks that overload their cognitive capacity. One example of such a task is asking subjects to explain or interpret their reports (which has been described above). Another explanation as to why subjects may produce incomplete reports may be that the information to be reported has already been transferred to the LTM and is difficult or impossible to be retrieved. Concluding, it is important to quote Ericsson and Simon (1980: 243), who emphasise that "[i]ncompleteness of reports may make some information unavailable, but it does not invalidate the information that is present."

It seems that the specifications presented above can undoubtedly help researchers to design sound think-aloud studies, securing the validity and reliability of their research attempts. The guidelines can also facilitate comparative analyses of think-aloud research.

Notes

1. It is not very clear what Ericsson means by normal reading. Ericsson (1988: 300) claims that this type of reading is a result of extensive practice and is characteristic of skilled readers. He also means reading texts that are well-formed, thus not presenting confusion to the reader. I would assume that he also means reading a continuous text, without any artificial pauses and tasks imposed from the outside, e.g., by the researcher. I think this concept of normal reading is similar to Carver's (1977) concept of rauding reading (see Part One, Chapter 2, Section 2.2.2.).
2. The question as to whether it is possible to think aloud without changing the course of thinking was the object of debate between Ericsson and Simon (1998) and Smagorinsky (1998), who wanted to use the method within the perspective of cultural-historical activity theory (CHAT). Drawing on Vygotsky (1962), Smagorinsky (1998, cited in Ericsson and Simon 1998: 178) claims that "verbalisation of thinking as speech is a process through which thinking reaches a new level of articulation" and questioned the validity of the method. In contrast, Ericsson and Simon (1998) explained circumstances under which subjects can think aloud without modifying their verbalisations.

2. A review of selected studies in the L1 reading context

Below, a review of empirical studies that focus on investigating text comprehension in the L1 context is presented. Although all the studies view reading as a cognitive process, they explore various aspects of reading comprehension. In the review, I focus on the symbiotic relationship of the think-aloud methodology and the aspects of reading the studies explore. I am particularly interested in how the studies conducted the protocol analysis and how this methodology facilitated the inquiry concerning reading. I also examine whether the think-aloud procedures applied in the studies managed to elicit the process of comprehension or simply subjects' efforts to overcome breakdowns in comprehension (the observation made by Ericsson 1988 in relation to think-aloud studies). The most important information concerning the studies is summarised in Table II.2.

Table II.2. Think-aloud text comprehension studies in the L1 context

Name	Type of text	Subjects	Aim	Results
Olshavsky 1976/1977; think-aloud protocols (partly retrospective)	short stories	24 American secondary school students	to identify strategies in relation to subjects' interest, reading proficiency and writing style	reading is a problem-solving process; strategy use depends on subjects' interest, reading proficiency and writing style
Collins, Brown and Larkin 1980; retrospection	five short but difficult-to-understand texts read to subjects	4 college students	to observe how subjects process texts and construct their own models of understanding	reading is an active process; skilled readers used a variety of strategies to construct a model that best fits the content of the text
Bereiter and Bird 1985; concurrent think-alouds	six 500-word passages	2 psychology students and 8 professionals	to investigate strategy use during reading	reading consists of elements which result from comprehension breakdowns; readers use a variety of strategies to cope with breakdowns in their comprehension
Baker (1986); immediate retrospection	two 800-word passages adapted from children's expository texts; each passage contained "problems"	primary school learners (10, 11 years old) and college students, identified as average and above-average readers	to identify standards applied by readers while evaluating comprehension	readers used a variety of different standards of evaluation, with mature readers using the whole array of standards
Lundeberg (1987); concurrent think-alouds and immediate retrospection	two three-page long legal cases	8 law professors, 2 attorneys, 10 students in fields beside law	to identify strategies used by expert and novice readers; to identify differences in strategy use between the two groups	expert readers demonstrated a better knowledge of the text type and law, and consequently greater flexibility in reading as well as a more critical approach to texts

Source: own study.

2.1. Reading as a problem-solving process

Olshavsky (1976/1977), in an often-quoted study, assumed that reading is a problem-solving process. Secondary school American students were instructed to read a short story silently. They stopped at each dot and talked about what happens in the story and about what they were doing and thinking as they read. The text was divided into clauses, at the end of which Olshavsky put a red dot. Olshavsky (1976/1977: 656) defined the strategy as "a purposeful means of comprehending the author's message." Strategy use was related to three factors: interest, reader proficiency and writing style (abstract or concrete). The following strategies were identified: **word related strategies** (e.g., use of context to define a word, synonym substitution); **clause related strategies** (e.g., inference, addition of information) and a **story-related strategy** – the use of information from a specific passage to develop an understanding of the whole story. The strategies identified were of two types: **problem identification** and **problem solving**. The findings led Olshavsky (1976/1977: 670) to the conclusion that "the types of strategies that were identified lend support to a theoretical position that reading is a problem solving process." As regards the three factors affecting reading behaviour, the findings indicate that readers tend to apply more strategies when they are interested in the text, when they are proficient readers and when they read abstract material. The greatest use of an inference strategy was observed among subjects who read abstract style material.

2.2. Reading as a process of constructing a text model

Collins, Brown and Larkin (1980) assumed that reading comprehension does not entail simply making sequential connections between events in the text but, as Bransford and Johnson (1973) suggest, constructing a complex model which is revised and evaluated during reading. The researchers read five difficult-to-understand short texts to four college students and asked the subjects to retrospect on how they had constructed their comprehension. In the interpretations of the protocols, the researchers applied their progressive-refinement theory of text understanding, which draws on the principles of means-ends analysis (see Note 1) as well as model-based views of inferences (see Part 1, Chapter 3, Section 3.1.2.).

While analysing the protocols, the researchers found evidence that the main aim of inferences is not to search for relations between text propositions (which is a claim of a text-based view of inference) but "to synthesise an underlying model, which organises and augments the surface structure fragments in the text" (Collins, Brown and Larkin 1980: 386). The researchers observed how subjects gradually refined their initial model of the text, a partial model formed from schemata activated by the first elements in the text. When readers proceeded in their reading, each new piece of information was assimilated to their initial models. When new information could not be assimilated, the model was restructured. The investigators claim that in the construction of their models readers attempted to answer a number of questions. Answering these questions led to a refinement of the model but also constrained the answers to other questions. The process which facilitates convergence on a model involves constraint satisfaction (Bobrow and Brown 1975), a heuristic omnipresent in human problem solving.

Subjects used the following strategies to revise their models:

- **rebinding**, which in simple terms means keeping most of the model constructed up to some point and changing only the last variable bound;
- **questioning a default interpretation**, i.e., realising that the interpretation readers accepted is wrong;
- **near** or **distant shift of focus**, which helps readers to see the same issue from a new perspective and start to build his/her representation of the text from a different angle;
- **case analysis**, i.e., a systematic process of considering all possible interpretations.

Subjects used the following strategies to evaluate the plausibility of the models they constructed while attempting to understand the texts:

- testing the plausibility of the assumptions and consequences of the model;
- considering the completeness of the model;
- evaluating the interconnectedness of the model, i.e., checking whether assumptions are supported by other parts of the model;
- evaluating the match of the model to the text, i.e., how well the model matched particular aspects of the text.

The results showed that although students check different elements of the model against each other, in order to accept the model they need to evaluate positively not only its parts but the whole model.

The results of the study showed that comprehension is an active process. Readers apply a variety of strategies to revise and evaluate different models, which finally leads to the construction of a model that "best accounts for the events described in the text" (Collins, Brown and Larkin 1980: 385).

2.3. Evaluating text understanding

In order to investigate how readers monitor comprehension, Baker (1985) proposed an interesting framework for conceptualizing the standards that readers use to evaluate their understanding. Seven different standards, each contributing to comprehension, were identified: (1) the **lexical standard** involving checking that the meaning of an individual word is understood; (2) the **syntactic standard** allowing one to evaluate the grammaticality of a sentence or phrase; (3) the **internal consistency standard** entailing checking that the ideas expressed in the text are logically consistent with one another; (4) the **external consistency standard** involving verifying that the facts presented in the text are true and consistent with respect to what one already knows; (5) the **propositional** (see Note 2) **cohesiveness standard**, which means checking that there is a cohesive relationship among propositions sharing a local context; (6) the **structural cohesiveness standard**, which involves evaluating the thematic compatibility of the ideas in a paragraph or text; and (7) the **informational completeness standard**, which enables the reader to check that the text provides all of the information necessary for full understanding.

Baker (1986, cited in Baker 1996) compared the effects of instruction, developmental level and reading ability on comprehension evaluation. The subjects in the study were primary school learners (10 and 11 years old) and college students, identified as average and above-average readers. They were asked to read two 800-word passages adapted from children's expository texts. Each passage contained problems that could be detected if readers applied the corresponding standards of evaluation. Half of the participants were told that the passages could be difficult to understand. The other half received specific instructions concerning the seven types of problems they would find in the passages.

The results showed that students who had received specific instructions identified more problems than those receiving general instructions. In addition, skilled readers identified more problems than less skilled readers; this was true even at the college level. Adults identified more problems than the children. The 10- and 11-year-old learners performed at comparable levels.

The study observed that readers had used a variety of different standards of evaluation, with most of the mature readers using all seven. The researcher found that all students, both children and adults, enriched an extent of standards and used them more effectively when given specific instructions to do so. It was encouraging to observe that both skilled and less skilled readers benefited equally from the instruction.

2.4. Strategies used by expert readers

Bereiter and Bird (1985) instructed expert readers (university students) to read aloud six difficult and ambiguous passages of text: an exposition, description, narration, personal opinion, discussion of controversy and the description of a process. The aim of the study was to identify on-line strategies, i.e., those used during the actual course of initial reading and then to teach them to less proficient readers.

To understand their study better, it is important to look at how the researchers define an online strategy. Following a cognitive perspective on reading, Bereiter and Bird (1985: 133) view strategies as "procedures for heuristic search through a space of possible text interpretations." They agree with Pearson, Hansen and Gordon (1979), who emphasising the role of readers' domain knowledge assume that fluent comprehension in a familiar domain involves mostly recognition and does not necessarily require using strategies. Bereiter and Bird strongly claim that strategies may be needed only when difficulties in comprehension occur due to insufficient domain knowledge and/or ambiguities in the text. Thus, they view think-aloud protocols as reports of mostly those elements of reading which result from comprehension breakdowns, those moments that are brought to consciousness and thereby can be reported. The researchers conclude that these observable behaviours caused by comprehension difficulties may be the most teachable.

It is useful to discuss the criteria the researchers accepted to describe behaviours they observed as teachable strategies. They drew on Newell and Simon's (1972) human problem-solving theory and decided to treat strategies as condition-action pairs. In their analysis, they specified both a set of conditions and a set of actions that readers must take to meet the conditions. For example, the strategy of restatement is defined by the condition of encountering unfamiliar expressions and the action of rephrasing by means of inferred equivalents. Bereiter and Bird claim that in strategy instruction it is vital to teach learners both to recognise conditions and to take appropriate actions.

It is interesting to note how careful the researchers were in distinguishing strategic from non-strategic behaviours. For example, they did not decide to classify predicting, imagery and recall of related information as evidence of strategic behaviour. They explained that the protocols from their study did not provide enough data to label prediction and imagery as strategies; quite the contrary, Bereiter and Bird argued that as routine activities they do not show any trace of purposeful strategic behaviour and may even impede comprehension. Similarly, the researchers warned that a single example of activating relevant prior knowledge may be of an automatic character and may not be related to attempts to solve comprehension problems.

The following four types of behaviour were identified and labelled as strategies: **restatement**, e.g., rephrasing the text to make it simpler; **backtracking**, e.g., re-reading the preceding text; **demanding relationships**, i.e., responses to missing information by asking questions and looking for links between topics; **problem formulation**, e.g., identifying comprehension problems and engaging in active problem solving. The researchers taught learners all the four strategies. The findings indicated that the strategy of demanding relationships proved to be the most difficult to teach.

2.5. Differences between expert and novice readers

Lundeberg (1987) investigated the reading strategies used by 10 expert lawyers and 10 novice volunteers in reading legal cases. The main purpose of the study was to identify the differences between strategies applied by the two groups and then teach the strategies used by experts to law students. After they finished reading, the subjects were asked a few questions that Lundeberg would normally ask when teaching first-year law students. Behaviours that seemed to be purposeful facilitators of understanding and which occurred in at least 20% of protocols were named strategies (see Note 3). The analysis revealed the following comprehension strategies: **use of context**; **overviewing the text** (applied before subjects become engaged in more careful reading, e.g., to estimate the length of the text, to mark the key words); **rereading analytically**, i.e., selective rereading, e.g., to check facts; **underlining** during the first reading; **synthesising**, e.g., facts and speculating on alternative outcomes of the cases presented in the texts; **evaluating** the quality of the judge's decision and stating whether one agrees or disagrees with this decision.

Below, I provide a table in which several examples of the differences found between the expert and novice subjects of the study are presented.

Table II.3. Differences between expert and novice readers of English as L1

Strategy	Expert readers	Novice readers
Use of context	Before reading they identified the type of text (i.e., a contracts case) and parties involved in the case.	They ignored the case title and consequently the parties involved in the case.
Overviewing the text	They previewed the text by "flipping to the end." Most of them marked the key words in the text. They stopped to summarise the facts and drew a diagram of the suit.	Only 4 out of 10 readers overviewed the length of the text, flipping to the end of the case did not help them a lot. None of the novice readers marked the key words in the case.
Rereading analytically	Both groups of readers used these strategies, although experts used them more frequently.	
Underlining	This strategy was used equally frequently by both groups.	
Synthesising	They demonstrated the ability of tying together the facts into a cohesive whole as well as the ability to infer from the text alternative legal situations.	They focused on only one element of the case, which resulted in less cohesive discussion; none of them inferred alternative legal situations from the case presented in the text.
Evaluating	They were more critical about the judge's decisions, showing an awareness of the judicial decision process.	They did not evaluate the judge's decisions, assuming that the law is not to be questioned.

Source: own study based on Lundeberg (1987).

Other differences concern the allocation of time during reading. Experts, unlike novices, spent more time on overviewing the text and reading the first page. This helped them to become acquainted with the structure and content of the texts, and adjust their reading rate in the further part of the task. In fact, expert readers showed greater flexibility in reading; they recognised parts of the text which contained irrelevant details. Lundeberg (1987: 417) concluded that "[l]ike experts in other studies (Berliner 1986), these experts were slower in the initial stages of their problem solving." Novice and expert readers differed in reference to their perceptions of their comprehension process. Novice readers often expressed dissatisfaction with their comprehension of the text. Most of them attributed their difficulties to themselves, e.g., their reading skills or concentration, rather than to the text. In contrast, expert readers rarely showed discomfort caused by comprehension problems.

2.6. A summary of research findings

In the section below, I focus on the studies reviewed earlier. For each study, I analyse how a think-aloud procedure applied in the study seems to influence the findings. I am particularly interested in the ecological validity of the studies, i.e., in the extent to which the conditions simulated in the studies reflect real life reading. Then, I discuss the conception of reading that each of the studies seems to elucidate, e.g., the aspects of reading emphasised. I also highlight the results that I find the most illuminating for reading instruction purposes.

Olshavsky (1976/1977)

Following strategy research on problem solving (Newell and Simon 1972) and reading (H. Clark 1975), Olshavsky identified strategies American students used while reading a short story. The results confirmed her assumption that reading is a problem-solving problem. As regards the ecological validity of the study, the use of a short story seems a good choice. However, asking readers to stop reading after every clause made it impossible to elicit and investigate the "whole" authentic process of comprehension. Observing how subjects read separate clauses slowed down the reading process (and made it more reportable) but we may assume that this procedure did not elicit a whole range of strategies that would have been used, had students been allowed to read as they normally read. The strategies the researcher identified were classified into problem identification and problem solving, which supports the theoretical framework accepted prior to the study. The other classification of strategies, i.e., into word-, clause- and story-related, seems to be a result of the way students were instructed to read the text, i.e., stopping after every clause. Dividing the text into clauses and observing how subjects read the text chunk by chunk highlighted the three aspects of text processing mentioned above. This shows how the type of a think-aloud method used in the study can influence the process of analysis and the interpretation of the results. As regards reading instruction, the result that I find most informative for teaching is the conclusion that readers infer more when they read abstract style text and that they use more strategies when they find texts more interesting.

Collins, Brown and Larkin (1980)

The study of Collins, Brown and Larkin is of particular interest to my reading comprehension research. Their study is an illustration of the authors' progressive-refinement theory of text understanding, whose principles draw on human problem-solving theories (Bobrow and Brown 1975; Newell and Simon 1963). Subjects listened to five authentic texts and were asked to retrospect on how they had constructed their comprehension, what problems they had encountered and what hypotheses they had made. This uninterrupted process of comprehension seems a real-life task, which indicates the study's relatively high degree of ecological validity. However, the fact that subjects listened to the texts (i.e., they were not exposed to texts in their written form) raises some doubts about the validity of the research. This procedure allowed the investigators to focus on only the higher levels of text processing, i.e., comprehension, excluding lower-level aspects of text processing, such as decoding. In fact, both the theoretical assumptions accepted before the study and the conclusions drawn from the study did not account for any aspects of lower-level text processing. For example, the protocols indicated that when encountering difficulty connected with particular words in the text, the subjects did not use strategies, such as guessing the meanings of words to connect events in a sentence but instead focussed on generating the understanding of words that best fit slots in the network of their model. Every effort made by the reader did not aim to understand separate successive sentences in the text, as was the case in Olshavsky's research, but to construct a representation of the whole text.

It is worth noting that because of the lack of focus on lower-level text processing, the choice of procedure seems appropriate for the purpose of the study, i.e., investigating how L1 readers construct a representation of the text. However, applying the same procedure to explore FL reading comprehension could produce a false, incomplete picture of reading.

This study offers important teaching implications. The researchers observed that their students asked a variety of questions while developing their models of texts. However, the protocols the students produced did not allow the investigators to explain what helped the readers to ask the right questions. Finding the answer to this question would be critical for teaching purposes.

Baker (1986)

Unlike Olshavsky (1976/1977) or Collins, Brown and Larkin (1980), Baker focuses on a more narrow aspect of reading comprehension, i.e., ability to evaluate text comprehension. To investigate this ability, the researcher accepted the view of reading as problem solving. Baker modified 800-word texts, introduced in the texts "problem" areas and asked her subjects to identify and explain them. This procedure made the reading task semi-authentic. Although subjects were asked to read complete texts and were free to read the texts as they liked, they were warned about possible problems in understanding texts, which could have influenced the way they read. The most valuable finding contributing to our understanding of reading is the list of standards Baker used to measure her subjects' reading skills. This framework of standards shows that the ability to evaluate comprehension operates on both lower- and higher-level components of reading, i.e., word, syntax and meaning level. Evaluating comprehension involves checking both internal and external consistency, i.e., evaluating relationships among propositions within a local context, e.g., a paragraph as well as checking the integration of text information with one's prior knowledge. As to its teaching implications, the study emphasises the role of instruction in developing evaluation skills. Baker shows that this ability develops with practice and is a factor distinguishing skilled from less skilled readers.

Bereiter and Bird (1985)

This study is interesting because of the way it defines a strategy. The investigators were very careful while classifying their subjects' behaviours as strategies. They did not label certain behaviours as strategic, e.g., they claimed that the prediction and imagery they observed in the protocols seemed automatic and were not purposeful enough to name them as strategies. Bereiter and Bird provide a good example for those who wish to investigate reading strategies. It shows that a clear definition of the construct of a study can increases the validity of the study and facilitates a comparison of the study with similar studies.

Another aspect of the study I find particularly revealing is the researchers' conclusion regarding reading instruction. Out of the four strategies they attempted to teach, the strategy of demanding relationships in the text was found the least teachable. The researchers did not find it surprising that the most sophisticated strategy was the most difficult to teach. Drawing on Newell and Simon's (1972) problem-solving theory and viewing strategies as condition-action pairs, the experimenters specified the condition that learners would have to recognise before applying this strategy. The application of this strategy requires recognising "specific informational lacks in order to be able to formulate appropriate *wh*-questions" (Bereiter and Bird 1985: 150). Bereiter and Bird, just like Collins, Brown and Larkin (1980), call attention to learners' ability to ask questions as a crucial element of proficient readers' competence.

Lundeberg (1987)

Lundeberg's study seems unique. All the subjects were put into the role of teacher assistants. They were asked to demonstrate how they read legal texts so that the experimenter could prepare a more efficient reading course for her law students. This made the task very authentic. The analysis of protocols revealed the strategies of using context, overviewing the text, rereading analytically, underlining, synthesising and evaluating – strategies identified also in other studies. The novelty of this research lies in the differences between novice and expert readers that the study underscores. Expert readers were more successful in integrating facts from the text into a cohesive whole and demonstrated a more critical approach to the text content. Another interesting observation is that experts were slower at the initial stages of reading, i.e., overviewing the case and reading the first page. An encouraging conclusion concerning reading instruction is that the strategies identified in the study turned out to be teachable.

2.7. Conclusions – reading in L1

The review shows that protocol analysis proved successful in eliciting many aspects of reading ability, not just readers' attempts to cope with comprehension breakdowns. Below, I look at the relationship between the TA methodology and the results the studies produce. In the next section, I discuss the view of reading that the studies seem to create.

2.7.1. The relationship between the think-aloud method and reading

The survey of think-aloud studies presented above shows the "symbiotic" relationship between the think-aloud method and the construct this methodology explores – reading. The studies applied various procedures. Differences referred to verbal reporting tasks, the degree of intactness of texts and the mode of text presentation. They are presented below.

Table II.4. The relationship between the think-aloud procedure and reading as investigated in the L1 reading context

Think-aloud procedure	Examples of studies
Verbal reporting tasks	reading aloud a text (Bereiter and Bird 1985) vs. silent reading (Lundeberg 1987) reading texts in an uninterrupted way and reporting on one's comprehension concurrently (Bereiter and Bird 1985) vs. stopping at the end of every sentence and reporting retrospectively (Olshavsky 1976/1977)
Degree of intactness of texts	reading complete unmodified texts (Lundeberg 1987) vs. reading texts with "problem" areas, identifying and explaining those areas (Baker 1986)
Mode of text presentation	reading texts vs. listening to texts (Collins, Brown and Larkin 1980)

Source: own study.

In all the studies, the think-aloud method seems appropriate for research purposes. Let us look at how the studies capitalised on the potential of the think-aloud methodology. Collins, Brown and Larkin (1980) exposed subjects to the oral version of texts, eliciting uninterrupted retrospective understanding of complete texts. This procedure created an excellent opportunity to observe how readers utilise information from texts and, driven by their prior knowledge, revise and evaluate their understandings of the text in the form of a model. This methodology "suits" the theory which serves as a framework for the study (the authors' progressive-refinement theory of text, which is a model-based view of reading). An oral presentation of texts to subjects induced the construction of a situation model representation of text, rather than a propositional representation (van Dijk and Kintsch 1983). It created an opportunity to observe readers who "do not simply connect the events in the text into a sequential structure. [But rather] they seem to create a complex scenario or model within which the events described might plausibly occur" (Bransford and Johnson 1973, cited in Collins, Brown and Larkin 1980: 385). It is worth noting that theories concerning inferencing point to the difference between a propositional representation and a mental model representation of text. Research (e.g., Jenkin *et al.* 1993) suggests that texts can be comprehended in two different manners: reading in L1 may result in creating a mental model representation of the text, while reading in L2 only in the construction of a propositional representation. I think that the technique applied in this study could have brought different results, had the aim of the study been reading in L2.

Baker (1986, cited in Baker 1996) investigated how readers monitor their comprehension. Preparing a passage with difficult-to-understand parts and asking subjects to identify these areas was a suitable choice to observe this aspect of metacognition.

Let us now compare the results of the study that applied a rather artificial technique of stopping reading at the end of clauses (Olshavsky 1976/1977) with the findings of the research in which readers were asked to read texts as they would normally have read (Lundeberg 1987). Also in these studies there is a noticeable link between the research method applied and what this method elicits. In the protocols which recorded clause-after-clause reading, Olshavsky identified three types of strategies: those related to word, clause and story. Slowing down the process of reading and dividing readers' text processing into clause-protocols shed light on these three levels of text comprehension. However, it is important to emphasise that although 9 strategies were identified within the word and clause types, only one of a very general nature within the story level was noted. The clause-by-clause technique did not manage to elicit behaviours reflecting text processing at a higher level, i.e., the discourse level. In contrast, Lundeberg's (1987) procedure is less structured, but more natural. Students were asked to read complete, unmodified texts; during the session the subjects were asked questions which were adjusted to their individual behaviours. This unstructured procedure yielded protocols which reflect strategies that readers used at all levels of text processing. For example, the researcher identified a word-level strategy of contextually defining words and a clause-level strategy of adding information. The bulk of strategies identified by Lundeberg is related to coping with a more global context, e.g., overviewing the text, synthesising to connect facts into a cohesive whole. As the only researcher in this overview, Lundeberg identified a group of strategies referring to readers' abilities to critically evaluate the facts and opinions presented in the text. It seems that this whole-text-based think-aloud procedure elicited a wide range of behaviours and enabled the researcher to identify a rich list of differences between novice and expert readers. An interesting finding is that expert readers "flip to the end of the text to preview the text" – a strategy impossible to elicit in a sentence-by-sentence procedure.

The discussion presented above has demonstrated how each study investigated reading in L1 and what methodology it used. It appears that various ways of organising think-aloud tasks have created various research conditions, which have allowed the researchers to investigate various aspects of reading. This has illustrated the potential of protocol analysis as a method providing a rich source of evidence and offering ample research possibilities.

2.7.2. The view of reading and the reader created by the studies

The next issue I discuss is the view of reading all the protocol analyses seem to develop. All the studies analysed above assume that reading resembles a problem-solving activity. Readers aim to understand the text but in this task they encounter difficulties – problems. Readers attempt to solve problems related to both a local context (the word- and clause-levels of text processing) and a more global context (the whole text-level). They experience difficulty in understanding the meaning of unknown words or the grammaticality of a sentence as well as comprehending facts presented in a paragraph or the whole text. To solve these problems, readers apply a variety of strategies. They use context to define unknown words, search for synonyms, reread, rephrase to make the text simpler and infer. They know what to do when they cannot comprehend the ideas conveyed in the text. They ask questions to link text ideas with one another and draw on their background knowledge to check whether these ideas are consistent with what they know about the topic. Sometimes readers do not succeed after the first trial. Asking the wrong questions about the text may lead to constructing a series of intermediate incomplete versions of understanding. The process of reaching the final stage of comprehension is similar to constructing a model of text. It is a data-driven process, which means that readers draw on the information given in the text and their prior knowledge.

Based on problem-solving theories, the studies offer insights into how skilled readers differ from less skilled ones. Good readers seem to use more strategies than poor readers. Skilled readers have sufficient language proficiency; they plan their reading, e.g., they prefer to spend more time at the beginning of their reading to overview the text. They are flexible and adjust their reading rate, recognising parts of text which contain irrelevant details. They use efficient monitoring skills, i.e., they check the logic and consistency of the model they develop and evaluate the effectiveness of their actions. They read critically, i.e., they evaluate facts and opinions from the text and are able to suggest alternative versions of the text message. They know how to draw on their prior knowledge related to the text form; they recognise a type of text and predict from text structure. They are careful while using their knowledge on the topic of the text; they integrate it with the knowledge presented in the text.

As regards reading instruction, the studies imply an encouraging conclusion that strategies are teachable. It is possible to improve readers' evaluating skills; readers can be taught how to identify comprehension problems and to engage in active problem solving. Learners can also develop the strategies of rephrasing the text to make it simpler. However, the skill that proved the most difficult to teach is being aware of gaps in one's understanding – an important aspect of metacognition and looking for links between topics – an ability that is an example of higher-level text processing.

The studies also point to the relationship between strategies and other learner factors, e.g., reader interest and the style of text. Texts evaluated as interesting elicit more strategies, which seems to imply that readers are cognitively more active while coping with such texts. Abstract texts require more inferencing – the observation indicating that abstract material is a more demanding problem to solve. These findings can prove useful in designing reading instruction.

The overview of the reading studies based on problem-solving theories described in this chapter points to a number of merits of this type of research. The conceptualisation of reading as problem solving has allowed the researchers to:

- identify reading strategies used in various types of texts, e.g., expository, descriptive and written in an abstract style;
- investigate strategies in relation to reading proficiency and reader interest;
- examine differences between skilled and less skilled readers;
- explore the possibility of teaching less skilled readers strategies used by more skilled readers and finding out which of the identified strategies may prove most difficult to teach.

I think that the advantages enumerated above seem encouraging and can inspire more research into L1 reading.

Notes

1. Means-ends analysis is a technique that was first used in Newell and Simon's (1963) model of problem solving. Solving a problem involves first defining the difference between the current state and the goal state, and gradually reducing differences between the two states. It is crucial to consider at every step in this process the means that one has at his/her disposal to achieve the goals. This helps one to define and achieve intermediate states (subgoals) that bring him/her closer to the goal state, i.e., the solution of his/her problem.
2. It is not clear what Baker (1985) means by propositions. Most probably they define propositions as "ideas that can be expressed in words, not the words themselves" (McNamara, Miller and Bransford 1991). See Part 1, Chapter 3, Section 3.1.1. for more information about proposition-based models of reading.
3. Although Lundeberg called the strategies described in the study as metacognitive, in my review I have deliberately avoided calling these strategies "metacognitive." In my opinion, the strategies the researchers identified are mainly cognitive, i.e. they are an integral part of task performance (as defined by O'Malley and Chamot 1990).

3. A review of selected studies in the FL/L2 reading context

In this chapter, several studies that explore reading in FL/L2 are discussed. The studies investigate various aspects of FL/L2 reading, which is indicated in the titles of the subchapters. The most important information concerning the studies is summarised in Table II.5.

Table II.5. Think-aloud text comprehension studies in the FL context

Name	Type of text	Subjects	Aim	Results
Hosenfeld (1977, 1979, 1984); concurrent think-alouds, immediate and delayed retrospection	a learning task	40 American students of French, Spanish and German (1977, 1984); one American student of French as FL (1979)	to compare strong and weak readers' behaviours (1977, 1984); to observe the effect of reading instruction on readers' performance (1984)	strong and weak readers read differently; reading instruction proved effective
Berman (1984); sentence-by-sentence think-alouds	two paragraphs of complex syntax from an academic article	20 Hebrew-speaking undergraduate students of EFL	to find out whether "language" or "conceptual" difficulty makes reading in EFL difficult for students	students' difficulty in reading was caused by syntactic, rather than lexical or conceptual factors
Zupnik (1985); think alouds*	not given	2 intermediate EFL students: a strong reader and a weak reader	to compare the strategies used by a strong and a weak reader	the weak reader used more strategies and a larger variety of strategies; strategies used by the weak reader and the strong reader were of a different type
Block (1986); concurrent think-alouds and immediate retrospection	two texts from a psychology textbook	college EFL students: 3 native speakers of Chinese and 3 native speakers of Spanish	to identify strategies used by non-proficient EFL readers;	the following were identified: extensive and reflexive approaches to text, general comprehension and local linguistic strategies and "integrating" and "non-integrating" readers

Name	Type of text	Subjects	Aim	Results
Yang (2002); concurrent think-alouds and immediate retrospection	a short 200-word text from a college-level textbook	6 strong and 6 weak FL readers (Chinese native speakers	to compare comprehension monitoring of strong and weak readers; to observe teacher instruction on students' monitoring	better readers operated at higher levels of comprehension monitoring; less able readers' monitoring was limited to lexical and syntactic levels; all subjects benefited from instruction

* this sign means that it is not possible to specify the kind of think-aloud procedure used in the study

Source: own study.

3.1. FL/L2 readers' approach to the text

Block (1986), drawing on Thorndike (1917), assumed that reading is a problem-solving activity and readers use a variety of strategies to find their way in the text. She investigated the comprehension strategies used by non-proficient EFL college students: 3 native speakers of Chinese and 3 native speakers of Spanish read two English texts from a psychology textbook. For one text, the subjects were instructed to read silently and after each sentence to say what they were thinking when they read and what they did not understand. For the other text, the students reported on the process of their comprehension after they had read the whole paragraph. Thereby, both concurrent and retrospective TA protocols were obtained. Reports were classified according to the mode of response (extensive and reflexive) and strategy type. In the **reflexive mode**, readers approached the text affectively and personally, and focused more on their thoughts than on the information in the text. Reflexive readers responded in the first or second person. In the **extensive mode**, readers tried to understand the message expressed by the author without relating the text to their feelings. They responded in the third person.

The strategies were divided into two types: general comprehension and local linguistic. **General comprehension strategies** included comprehension-gathering and comprehension-monitoring strategies. General comprehension strategies included, e.g., anticipating content, integrating information, interpreting the text, using general knowledge or monitoring comprehension. **Local linguistic strategies** aimed to solve specific language problems; they involved, e.g., paraphrasing, rereading, solving vocabulary problems. It was interesting to observe that all local strategies occurred in the extensive mode.

Apart from identifying and describing strategies, Block measured the amount of time subjects spent on the think-aloud task and on each instance of strategy use. This allowed her to prepare timelines which showed the patterns within the process of comprehension of individual readers. Block distinguished two patterns of strategy use: one that she called "**integrators**" and the other – "**non-integrators**." The first group approached the text in the extensive mode (i.e., comprehended the text without relating the message to themselves). Students showed an awareness of text structure and monitored their understanding successfully. When expressing personal experiences, they linked them with the information in the text so that a connected version of the text was constructed. Non-integrators, in contrast, relied much more on their thoughts and experiences and failed to connect them with the text message. Block seems to agree with Stanovich (1980), who claims that personal associations during reading may serve a compensatory function.

3.2. Strategies used by successful and unsuccessful readers

Hosenfeld (1977, cited in Cohen and Hosenfeld 1981) looked at the behaviours of successful and unsuccessful readers. The subjects were 20 students who scored high on a reading proficiency test and 20 students who scored low on this test. All subjects were American students attending French, Spanish and German classes. The findings showed that the two groups of readers use different strategies to understand texts. **Successful readers** read in broad phrases, remember the meaning of the sentences they have read, ignore unessential words and use context to guess the meaning of new words. **Unsuccessful readers** read word-by-word, tend to forget the meaning of sentences as soon as they decode them, rarely skip words that are not essential for understanding and prefer to check the meaning of unknown words in a dictionary. For the sake of clarity, Hosenfeld (1977) presented the results of her research in the form of "reading maps," which effectively portrayed the differences between the two types of readers. Further analysis of the above described protocols led Hosenfeld (1984) to identify the following strategies of successful reading: identifying the grammatical category of words, sensitivity to a different word order in FL, examining illustrations, paying attention to the title and using it to make inferences, using orthographic information (e.g., capitalisation), referring to the side gloss, using the glossary as a last resort, looking up words correctly, continuing after the unsuccessful decoding of a word or phrase, recognising cognates, using knowledge of the world, going on with a proposed solution to a problem and evaluating guesses.

Hosenfeld conducted a few studies which aimed to check whether it is possible to teach an unsuccessful reader strategies of successful reading. In one of them (Hosenfeld 1979, cited in Hosenfeld 1984), a 14-year-old girl learning French as FL was first shown a protocol of a successful reader and asked to compare her reading with that from the verbal report. Then, she practised new reading strategies. The girl improved her style of reading and began to apply a number of successful reading strategies. However, there were strategies she did not manage to learn. These were: identifying the grammatical function of words, skipping inessential words and changing the form of words, e.g., verbs, before looking them up in a glossary.

Zupnik (1985, cited in Cohen 1986) compared two intermediate EFL readers, a strong one and a weak one. In the analysis of the moves (i.e., strategies) used by the readers, the researcher applied Sarig's (1987) taxonomy (described in Section 4.4. below). The results revealed that the weak reader used more moves and a larger variety of moves than the strong one. This seemed to contradict Olshavsky's findings that stronger readers use more strategies. However, a closer analysis showed that most of the moves used by the weak reader were clarification and simplification (e.g., the analysis of vocabulary), whereas most of the moves applied by the strong one were monitoring moves (e.g., the ability to identify failure in comprehension). Moreover, most of the strong reader's moves were comprehension-promoting, while most of the weak reader's moves deterred comprehension.

3.3. Monitoring comprehension by proficient and less proficient readers

Yang (2002) aimed to compare comprehension monitoring of proficient and less proficient FL readers as well as to observe the influence of teacher intervention on subjects' comprehension monitoring. The researcher defines comprehension monitoring not as strategies or skills but as a general competence or higher-level ability which controls readers' understanding and enables them to use specific monitoring strategies. After a think-aloud session, the subjects were asked to answer a set of multiple choice questions without referring to the text. Five days after the main experiment, the subjects were asked to read and evaluate their protocols.

To analyse the subjects' protocols, a taxonomy of evaluation standards proposed by Baker (1985, cited in Baker 1996) was used; Yang calls them levels of cognitive process in comprehension monitoring. (All the seven standards are presented in Chapter 2, Section 2.3. in this part). The levels of monitoring adapted from Baker (1985, cited in Baker 1996) showed how the lexical and syntactic levels were utilised to monitor the lexical and syntactic comprehension of the text. They also indicated how the other levels were used to integrate this linguistic knowledge with the subject's prior knowledge internal and external to the text. Thus, Yang (2002: 16) concluded that "[t]he emergence of higher standards of comprehension monitoring follows the comprehension of a large portion of the text at the lexical and syntactic levels." To achieve higher levels of comprehension of the text, it is necessary to operate at a higher level of comprehension monitoring.

The results indicated that both proficient and less proficient subjects could monitor their comprehension. The better readers operated more frequently at the higher levels of comprehension monitoring and seemed to monitor their on-line reading retrospectively. For example, although they were not able to grasp the meaning of certain words as they appeared in the text, they managed to successfully "guess" what the words mean as they progressed to the end of the text. In contrast, the less able readers' monitoring was limited to the lexical and syntactic levels. The author of the study attributed it to the readers' poor language knowledge and inability to integrate it with their prior knowledge related to the text.

As regards the second part of the study, i.e., the instruction session, the results showed that all the subjects benefited from teacher intervention. All the readers began to apply a richer repertoire of cognitive levels; even the less proficient readers got engaged in the levels other than the two most basic ones, i.e., lexical and syntactic. The reading teacher directed the subjects' monitoring, helped them to distinguish relevant from irrelevant information as well as prompted them to evaluate their interpretations of words.

3.4. Factors that make texts difficult to read

Berman (1984) conducted an informal study with her students at Tel Aviv University. The material for the study was taken from the academic text her students found difficult. The main aim was to find out what factors made the text difficult: linguistic or conceptual. Subjects read the passage sentence-by-sentence, explaining what they had not understood. To explain unclear aspects of the text, students resorted to translating sentences into Hebrew; in some sentences they were asked by the researcher to reword the sentence or indicate the subject and main verb. The analysis of students' protocols revealed a number of sources of difficulty caused by syntactic, rather than lexical or conceptual, factors. Berman identified areas of difficulty which in many cases were attributed to differences between Hebrew and English grammar. For example, subjects were confused by the deletion of grammatical markers or lack of overt pronominalisation of the complex subject in the sentence they read.

3.5. Conclusions – reading in FL/L2

In this section, the following questions are answered:

- What are the differences between skilled and less skilled readers?
- What is the conception of FL reading depicted by the studies and is this picture similar to the one implied by L1 reading research?

At the end, the TA methodology used in the studies is discussed. In this section, the terms "skilled," "strong," "successful" and "good" are used interchangeably.

3.5.1. Skilled vs. less skilled FL/L2 readers

Strategies used by strong and weak readers were investigated by Block (1986), Hosenfeld (1977, 1984), Yang (2002) and Zupnik (1985). Hosenfeld managed to identify strategies that distinguish successful from unsuccessful readers. Successful readers apply a range of strategies related to lower-level processing: they identify the grammatical category of words, show sensitivity to a different word order in FL, use orthographic information, decode word meaning correctly, read in broad phrases, recognise cognates and skip irrelevant words. They also use the following higher-level strategies: paying attention to the title and illustrations and using them to make inferences as well as using knowledge of the world. Hosenfeld laid emphasis on the role of memory in reading – successful readers remember the meaning of a phrase or sentence they decode, in contrast to unsuccessful readers, who tend to forget the meaning of a chunk of language as soon as they decode it. This shows that successful readers are better at word recognition and consequently read more fluently.

Zupnik's (1985) research confirms Hosenfeld's (1977) findings. She implies that weak readers use more clarification and simplification moves (those operating at the lower level of text comprehension), whereas strong readers – more monitoring moves (which are examples of higher-level reading strategies). Similarly, Berman's (1984) research underlined the role of lower levels of text processing. She identified syntactic factors as potential sources of FL reading difficulty.

Block (1986) highlights the role of background knowledge in reading. In her study, the most successful readers seemed to be so called Integrators responding to text in the extensive mode. This means that they concentrated on comprehending the ideas conveyed by the author of the text they read, rather than on relating the text to their personal experiences. When they made associations while reading, they integrated this information to the information in the text. In contrast, less successful readers, Nonintegrators, responded in the reflexive mode. They related text message to their emotions and personal experiences. Block (1986: 486) concludes the following: "Although their associations with their own lives were initiated by information in the text, Nonintegrators usually failed to reconnect these associations with the information in the text. Thus, these associations became ends in themselves, rather than a means for extending and explaining the text."

Yang (2002) focused on readers' ability to monitor comprehension. The study implied that both weak and strong readers are able to monitor their comprehension. However, better readers operate more frequently at higher levels of cognitive processing, such as checking cohesiveness among propositions that share a local context or checking the completeness of the information extracted from the text. Weak readers' evaluation, on the other hand, is limited to the lexical and syntactic levels, i.e., the checking of word understanding and evaluating the grammaticality of a sentence.

As demonstrated above, the studies reviewed in this section highlight the role of both lower-level and higher-level components of text processing in proficient reading. A successful FL reader has developed functioning at both levels, especially efficiency and automaticity at the lower decoding level. This facilitates his/her processing at higher levels and enables him/her to control understanding. A good reader knows how to use his/her background knowledge; while comprehending the text message the reader does not use it as a factor to fill in gaps in his/her incomplete language competence (which characterises weak readers) but is able to integrate this knowledge with the information from the text. A skilled reader evaluates his/her understanding at both lexical and syntactic as well as text information level. While coping with a larger portion of text, he/she examines the thematic compatibility of the ideas in a paragraph or text and checks the relation of this information with what he/she knows about the topic.

The studies contribute to the debate concerning the role of FL/L2 competence in FL/L2 reading – known as the Linguistic Threshold Hypotheses (see Part 1, Chapter 1, Section 1.1.). They also discuss other questions related to the one posed in the above mentioned hypothesis. Namely: what is the role of FL/L2 reading strategies and FL/L2 competence in FL/L2 reading and whether the effectiveness of FL/L2 reading strategies depends on readers' FL/L2 competence. Yang's (2002: 18) words best summarise the studies' findings concerning this question:

> For many years, researchers only focused on seeking either 'efficient reading strategies' to help readers solve problems, or the so-called 'metacognitive strategies' to build up readers' comprehension monitoring. However, the truth is that if readers do not possess sufficient basic language skills, then no matter how many diversified reading strategies they are equipped with ... the process will turn out to be fruitless if they have no basic resources to access when attempting to solve problems.

Several studies reviewed in this section examined the effectiveness of reading strategy instruction. All of them show that reading strategies are teachable. However, they indicate that there are strategies that the instruction did not manage to teach. These are: identifying the grammatical function of words, changing the form of words, e.g., verbs, before looking them up in a glossary and skipping inessential words while reading. I think that all these strategies can be taught only if the reader improves his/her language competence, which is in line with the above quotation emphasising the role of FL/L2 competence in FL/L2 reading.

3.5.2. FL/L2 reading vs. L1 reading

Let us look at the conception of FL reading that the studies create. FL reading is viewed as a language skill that is a source of difficulty for its users. It is a process in which the reader applies strategies to solve the problems he/she encounters while reading. This view is similar to the view of L1 reading described in the previous chapter. However, in comparison with L1 reading, FL reading seems to be more focused on the lower level of text comprehension; it is this level that makes a language a problem. This difference between L1 and FL reading is reflected in the strategies that have proved to be the least teachable in L1 and FL reading instruction. In teaching L1 readers the least teachable strategy was the strategy of demanding

relationships in a text (which is a higher-level skill). In FL instruction: identifying the grammatical function of words, skipping inessential words and changing the form of words, e.g., verbs, before looking them up in a glossary (which are lower-level abilities). This comparison elucidates the difference between what L1 and FL readers find challenging in reading.

As regards other reading aspects, it is worth noting that background knowledge and metacognitive strategies seem to play a similar role in L1 and FL reading. A most revealing finding concerning L1 readers' perceptions of their reading comprehension was suggested by Lundeberg (1987). Native reader novice and expert readers differed in reference to their perceptions of their comprehension process. This affective aspect of reading was also tackled in comparative studies of L1 and FL reading, which are discussed in the next section of this chapter.

To conclude, L1 and FL reading studies seem to shed light on the same aspects in the two reading processes, thus emphasising similarities between the two processes. Research also highlights differences, suggesting, however, that FL reading is not a poorer version of L1 reading, but a separate language phenomenon worth investigating. The review of reading research reveals some gaps in FL reading research. What calls for more attention is a model-based perspective on FL reading, similar to the one conducted by Collins, Brown and Larkin (1980) in their study of L1 reading. Such an approach would look at reading as a holistic integrative process in which the reader concentrates on constructing a model of the text, i.e., his/her understanding of the text. It is the approach that I have adapted for the TA study I present in this book. It facilitated my attempts to look at reading as a whole process, not only at a series of reading comprehension breakdowns (see Ericsson 1988).

4. A review of selected comparative studies in L1 and FL/L2

Of particular interest to this discussion are think-aloud studies that investigate both L1 and FL/L2 reading. Because of the focus of this book, most of the studies reviewed here explore reading in FL. Only one study, i.e., the one by Pritchard and O'Hara (2008), looks at the reading of sequential bilingual learners, those who read in L1 and L2 (see Note 1). The summary of the studies discussed in this chapter is presented in Table II.6.

Table II.6. Think-aloud text comprehension studies in the L1 and FL/L2 context

Name	Type of text	Subjects	Aim	Results
Nevo (1985); immediate retrospection	a multiple choice test in Hebrew (L1) and French (FL)	42 Hebrew secondary school students	to compare the test-taking strategies of readers while answering questions in their L1 and FL	FL students transferred test-taking strategies from their L1 to FL
Zupnik (1985); think-aloud*	an English text and two test tasks: in Hebrew (L1) and English (FL)	two Hebrew students: a weak and a strong reader	to compare the test-taking strategies of readers while answering questions in their L1 and FL	the weak reader used more strategies; the weak reader used different strategies than the strong reader
Block (1986); concurrent think-alouds and immediate retrospection	two texts from a psychology textbook	college students: 3 native speakers of Chinese, 3 native speakers of Spanish and 3 native speakers of English	to compare the strategy use of FL readers with those of native speakers of English	reading is a strategy driven process; strategy use is a stable phenomenon in both L1 and FL reading; no differences in strategy use in L1 and FL were found
Cavalcanti (1987); pause protocols	two introductions to academic articles: one in Portuguese and one in English	Brazilian readers read in their L1 (Portuguese) and FL (English)	to identify the pragmatic interpretation problems of FL readers and L1 readers	EFL readers used the same reading style regardless of the language of text; readers read faster and made fewer pauses in their L1
Sarig (1987); concurrent think-alouds	two academic texts of equivalent difficult level	10 secondary school students: native speakers of Hebrew reading in EFL	to identify the reading moves used by EFL readers; to compare the reading moves of subjects reading in L1 and reading in FL	4 types of moves were identified: technical-aid, clarification-simplification, coherence-detecting and monitoring; all moves were divided into comprehension-promoting and comprehension-deterring; readers were more critical of reading in their L1
Davis and Bistodeau (1993); think-alouds, a sentence-by-sentence technique	two newspaper articles: an English and a French version	8 native readers of English and 8 native readers of French	to identify and compare the reading moves used in L1 and FL	in L1 reading more top-down strategies were found, in FL reading – more bottom-up strategies were observed; affective differences were found: readers were more critical of reading in their L1

Name	Type of text	Subjects	Aim	Results
Pritchard and O'Hara (2008); immediate retrospection	a passage from a science textbook: an English and a Spanish version	20 students: all native Spanish speakers (sequential bilinguals)	to compare the strategy use of proficient bilingual readers in L1 and L2 reading	in L1 students relied more on intersentential strategies, while in L2 they used more intrasentential strategies; students used different strategies when facing reading problems; no transfer between L1 and L2 was observed

* this sign means that it is not possible to specify the kind of think-aloud procedure used in the study

Source: own study.

4.1. Processing strategies in L1 and FL/L2 reading

Davis and Bistodeau (1993) investigated eight native readers of English and eight native readers of French. Two newspaper articles on the same topic were selected, each in two versions: an English and a French version. Each subject read one text in the FL and the other in the L1. Subjects were shown the texts sentence by sentence and asked to think aloud. After reading each passage, they were asked to write down everything they remembered from the text. This task gave subjects a clear purpose to read the texts for global understanding. After the think-aloud session, subjects were interviewed about whether and how their L1 and FL reading differed as well as what they thought about the think-aloud task itself. Thirteen strategies were identified: 3 **bottom-up strategies**, e.g, individual word focus, focus on intrasentential features; 10 **top-down strategies**, e.g., prediction, making inferences, drawing on prior knowledge, evaluative comments and self-questioning; and 2 **metacognitive strategies** – comments on the task itself and comments on the subjects' own behaviour.

The analysis concerning native readers of English revealed that when subjects read in their L1 (i.e., English), they used significantly more top down strategies than in their FL (i.e., French). For example, subjects made significantly more evaluative comments in their L1 than FL. Exactly the opposite was observed in their FL reading, i.e., greater frequency of bottom up strategy use in the FL than in the L1. For example, focusing on individual words was reported more frequently in the FL than the L1. The number of metacognitive comments did not differ according to the language. As regards the group of native readers of French, no statistically significant differences were found between the use of bottom-up and top-down strategies. An interesting finding was that the more linguistically proficient readers produced more top down comments in both their L1 and the FL.

The comparison of the two groups, native readers of French and native readers of English, revealed two common trends between the groups. First, it was found that when subjects read in their FL, there was a positive correlation between the reported use of restatement (one of the bottom-up strategies) and the number of units recalled. To explain this result, Davis and Bistodeau quoted Kern (1988), who claims that due to weaker memory traces in a non-native language restatement may be more useful in one's FL. The other trend refers to affective differences between L1 and FL reading. Subjects seemed to react differently to comprehension difficulties depending on whether they read in their L1 or FL. Readers' comments implied that subjects were more critical of reading in their L1. The researchers concluded that when reading in the L1 readers were more likely to blame the author for any misunderstandings and when reading in their FL – themselves.

Pritchard and O'Hara (2008) aimed to identify patterns of strategy use amongst Spanish-English bilinguals. The subjects read two texts: a passage taken from a Spanish science textbook and the other taken from the English version of the same book. The students were asked to read the texts and at the pre-determined points in the passage to stop and describe their strategies and thoughts connected with their reading. The researchers identified four categories of strategies serving the following functions: monitoring, establishing intrasentential ties, establishing intersentential ties, establishing intertextual ties. Although no differences were found in the type and range of strategies used in reading the two texts, differences in the frequency of strategy use were observed. Students used more strategies that served establishing **intrasentential ties** in reading in English (their L2) than in reading in Spanish (their L1). They used more strategies that served to establish **intersentential ties** in reading in Spanish (their L1) than in reading in English (their L2). Additionally, Pritchard and O'Hara (2008: 635) concluded that "when reading in their L2, even proficient, bilingual readers process text in a more word-by-word manner. … [W]hen reading in their L1, proficient, bilingual readers are better able to integrate information throughout a passage."

Pritchard and O'Hara were also interested in how the students behaved when confronted by reading difficulties (identified in TA protocols as the intervals students made when developing text comprehension). More prolonged intervals were observed in protocols concerning reading the English text (students' L2) than in reports concerning reading the Spanish text (students' L1). It was found that the students used different solutions when facing difficulties. In reading in Spanish students resorted to comprehension monitoring strategies; in reading in English they relied on sentence-specific strategies (i.e., those establishing intrasentential ties). Additionally, Pritchard and O'Hara (2008: 636, 637) raised the question about transfer between the two languages and drew the following conclusions:

> The differential use of comprehension monitoring strategies that was evident in this study needs to be investigated to determine why readers who had achieved a high level of cognitive literate proficiency in both Spanish and English did not transfer those strategies when reading in English. One possible explanation may be that students are more likely to make that transfer when reading narrative texts rather than the expository ones used in this study.

4.2. Interpretation problems of L1 and FL readers

Cavalcanti's (1987) study aims to identify pragmatic interpretation problems related to key lexical items of FL Brazilian-Portuguese native speakers and native speakers of English. Subjects read the introductions to academic papers: one in Portuguese and one in English. At the end of their reading they summarised the text. Brazilian readers read in their L1 and their FL; while speakers of English only in their L1. Cavalcanti introduced several control measures. Before the think-aloud session subjects were asked to read the title of the passage and predict the content of the text. The next control step was an interventionist procedure – a pause in the text, the same for all subjects, which induced readers to retrospect on their reading process. Additionally, at the end of each paragraph and at the end of the text readers were asked to summarise the text they had read. The last control measure was a selection-of-key-lexical-item task, which required readers to choose a few words from the text that could help them to recall the text later. All these measures produced material for comparison among the subjects.

The results indicated that EFL readers applied the same reading style regardless of the language in which they read. Subjects were found to read faster in their L1; they also made fewer pauses in their L1 than the FL. It was interesting to observe that the Brazilian native speakers made more pauses in their L1 reading than the native speakers of English did in their reading. Moreover, the findings revealed that protocols based on L1 reading were less informative than protocols based on FL reading.

4.3. Test-taking strategies in L1 and FL reading

Research into how students take reading comprehension tests reveal interesting insight into L1/FL reading differences. Zupnik (1985, cited in Cohen 1986) compared strategies used by a weak and a strong reader while reading an English text (students' FL) and answering questions in English (FL) and in Hebrew (L1). Subjects were asked to think aloud and then provide answers in writing. It was found that on the Hebrew test the two readers reported almost the same number of moves (i.e., strategies). On the English test the poor reader reported four times as many moves as the good reader did. The analysis of types of strategies, based on Sarig's (1987) taxonomy, revealed that the poor reader used mostly clarification and simplification moves with very limited reliance on monitoring strategies. As regards comprehension success, most of the strong reader's moves were comprehension-promoting, whereas the weak reader's moves were often comprehension-deterring.

Nevo (1985, cited in Cohen 1986) was interested in what strategies her subjects use while answering reading comprehension questions. To elicit feedback, Nevo prepared a checklist of 15 strategies students were likely to use. Among the strategies in the checklist were, e.g., using background knowledge, using clues in the text, matching the question with the text, etc. She administered a multiple-choice test in Hebrew (students' L1) and French (students' FL), and asked students for each test item to select two strategies that helped them to answer the question. The researcher found that students transferred test-taking strategies from the first language to the foreign language. Nevo also investigated whether the strategies students chose facilitated the choice of the correct answer. She pointed out that it was in the foreign-language test where students more often selected strategies that did not promote the choice of the correct answer.

4.4. Transfer of reading processes from L1 to FL

The researchers discussed below were interested in whether reading processes in the first language transfer over to the foreign language. Block (1986) compared L1 and FL readers. The study is described in detail in the previous section, devoted to L1 reading studies (see Chapter 3, Section 3.1. in this part). Here only conclusions concerning differences between L1 and FL reading are presented. Her findings suggested that there were no significant differences between the reading times of L1 and FL readers. Similar conclusions were drawn for strategy use; both L1 and FL readers used similar strategies and patterns of strategies. Block (1986: 485) implies that "strategy use is a stable phenomenon which is not tied to specific language features." Drawing on similar results suggested by Cummins (1980) and Hudson (1982), Block (1986: 485) claims that "the development of strategy use, particularly as it is applied to informative text, does not seem to depend on language-specific features" and "some aspects of reading ability are readily transferred from one language to another."

Sarig (1987) investigated reading in Hebrew as L1 and reading in EFL. Ten secondary school seniors read a Hebrew and an English text – two academic texts of equivalent difficulty levels. The tasks resembled problem-solving tasks; they required main idea analysis and synthesis of the overall message. While analysing the data, the experimenter identified reading moves which referred to each separate action the reader took. All moves were classified according to their function, i.e., comprehension promoting and comprehension deterring moves as well as according to stages in the problem-solving process, i.e., the proposition identification stage, the identification of main proposition stage and the synthesis of the overall message stage. Moreover, four types of reading moves were identified: technical-aid moves, e.g., skimming, scanning; clarification and simplification moves; coherence-detecting moves, e.g., identifying the macroframe of the text, effective use of prior knowledge; monitoring moves, i.e., conscious change of planning, identification of misunderstanding.

On the basis of the protocol data, Sarig found conditions under which the above mentioned moves facilitate comprehension. The cross-lingual analysis showed that the move types functioning across the task performance stages are almost identical in the two languages. Out of the four moves, it is coherence-detecting that contributes most to both success and failure in comprehension (about 1/3). The clarification and simplification moves proved the least important in both L1 and FL. Correlations between the frequency of moves in L1 and FL indicated that readers handled high-level tasks in both languages in a very similar way. Sarig (1987: 115) concluded that

> [t]he same factors explain success and failure to almost the same extent. In addition, there appears to be a considerable relation between the frequency of comprehension-promoting and deterring moves. One may conclude, then, that reading processes do transfer crosslingually, as far as main idea analysis and overall message synthesis tasks in an academic text are concerned.

To investigate transfer of reading strategies, Sarig also examined students' individual reading styles. The data showed that reading is a highly individual process; readers use a unique personal combination of strategies. Sarig (1987: 117) concluded that "readers do not differ as greatly in the number of moves they use ... as they do in the particular strategy selection which characterizes them." The researcher claims that her results seem to contradict the traditional dichotomy (e.g., Hosenfeld 1977) between poor and good readers, the view that implies that these two groups use different sets of strategies. Instead, she suggests that readers seem to use the same strategies in situations that may lead to success or failure in their comprehension. As regards transfer, the finding that reading seems to be a highly individual process to almost the same extent in both languages supports the conclusion that "reading processes from the first languages do appear to transfer to the foreign language" (Sarig 1987: 118).

The analysis of students' individual reading styles led Sarig to conclude that an ability to transfer reading skills does not depend on FL proficiency or the level of FL reading competence but is an individual cognitive trait. Similar performance was observed in both an intermediate and a lower FL proficiency learner. Both poor and good readers were found to transfer moves that facilitate and deter comprehension. Subjects differed with regard to the extent of transfer of reading strategies and whether it promoted or hindered understanding.

4.5. Conclusions – reading in L1 and FL/L2

This section looks again at the comparative studies reviewed above and aims to address the following questions:

- Do FL/L2 readers read in a similar way in their L1 and FL/L2?
- Do FL/L2 readers transfer their L1 reading strategies to FL/L2 reading?

The questions will be discussed in relation to reading fluency, reading strategies and the transfer between L1 reading and FL/L2 reading.

Block (1986), Cavalcanti (1987), and Pritchard and O'Hara (2008) provide a basis for discussing the issue of reading fluency. Block (1986) found that there are no significant differences between the reading times of L1 and FL readers, which may suggest that both groups were equally fluent in reading. In contrast, Cavalcanti (1987) observed that her Brazilian native speakers read faster in their L1 than in their FL; they made fewer pauses in their L1 reading. This difference between the two studies presented above may be due to the procedure and elicitation techniques applied in the studies. Asking readers to stop after every sentence (Block 1986) and allowing subjects to decide where to pause (Cavalcanti 1987) could elicit different processes. Besides, the reading times measured by Block include both silent reading times and reporting times, which makes the two studies difficult to compare. The results of Pritchard and O'Hara's (2008) study are consistent with those of Cavalcanti. Pritchard and O'Hara looked at how bilingual readers make connections between their local understandings of the text in order to construct an integrated comprehension of the whole text. They measured the length of intervals between these connections. Their study showed more prolonged intervals between connections when the learners read in their L2 (i.e., English), as compared to their reading in their native language (i.e., Spanish). This implies that the process of reading in L2 was more demanding for the students and took more time. To sum up, most of the studies discussed here indicate that reading in L1 is faster and more fluent than reading in FL/L2, which may be explained by the fact that reading in L1 is more automatic and as such can result in less verbalization and more pauses during think-aloud research.

A number of issues concerning reading strategies were investigated, e.g., similarities and differences between strategies applied in L1 and FL/L2 reading, the possibility of transfer between L1 reading and FL/L2 reading, the relationship between the transfer of strategies and the level of FL/L2 proficiency as well as the relationship between the transfer and the level of FL/L2 reading skill. Studies that explored these questions are discussed below.

The most illuminating results refer to the **types of strategies** used in L1 and FL/L2 reading. Davis and Bistodeau's (1993) study showed that native readers of English when reading in their L1 used more top-down strategies than when reading in their FL (French). For example, they made more evaluative comments when reading an English text than reading a French text. In their FL reading, the opposite was observed – subjects used bottom-up strategies more frequently than in their L1. It may be interesting to note that the abovementioned differences between the use of top-down and bottom-up strategies in L1 and FL reading were found only in the reading of the native speakers of English. In the reading of the native readers of French, these differences were not statistically significant. I think that this lack of correspondence may be due to differences between the two languages and how they are processed.

The same regularity concerning differences between the use of top-down and bottom-up strategies was found by Pritchard and O'Hara (2008), who investigated strategies used by bilingual native Spanish speakers reading Spanish and

English texts. The study showed that when reading a Spanish text (their L1), the learners used more strategies that establish intersentential connections; when reading an English text (their L2), they were more likely to look for intrasentential connections.

In contrast, Sarig's (1987) cross-linguistic analysis showed that different types of strategies function in the two languages in an almost identical manner. It was top-down moves (called in Sarig's taxonomy coherence-detecting) that proved the most important in comprehension in both L1 and FL; they contributed most to both the success and failure in text understanding. The study indicated that bottom-up moves (clarification and simplification) contributed the least in both L1 and FL contexts. I would argue that these findings can be attributed to the reading tasks assigned to the subjects, i.e., the main idea analysis and overall message synthesis. This type of task requires approaching the text from the above, i.e., reading for the gist, which may involve activating lower-level strategies to a lesser extent.

Summing up, the studies do not provide unequivocal results, which can be explained by differences in the research procedures. Following Pritchard and O'Hara's (2008) findings, we can conclude that top-down and bottom-up strategies are factors distinguishing L1 and FL/L2 reading. Reading in L1 seems to be more efficient, more automatised; therefore, bottom-up strategies are not reported in think-aloud studies. Native readers, equipped with more advanced language proficiency, read more effortlessly, which results in fewer bottom-up and more top-down strategies in their protocols.

Empirical studies also elucidated the importance of **language proficiency** in reading. The relationship between language proficiency and types of strategies was explored by Davis and Bistodeau (1993), who observed that the more linguistically proficient readers (in their FL) produced more top-down comments in both their L1 and FL. Similarly, Sarig (1987) found that in her subjects' reading bottom-up strategies depended more than top-down strategies on readers' language proficiency. She called the bottom-up strategies identified in her study "the most language dependent move type" (Sarig 1987: 113), explaining that the successful use of these strategies depended on "effective lexical, morphological, syntactic and rhetorical recognition of utterances in context" (Sarig 1987: 111), abilities that are commonly considered to constitute FL competence. The role of lower-level skills were also emphasised by Pritchard and O'Hara (2008), who observed that even proficient bilingual readers relied more heavily on the use of bottom-up strategies when reading in their L2. To sum up, the findings imply that readers' language proficiency is related to the levels of processing that reading tasks activate. Language proficiency seems to be critical in lower-level text processing. This seems to be true especially for FL/L2 reading.

The studies also focussed on the role of **metacognitive strategies** in L1 and FL/L2 reading. Davis and Bistodeau (1993) did not find differences in the number of metacognitive strategies according to the language. Zupnik (1985) observed very limited use of monitoring strategies in the poor FL reader's behaviour. Pritchard and O'Hara (2008) identified monitoring comprehension as an effective strategy applied in L1 reading, which was not the case in L2 reading. The studies seem to suggest that metacognitive strategies characterise successful L1 reading and its use may facilitate FL/L2 reading.

The next issue explored in comparative analyses is **readers' perceptions** of their reading comprehension in L1 and FL. The findings of comparative studies complement the results of L1 reading research. In Lundeberg's (1987) study, native novice readers and expert readers differed in reference to their perceptions of their comprehension process. Novice readers often expressed dissatisfaction with their comprehension of the text; most of them attributed their difficulties to themselves, e.g., their reading skills or concentration, rather than to the text. In contrast, expert readers rarely showed discomfort caused by comprehension problems. In their cross-linguistic study, Davis and Bistodeau (1993) indicated that subjects seemed to react differently to comprehension difficulties depending on whether they read in their L1 or FL. When reading in the L1, readers were more critical of the text and more likely to blame the author for any misunderstandings and when reading in their FL they blame themselves. The two studies seem to imply that native speaker novice readers perceive their comprehension problems in a similar way to FL readers. Both groups attributed their difficulty to themselves, i.e., their insuficient language competence.

Let us focus on the issue of **transfer** of strategies between L1 and FL/L2 reading. The studies do not provide a single unequivocal answer. Block (1986) and Sarig (1987: 118) suggest that "reading processes from the first languages do appear to transfer to the foreign language." Block claims that both L1 and FL readers used similar strategies and patterns of strategies, suggesting (Block 1986: 485) that "strategy use is a stable phenomenon which is not tied to specific language features" and "some aspects of reading ability are readily transferred from one language to another." Sarig (1987: 115) drew similar conclusions from her cross-lingual analysis, claiming that "[o]ne may conclude ... that reading processes do transfer crosslingually as far as main idea analysis and overall message synthesis tasks in an academic text are concerned." Also studies concerning test taking support the assumption that FL/L2 readers do seem to transfer their L1 strategies to FL/L2 reading. Nevo (1985) found that subjects transferred test-taking strategies from their L1 (Hebrew) to the FL (English). In contrast to the above-mentioned conclusions, Pritchard and O'Hara (2008) did not observe transfer of reading strategies between the two languages. They concluded that even proficient bilingual readers did not seem to transfer strategies from their L1 to L2. I think that the differences between the research findings can be attributed to differences in how the studies operationalised transfer and the status of the non-native language, i.e., whether it was the subjects' FL or L2.

The next issue explored in think-aloud research is the **relationship of interlingual transfer with the level of FL/L2 proficiency and the level of FL/L2 reading skill**. Sarig (1987) concluded that the ability to transfer does not depend on readers' FL proficiency nor on their level of reading competence. Both learners at lower and higher FL proficiency levels performed in a similar way when reading in FL. Both poor and strong readers were found to transfer strategies that facilitate and deter their comprehension. Last but not least, reading research presents transfer of L1 reading strategies to FL/L2 reading as a very individual process. The analysis of the reading styles of individual readers conducted by Sarig (1987) underscores a unique character of strategy use. Similarly, readers differ with regards to the extent of transfer.

To sum up, the think-aloud studies exploring reading in L1 and FL/L2 discussed above seem to imply the following:

- readers are more fluent in their L1 than their FL/L2;
- L1 readers and FL/L2 readers use similar strategies and patterns of strategies; reading processes transfer from the L1 to the FL/L2;
- in L1 readers use more top-down strategies than in their FL/L2; whereas in FL/L2 readers use more bottom-up strategies than in the L1;
- FL/L2 learners transfer their test-taking strategies from their L1 to the FL/L2;
- ability to transfer does not depend on the level of FL/L2 proficiency nor on the level of FL/L2 reading competence;
- strategy use is individual; readers differ with regard to the extent of transfer.

The review of studies presented here has produced a wealth of evidence indicating how complex L1 and FL/L2 reading are. There are comparative studies that seem to echo the results obtained in L1 reading research and FL/L2 reading studies. There are also studies that seem to contradict the research conducted within L1 or FL/L2 context. For example, Sarig (1987) did not agree with Hosenfeld's (1977) conclusion concerning differences between successful and less successful readers. It is worth pointing out that any comparison of studies and their results seems difficult because of the differences in research design, such as the number of subjects, languages that were the object of investigation and techniques used to elicit think-aloud data. More comparative research is needed to explore further the relationship between L1 and FL/L2 reading by means of more homogenous research paradigms.

Notes

1. For most insightful studies which explored the reading competence of Latina/o students, see, e.g., Jiménez (1997); Jiménez, Garcia and Pearson (1996) and Hardin (2001). Their attempts concentrate on specifying a bilingual literacy schema, which includes the capability of applying and transferring literacy knowledge and abilities from one language to the other as well as transferring information across languages. As Jiménez, Garcia and Pearson (1996: 90) emphasise, all the studies examine "bilingualism as a potential strength, which might facilitate literacy development, rather than an inherent weakness."

Part III THE THINK-ALOUD STUDY

1. Description of the study

1.1. The goal of the study

Assuming that students are more skilled readers in their mother tongue than in a FL I wanted to investigate whether there was any aspect of reading in which students show more skill in Polish and which students could improve upon in the process of reading in English. I considered the think-aloud (TA) procedure appropriate for this purpose. My assumption was that gaining insight into subjects' reading processes could provide an excellent opportunity to observe how students approach text in both languages and what difficulties they encounter and how they handle them. I believed that applying an "on-line" method would facilitate a comparison of students' reading in the two languages. The following general questions were investigated:

- Do proficient readers of Polish (L1) and advanced readers of English (FL) read in the same manner in their L1 and FL?
- If they do not, what is the difference in the way they read in Polish (L1) and English (FL)?

It is important to emphasize that the above questions took on a more specific form at various stages of the study. The study consists of six stages, which are presented below (Table III.1.).

It is important to emphasise that the main study was preceded by a pilot study, which aimed to pre-test the think-aloud procedure and to find texts at the appropriate level of difficulty. In the pilot study, five undergraduate students were asked to read a Polish and an English text, and to think aloud when reading. The results of the pilot study had an important influence on the final version of the texts and the think-aloud procedure applied in the main study.

Table III.1. Stages of the study

Stage of the study	Focus of the analysis	Source of data
Stage 1	Analysis of reading strategies	TA protocols
Stage 2	Analysis of problems and solutions	TA protocols
Stage 3	Analysis of propositions	TA protocols
Stage 4	Analysis of idiosyncratic patterns of constructing comprehension	TA protocols
Stage 5	Evaluation of students' comprehension	TA protocols
Stage 6	Interviews with students	Interviews conducted with each student by the author of the study

Source: own study.

1.2. Subjects

The subjects chosen for the study were ten undergraduate students of a foreign language teacher training college: 6 women and 4 men. All the subjects volunteered to participate in the study; some explained that they had decided to take part in the study because they were interested in linguistic research. All the subjects were in their early twenties. Their foreign language competence was assessed as advanced – C1 (according to *Common European Framework*, Coste *et al.* 2003). As regards the students' L1 reading skill, I considered the subjects to be a homogenous group of competent L1 readers. This was concluded on the basis of the information obtained from the questionnaire that had been administered before the think-aloud study. The questionnaire is not discussed in this book; it was the main method in another study which explored the role of L1 in foreign language learning (see Kusiak 2009 for more details). The subjects were my students; thus, I assumed that they would feel comfortable with me as a researcher conducting the study.

1.3. Texts

Both texts were authentic news magazine articles: a Polish one taken from *Newsweek* (the Polish edition) and an English text – from *Time*. The texts are one-page long; both are accompanied with photos. The Polish text consists of 9 paragraphs; the English text has 10 paragraphs. Since the pilot study showed that the task of reading complete texts could be too time-consuming and thus tiring for the subjects, the students were asked to read the first 6 paragraphs in the Polish article and the first 7 paragraphs in the English article. The passages prepared in this way were evaluated to be in themselves self-contained and complete. The English text, entitled *Is progress obsolete*? (Lasch 1992), discusses the issue of progress, its advantages and limits; the Polish text *Materia ducha* (Pinker 2004) asks questions concerning the dichotomy of brain and soul. In selecting the texts no readability formula was used to assess the texts. Since the study was based on a theory which views reading as a problem-solving activity, I assumed that the texts should be challenging for the students. I decided that this challenge should be present not in the topic itself but in how it is discussed. This means that I had looked for texts that develop their main topics in an "intricate" way, which would be reflected in their complex propositional network. However, I assumed that the topics of the texts were ones of general interest and that the subjects would find the texts interesting enough to continue reading. The main reason why expository texts were chosen for the study was that expository text is the main genre of textbooks and other texts that college students read for their study purposes.

1.4. Tasks

I intended to elicit simultaneous verbalisation produced by the subjects at the moment of their performance. My purpose was to elicit a natural way of reading a complete text, "the overall approach of the subjects towards the task, in which the whole process of the task fulfilment is verbalised" (Gabryś-Barker 2009: 31). In order to slow down the process of readers' attending to a text, the think-aloud task directed subjects to read the texts paragraph after paragraph. This procedure served to elicit reading for main ideas and to observe how the students construct their models of text, which would correspond to the particular paragraphs (see Part One, Chapter 3, Section 3.1.2. for a model-based theory of comprehension). Another aim of asking the subjects to read paragraph by paragraph was to introduce breaks in the same places in the texts, whereby to impose on the students a similar manner of reading. This was meant to facilitate a comparison of students' protocols. It is interesting to add that the main study did not repeat the think-aloud procedure applied in the pilot study, which was: (1) to ask students to read each text paragraph by paragraph; (2) to summarise each paragraph they had finished reading and (3) to predict what the next paragraph would be about. This was evaluated as a procedure that could hinder students' natural way of reading.

The subjects read two texts: an English and a Polish text. Five students initially read the English text, then the Polish one. The other five read the texts in the reverse order. They all followed the same think-aloud procedure for both texts. To decrease the cognitive load of the task (see Part Two, Chapter 1, Section 1.5.), the subjects were instructed to report in Polish while reading both texts. The subjects were informed that the session would be recorded. My role during the think-aloud session involved fostering verbal reporting. When the subjects were silent for particularly long, I asked them questions about what they were thinking. Additionally, as I was following the text while the students were thinking aloud, I sometimes asked the students to clarify, e.g., which line or words in the text they were talking about. However, I attempted to minimise any social interaction with the subjects so that they could focus their attention on the task.

The think-aloud session was followed by an semi-structured interview, during which the students were asked to comment on the way they had read each text and on their general reading styles in Polish and English. The subjects were also asked to comment on the think-aloud task.

1.5. Directions to subjects

The students were not familiar with the think-aloud methodology. To make the task easier, I demonstrated what a think-aloud task is like, i.e., I thought aloud while reading an extract from an article in Polish selected from *Newsweek* (the Polish edition). Additionally, I presented several examples of aspects of reading which the students could report on while reading the texts, such as problems with difficult vocabulary, paying attention to illustrations, etc. Prior to the think-aloud task, the students were told that they would be asked to read silently two texts: an English text and a Polish one and describe in detail what they were "doing" during the process of reading the texts. Each student was told which text he/she should read first. The students were instructed to read each text paragraph by paragraph and to report back in Polish. They were informed that the texts they were going to read were newspapers articles. I made sure that the students did not know the articles they were going to read.

During the interview, the subjects were asked general questions, such as "Would you like to add anything about how you read the texts?" and "What do you think about the think-aloud task?" Additional questions were asked to encourage the students to develop their comments.

1.6. Transcription process

Both the think-aloud session and the interview were recorded by means of a digital voice recorder. The material was transcribed. The subjects' recorded verbalisations were matched with the corresponding paragraphs in the texts. While transcribing, I wrote down everything that the subjects produced. The data was parsed into clause-length sentences. I also transcribed signs of indecision or reflection, e.g., "uhm." I also indicated in brackets the meaning of such words, e.g., if I interpreted them as expressions of surprise, disappointment, etc. Pause time was indicated by dots placed in brackets; the number of dots reflecting the length of the pauses – the more dots, the longer the pause. Certain types of nonverbal behaviour which were possible to identify through a listening to the tape were indicated, e.g., subvocalisation of text or laughter.

1.7. Process of analyzing the protocols

In the present study, reading is viewed as a cognitive process that involves strategic problem solving (e.g., Olshavsky 1976/1977). It is accepted, as is often distinguished in theory and empirical research, that reading consists of two levels of cognitive processing. One level, called the "lower," focuses on letter identification, word recognition and syntactic parsing; the other one, referred to as the "higher," involves discourse processing and knowledge about text characteristics, which enable readers to construct their representation of the text. To explore the reader-text interaction, the main principles of mental model theories are drawn on. Two theoretical perspectives which have contributed to the conceptualization of reading in the present study are: the van Dijk and Kintsch (1983) model and Britton's (1994) theory of grammar exposition and the process of understanding expository texts. (Both are described in detail in Part I, Chapter 3, Section 3.4.3.) According to the first model (van Dijk and Kintsch 1983), text information is represented in memory at three levels: surface form, which refers to the representation of the exact wording and syntax; propositional textbase, which corresponds to a multileveled, locally coherent propositional network of semantic text information and a situation model, which depicts real-life situations presented in the text as perceived by the reader, i.e., the reader's interpretation of the text. According to Britton (1994), the author of an expository text directs the reader in his/her comprehension. The reader develops the representation of the text in the form of network of idea nodes derived from the text and his/her prior knowledge. After Kintsch (1988, 1998) and Britton (1994), it was accepted that the reader constructs in his/her mind mental structures (units of knowledge) which correspond to propositions (units of information) expressed in the text. In the TA study described below, I looked at the role of higher-level and lower-level skills of reading as well as the learners' ability to construct the representation of the texts they were asked to read.

The process of analyzing the protocols comprised several stages. At subsequent stages of the analysis, the general research question as to whether proficient readers of Polish (L1) and advanced readers of English (FL) read in the same manner in their L1 and FL became more specific. Stages 1–6 explain how at each stage of the study the main concept of the study, which is reading, was operationalized and how the data was analysed. To check the reliability of the coding scheme at stages 1–5, the coding process was conducted three times at intervals of a few months. Intrarater reliability averaged 90%, which was considered as satisfactory.

2. Analysis of students' strategies: Stage 1

2.1. Research questions

The first stage of analyzing the data involved distinguishing strategies the students took while reading the texts. An individual strategy was considered an action the student took in order to complete the task of reading. At this stage of the study, the following research questions were investigated:

1a) What strategies do proficient readers of Polish (L1) and advanced readers of English (FL) use when reading texts written in their L1 and FL?

1b) Do proficient readers of Polish (L1) and advanced readers of English (FL) use different strategies when reading texts written in their L1 and FL?

1c) Are there any differences in the frequency with which the subjects use particular strategies when reading texts written in their L1 and FL?

1d) Are there any patterns which reflect the manner in which the subjects use the strategies to construct their comprehension of the texts?

1e) If so, are the patterns the same in reading both texts?

2.2. Results

Question 1a)
What strategies do proficient readers of Polish (L1) and advanced readers of English (FL) use when reading texts written in their L1 and FL?

A range of actions was identified in the protocols. Strategies were grouped and named. This resulted in the identification of four categories of strategies which, as had been inferred, represented the learners' purpose in using particular strategies. Below are given the four categories with examples of each type of strategy (see Table III.2.).

Technical strategies seemed to serve as the most basic actions adopted by the students to talk about their reading. They involved dealing directly with the text. In **emotional strategies**, the readers showed their emotional reactions and involvement in relation to the text; they expressed their surprise or disappointment concerning both the ideas and organization of the text. **Rational/logical strategies** were actions which reflected the students' attempts to manipulate the text, e.g., to compare or link different parts of the text in order to construct comprehension. This group also contained strategies that involved predicting the development of ideas. **Evaluating/critical strategies** entailed actions which showed students' critical approach to both the text and their process of reading. The students were aware of whether they could understand the text or whether their understanding was not right; they evaluated the results of their understanding, commented and reflected on it, e.g., by asking themselves questions about the text and their own reading.

Table: III.2. A taxonomy of reading strategies established on the basis of the data

A. **Technical** strategies:
1. Paraphrasing – simple repetition of parts of the recently processed text – PA 2. Reading aloud parts of the text – RA 3. Rereading – RR 4. Referring to earlier parts of the text; linking different parts of the text; comparing different parts of the text, which does not result in an explanation of current text information – LINK
B. **Emotional** strategies:
5. Expressing surprise with text information – SUR 6. Expressing interest or lack of interest in the text information – INT 7. Dialoguing with oneself, e.g., by asking questions such as "Prawda"? (Pol.) , which in English means "Really"? – DIAL 8. Expressing disappointment with text information or how the information develops – DIS
C. **Rational/logical** strategies:
9. Making backward inferences to explain current text information by drawing on prior knowledge – BKNOW 10. Predicting the development of ideas; speculating about the implications of the given text information – PRED 11. Making backward inferences to explain current text information by drawing on previously given text information; identifying the main idea – IMI 12. Summing up information to capture the essential information (main ideas) presented in the text with the reader's own words; drawing conclusions – SUM 13. Focusing on certain parts of the text; emphasizing certain words, etc. – FOC 14. Identifying the purpose of parts of the text, e.g., the introduction, the main idea, examples to support the main idea, the conclusion, etc. – IPUR 15. Making associations, i.e., lateral inferencing, elaborating on the text information, which does not improve the coherence of one's representation (after Kaakinen and Hyona 2005; see Part I, Chapter 3, Section 3.3.)
D. **Evaluating/critical** strategies:
16. Stating understanding; accepting one's own state of understanding – UND 17. Stating lack of understanding – NO UND 18. Correcting understanding – COR UND 19. Stating uncertainty about one's comprehension – UND? 20. Looking for confirmation of predictions – CPRED 21. Stating no confirmation of predictions – NCRED 22. Stating confirmation of predictions – SCPRED 23. Commenting on one's way of reading the text – WAY 24. Evaluating the difficulty of a part of the text – DIFF 25. Evaluating a part of the text as important for one's comprehension – PART 26. Asking questions about the text information – QUEST 27. Commenting on the author of the text – AUT 28. Identifying a type of text – TYPE 29. Criticizing the text for lack of information, linkage, poor cohesion, etc. – CRIT 30. Stating not understanding certain vocabulary – VOC 31. Stating that one knows the meaning of certain vocabulary – VOC+ 32. Commenting on one's way of guessing an unknown word – WAY VOC 33. Discussing the text information; explaining to oneself; expressing agreement or disagreement with the text information; extrapolating – DISCUS 34. Evaluating a part of the text as, e.g., controversial, subjective – EVTEXT

Source: own study.

Question 1b)
Do proficient readers of Polish (L1) and advanced readers of English (FL) use different strategies when reading texts written in their L1 and FL?

The results of a quantitative analysis are presented in the tables below (Table III.3. and III.4.). It is important to comment on the strategies of paraphrasing and reading aloud applied by the students in reading the texts. These strategies are not presented in the tables. It was decided that the two strategies would not be analyzed as it was impossible to identify separate examples of these strategies. In analyzing how the students read a Polish text, it was only possible to indicate which of the two strategies was more frequently used by each reader. As regards an English text, a combination of the two strategies was identified: the readers paraphrased the English text in Polish (which was the language of reporting) and occasionally code-switched to English, thereby quoting the text. The strategy of reading aloud parts of the text helped the subjects to slow down the reading itself and focus on the difficult text again.

As explained above, this stage of analysis involved the identifying and enumerating of strategies. It was accepted that one strategy involves an action of one kind taken by the reader to process a text, regardless of how extensive the strategy was, i.e., regardless of the amount of text processed by the reader while applying a given strategy. This means that strategies of one type adopted by two different students could relate to different amounts of text.

Table III.3. Strategies applied in reading the Polish text

Subjects	A	B	C	D	E	F	G	H	I	J	ALL	%
Technical												
RR	3	0	2	1	0	0	1	0	1	0	8	2
LINK	9	2	9	2	1	2	3	1	0	1	30	6
ALL TECHNICAL	**12**	**2**	**11**	**3**	**1**	**2**	**4**	**1**	**1**	**1**	**38**	**7**
Emotional												
SUR	3	0	3	1	0	0	0	0	0	0	7	1
INTR	1	2	7	2	0	0	4	1	5	0	22	4
DIAL	2	1	6	0	0	1	15	0	4	7	36	7
DIS	2	5	2	0	0	0	1	0	0	0	10	2
ALL EMOTIONAL	**8**	**8**	**18**	**3**	**0**	**1**	**20**	**1**	**9**	**7**	**75**	**15**
Rational/logical												
BKNOW	3	0	3	0	0	0	6	1	1	4	18	4
PRED	5	3	3	4	2	0	4	2	0	1	24	5
IMI	11	6	7	2	5	5	15	10	2	7	70	14
SUM	10	1	8	1	2	3	1	2	0	4	32	6

FOC	4	4	5	2	3	3	3	1	6	5	36	7
IPUR	1	0	0	2	0	0	2	8	1	1	15	3
ASS	0	3	0	0	0	0	0	0	13	0	16	3
ALL RATIONAL	**34**	**17**	**26**	**11**	**12**	**11**	**31**	**24**	**23**	**22**	**211**	**41**
Evaluating/critical												
UND	5	0	5	1	0	2	6	3	0	1	23	4
NO UND	0	3	2	2	1	1	7	4	3	0	23	4
COR UND	1	0	0	0	0	0	2	0	0	0	3	1
UND?	0	0	0	0	0	0	0	0	0	0	0	0
CPRED	3	1	2	0	0	0	0	0	0	0	6	1
NCPRED	2	3	7	0	0	0	3	0	0	0	15	3
SCPRED	1	0	0	1	0	0	0	0	0	1	3	1
WAY	0	0	0	0	0	2	2	2	1	0	7	1
DIFF	0	0	0	0	0	0	0	0	0	0	0	0
PART	0	0	0	0	0	0	0	0	1	0	1	0
QUEST	5	8	9	0	0	0	11	0	3	0	36	7
AUT	0	0	0	0	0	0	0	0	0	1	1	0
TYPE	0	0	0	1	1	0	0	0	0	0	2	0
CRIT	2	7	2	0	0	0	7	1	0	0	19	4
VOC	0	0	0	0	0	0	0	0	0	0	0	0
VOC+	0	0	0	0	0	0	0	0	0	0	0	0
WAY VOC	0	0	0	0	0	0	0	0	0	0	0	0
DISCUS	4	4	9	0	1	1	8	1	9	10	47	9
EVTEXT	0	0	2	0	0	0	1	0	1	0	4	1
ALL CRITICAL	**23**	**26**	**38**	**5**	**3**	**6**	**47**	**11**	**18**	**13**	**190**	**37**
ALL STRATEGIES	**77**	**53**	**93**	**22**	**16**	**20**	**102**	**37**	**51**	**43**	**514**	**100**

Source: own study.

Table III.4. Strategies applied in reading the English text

Subjects	A	B	C	D	E	F	G	H	I	J	ALL	%
Technical												
RR	8	4	9	0	0	0	5	0	6	0	32	5
LINK	23	1	7	1	1	1	0	1	0	3	38	6
ALL TECHNICAL	**31**	**5**	**16**	**1**	**1**	**1**	**5**	**1**	**6**	**3**	**70**	**12**
Emotional												
SUR	1	0	0	0	1	0	1	0	0	1	4	1
INTR	0	1	3	2	1	0	1	0	1	1	10	2

DIAL	5	0	3	0	0	0	7	0	2	1	18	3
DIS	0	0	0	0	0	0	0	0	0	0	0	0
ALL EMOTIONAL	**6**	**1**	**6**	**2**	**2**	**0**	**9**	**0**	**3**	**3**	**32**	**5**
Rational/logical												
BKNOW	2	3	1	0	1	2	2	1	3	2	17	3
PRED	6	3	4	2	1	0	7	2	3	1	29	5
IMI	14	8	7	5	6	11	25	0	12	14	102	17
SUM	8	1	3	1	0	5	4	9	5	2	38	6
FOC	12	3	15	2	6	4	1	1	6	7	57	10
IPUR	3	5	1	2	3	2	0	2	4	3	25	4
ASS	1	0	0	0	0	0	0	0	8	0	9	2
ALL RATIONAL	**46**	**23**	**31**	**12**	**17**	**24**	**39**	**15**	**41**	**29**	**277**	**46**
Evaluating/critical												
UND	9	2	4	1	0	0	4	4	1	1	26	4
NO UND	2	2	6	0	1	0	4	1	7	3	26	4
COR UND	0	0	0	0	0	0	1	0	1	1	3	1
UND?	1	0	1	0	0	1	2	0	2	0	7	1
CPRED	2	3	0	0	0	0	1	0	1	0	7	1
NCPRED	1	1	1	0	0	0	0	0	0	0	3	1
SCPRED	1	2	0	0	0	0	1	0	1	0	5	1
WAY	10	0	10	1	2	0	4	4	4	4	39	7
DIFF	2	0	0	0	0	0	2	0	0	1	5	1
PART	0	0	0	0	1	0	1	0	0	0	2	0
QUEST	6	0	6	0	0	0	1	0	0	0	13	2
AUT	0	0	0	0	0	0	0	0	2	1	3	1
TYPE	0	0	0	1	0	0	0	0	0	0	1	0
CRIT	0	0	0	0	0	0	0	0	0	0	0	0
VOC	4	1	9	0	0	0	4	7	3	1	29	5
VOC+	0	1	0	0	0	1	0	0	0	0	2	0
WAY VOC	1	1	3	0	0	0	0	4	3	0	12	2
DISCUS	2	0	1	0	1	2	5	1	11	6	29	5
EVTEXT	0	2	0	0	1	2	0	1	0	0	6	1
ALL CRITICAL	**41**	**15**	**41**	**3**	**6**	**6**	**30**	**22**	**36**	**18**	**218**	**37**
ALL STRATEGIES	124	44	94	18	26	31	83	38	86	53	597	100

Source: own study.

The analysis (see Table III.3. and III.4.) showed that almost all the strategies occurred in reading both texts. The main difference was observed in the use of strategies that involve coping with vocabulary and commenting on the difficulty of the text. When reading the Polish text, the students did not report using strategies indicated as VOC, VOC+ and WAY VOC. So they did not comment on not understanding vocabulary, knowing the meaning of certain words or how they guessed unknown words. Similarly, the strategies that involve stating uncertainty about one's comprehension (UND?) and evaluating the difficulty of a part of the text (DIFF) did not appear in the students' reports on the Polish text. As regards reading the English text, the students did not express disappointment with the text information or how the information is developed (DIS), nor did they criticize the text for a lack of information, linkage, poor cohesion (CRIT).

Additionally, the results of the analysis indicated differences between the individual students in their use of strategies. Some students reported more extensively; therefore, their reports are more verbose. Subjects A, B, C, G, I and J reported in just such a wordy manner. The other four students were much more "economical;" many strategies were not observed in their reporting. This observation will be explained in a further discussion concerning this stage of the study.

Question 1c)
Are there any differences in the frequency with which the subjects use particular strategies when reading texts written in their L1 and FL?

Comparison of the use of strategies in reading in Polish and in reading in English
A comparison of the frequencies of strategy use across the two texts showed differences (Table III.5. and III.6.). For example, more emotional strategies were observed in reading the Polish text than in reading the English text; whereas more rational strategies were found in reading the English text than in reading the Polish text. To see whether those differences were statistically significant, the Wilcoxon signed-rank test was applied (see Table III.5.). By way of explanation, this non-parametric test allows one to compare paired samples when the population under investigation cannot be assumed to be normally distributed. Calculations are based on median, not mean values; therefore, quartile and median values are given in the table. P values that are lower than .05 indicate differences that are statistically significant. Thus, the results show that in reading the Polish text more emotional strategies were used, whereas in reading the English text more rational strategies were applied. No statistically significant differences were found in the use of technical and critical strategies, which means that these types of strategies were applied with the same frequency in reading both texts. Additionally, the analysis showed differences in the use of two strategies – commenting on one's way of reading the text (WAY) and stating not understanding certain vocabulary items (VOC). Both strategies were observed more frequently in reading in English.

Table III.5. Strategies applied in reading in Polish and English – comparison

Strategy	Polish text			English text			Wilcoxon test	
	Median	Lower quartile	Upper quartile	Median	Lower quartile	Upper quartile	S	p
RR	.5	0	1	2	0	5.75	20	.058
LINK	2	1	2.75	1	1	2.5	11.5	.733
ALL TECHNICAL	**2**	**1**	**3.75**	**4**	**1**	**5.75**	**31**	**.079**
SUR	0	0	.75	0	0	1	7.5	.590
INTR	1.5	.25	3.5	1	.25	1	6	.098
DIAL	1.5	.25	5.5	.5	0	2.75	4.5	.127
DIS	0	0	1.75	0	0	0	0	.098
ALL EMOTIONAL	**7.5**	**1.5**	**8.75**	**2.5**	**1.25**	**5.25**	**4.5**	**.021**
BKNOW	1	0	3	2	1	2	17.5	1.000
PRED	2.5	1.25	3.75	2.5	1.25	3.75	15	.395
IMI	6.5	5	9.25	9.5	6.25	13.5	37	.096
SUM	2	1	3.75	3.5	1.25	5	22	.619
FOC	3.5	3	4.75	5	2.25	6.75	23	.149
IPUR	1	0	1.75	2.5	2	3	32.5	.256
ASS	0	0	0	0	0	0	1	.423
ALL RATIONAL	**22.5**	**13.25**	**25.5**	**26.5**	**18.5**	**37**	**48**	**.041**
UND	1.5	.25	4.5	1.5	1	4	16	.797
NO.UND	2	1	3	2	1	3.75	26.5	.677
COR.UND	0	0	0	0	0	.75	5	1.000
UND?	0	0	0	.5	0	1	15	.053
CPRED	0	0	.75	0	0	1	8.5	.890
NCPRED	0	0	2.75	0	0	.75	0	.100
SCPRED	0	0	.75	0	0	1	10	.572
WAY	0	0	1.75	4	1.25	4	41.5	.027
DIFF	0	0	0	0	0	.75	6	.174
PART	0	0	0	0	0	0	4	.773
QUEST	1.5	0	7.25	0	0	.75	1	.104
AUT	0	0	0	0	0	0	1	1.000
TYPE	0	0	0	0	0	0	0	1.000
CRIT	.5	0	2	0	0	0	0	.057
VOC	0	0	0	2	.25	4	28	.022
VOC+	0	0	0	0	0	0	3	.346
WAY.VOC	0	0	0	.5	0	2.5	15	.057
DISCUS	4	1	8.75	1.5	1	4.25	3.5	.090
EVTEXT	0	0	.75	0	0	1	17	.665
ALL CRITICAL	**15.5**	**7.25**	**25.25**	**20**	**8.25**	**34.5**	**31.5**	**.313**

Source: own study.

Question 1d)

Are there any patterns which reflect the manner in which the subjects use the strategies to construct their comprehension of the texts?

Patterns of strategy use in Polish

To check whether there is any statistically significant pattern of strategy use in reading the Polish text, the Friedman test was applied. The results ($\chi^2 = 25.102$; $p = .000$) indicated that there is a consistent pattern. To find the exact pattern of strategy use, i.e., to see which types of strategies were used more frequently, the Dunn test was used. The results (Table III.6., Figure III.1) showed that when the students were reading in Polish, they used technical and emotional strategies significantly less frequently than rational and critical strategies. Figure III.1 shows the median values for each type of strategy. It indicates the following median ranking of strategies: rational (22.5), critical (15.5), emotional (7.5) and technical (2).

Patterns of strategy use in English

The same procedure was applied to investigate the pattern of strategy use for students reading the English text. The application of the Friedman test ($\chi^2 = 25.606$; $p = .000$) indicated that there is a statistically significant pattern of strategy use. The Dunn test (Table III.6., Figure III.2.) showed that, similarly to reading in Polish, in reading the English text technical and emotional strategies were used significantly less frequently than rational and critical strategies. Figure III.2. shows the median values for each type of strategy. The median ranking of strategies for the English text is as follows: rational (26.5), critical (20), technical (4) and emotional (2.5).

Table III.6. The use of the types of strategies in reading in English and Polish

Comparison	Difference in rank sum	p
Polish text		
ALL TECHNICAL vs. ALL RATIONAL	–173	.035
ALL TECHNICAL vs. ALL CRITICAL	–152	.035
ALL EMOTIONAL vs. ALL RATIONAL	–136	.035
ALL EMOTIONAL vs. ALL CRITICAL	–115	.012
English text		
ALL TECHNICAL vs. ALL RATIONAL	–207	.035
ALL TECHNICAL vs. ALL CRITICAL	–148	.035
ALL EMOTIONAL vs. ALL RATIONAL	–245	.035
ALL EMOTIONAL vs. ALL CRITICAL	–186	.035

Source: own study.

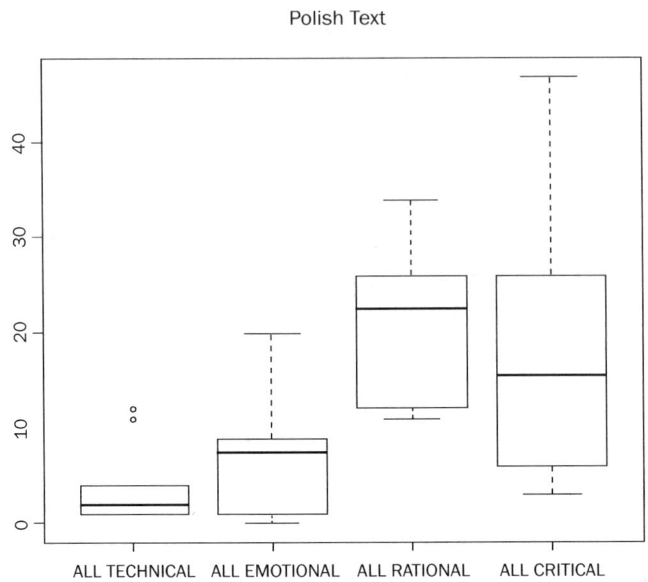

Figure III.1. Median ranks for the Polish text

Source: own study.

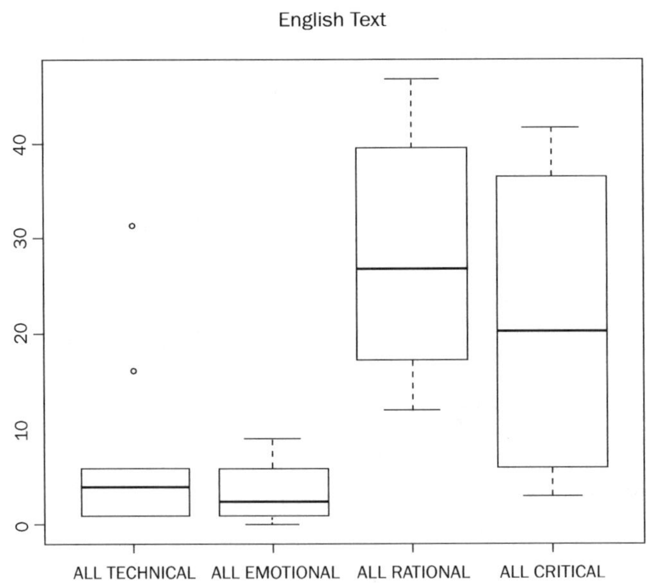

Figure III.2. Median ranks for the English text

Source: own study.

Question 1e)
If the students follow some patterns in their use of strategies, are the patterns the same in reading both texts?

Since it was found that there was a consistent pattern of strategy use when the students were reading the English text and when the students were reading the Polish text (see Question 1d), the next question was whether that pattern was the same in reading in English as in reading in Polish. The difference in the use of strategies was calculated by means of the following formula: the frequency when reading in Polish minus the frequency when reading in English. Figure III.3. shows the results of the calculations. The differences are represented by means of rectangular boxes. Differences are statistically significant when the box does not "touch" the 0 axis. Positive values (those placed above the 0 axis) indicate strategies that were more frequently used in reading the Polish text; negative values (those placed below the 0 axis) represent strategies that were more frequently applied in reading the English text. Thus, it was found that the students were more likely to use emotional strategies when reading in Polish than when reading in English. However, they were more likely to apply rational strategies when reading in English than when reading in Polish. This confirms the results of the analysis presented in Table III.5.

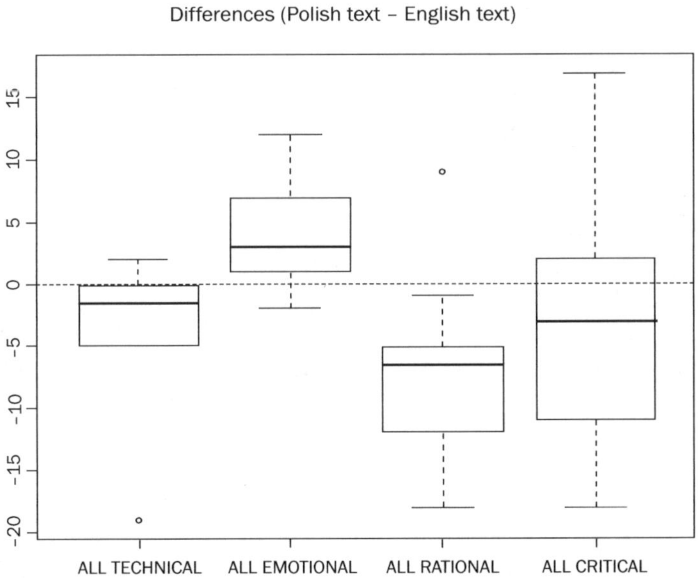

Figure III.3. Median ranks for Polish/English differences

Source: own study.

2.3. Discussion

The analysis of the students' actions indicated differences in strategy use between the students' reading in English and in Polish. In the discussion below, those differences that were not statistically significant are also taken into account. It is believed that they represent tendencies that are worth pointing out. The following was observed:

1) only in reading in English did the students apply actions taken in relation to encountering unknown vocabulary, such as stating their not understanding of certain vocabulary items (VOC), stating that they knew the meaning of certain vocabulary items (VOC+) and commenting on their way of guessing an unknown word (WAY VOC);
2) only in reading in English did the students report uncertainty about their comprehension (UND?) and evaluation of the difficulty of a part of the text (DIFF);
3) in reading in Polish more emotional strategies than in reading in English were found; only in reading in Polish did the students report an expression of disappointment with text information or with how the information is developed (DIS) (which is an example of an emotional strategy);
4) the following three critical strategies were more frequent in reading in Polish: asking questions about the text information (QUEST), discussing the text information and extrapolating (DISCUS) and criticizing the text for a lack of information, linkage, poor cohesion etc. (CRIT) – this strategy appeared only in reading the Polish text;
5) in reading in English there were more comments on the way of reading (WAY) than was the case in Polish;
6) in reading in English more rational/logical strategies were found than in reading in Polish;
7) in reading in English the students applied more rereading (RR) than when reading in Polish.

Let us discuss all the conclusions in more detail. The students experienced **vocabulary problems** while reading the English text. Coping with vocabulary is a strategy taken during a development of the surface form of a text. This finding shows that while reading in a foreign language the students focused more on constructing this basic level of their comprehension than while reading in their L1.

The fact that only in reading the English text did the subjects state **uncertainty about their comprehension** (UND?) and evaluated the difficulty of the text they were reading (DIFF) may be explained in a similar way. It seems that the students perceived reading in a FL as more difficult than reading in their L1 and consequently were more conscious of their reading problems when reading in the FL.

The students used more **emotional strategies** while reading in Polish. By way of repetition, emotional strategies involve expressing surprise, interest and disappointment about the information presented in the texts. They also mean the dialoguing with the text about one's comprehension by asking questions like "OK?," "Really?,"

"No?". In fact, the strategy of expressing disappointment appeared only in reading the Polish text. The example quoted below shows the nature of emotional strategies. While reading the Polish text, the following comment was made:

> *well, but do they really change the brain? They change our behavior, but do they change the brain? I demand some evidence! Perhaps, there will be some evidence later that meditation and education (..) change the brain, is that so? We will see!*
>
> (this example is taken from Student G's protocol)

The larger number of emotional strategies in reading the Polish text than in reading the English text seems to demonstrate more personal engagement on the part of the readers when reading in Polish. This may indicate students' ability to focus not only on the textbase, but also the situation model of the text.

The students produced **critical comments concerning the text** (CRIT) only while reading in Polish. The students criticized the following aspects of the Polish text:

- its complexity and chaotic presentation of ideas;
- lack of clarity and not enough arguments to support the main ideas that the readers managed to identify;
- lack of text coherence.

The readers also blamed the author of the text for his "attempts" to impose his opinions on them without providing enough arguments; some students even said that "the author is wrong" in what he tries to present. All the comments reflected students' attempts to comprehend the text, both to identify the main ideas of the paragraphs and to accept the correctness of this identification. It was very easy to observe how this behaviour accompanied the readers in their construction of the propositions of their models; how important it was for them to find a sufficient amount of evidence to support the correctness of their propositions before accepting them as the "reliable" scaffolds of their comprehension. This finding indicates that while reading in their L1 the students demonstrated certain aspects of a "deeper," more critical and self-conscious level of understanding. The subjects were more active and "cautious" in forming propositions of their models of the text. The process of comprehending involved not only identifying the main ideas, but also verifying their correctness. The readers were able to look at the process of reading the text as if from a distance; they became engaged with the text, which resulted in more monitoring. This stage of the analysis does not allow us to draw similar conclusions about reading in English.

The students asked more direct questions about the information contained in the text while reading the Polish text (more QUEST strategies). In these questions, the readers focused on the ideas that they found unclear or difficult to comprehend. It seems that the students used this technique to emphasize the ideas which they wanted to know more about in order to develop their understanding. For example, Student B asked: "But again what is determination in this context? Why is the brain called our computer, the computer of our soul, so what is it anyway?".

It is important to explain that the fact that the students did not ask so many direct questions while reading the English text does not mean that they did not seek information while reading in English. They realised the same need by means of indirect questions, e.g., "I was wondering" and indirect statements, e.g., "It is written here that;" "the text does not say." It is difficult to explain this difference in the reporting of the reading of the two texts. The higher frequency of asking direct questions while reading in Polish may mean that the students became more personally involved when reading in their native language. They were able to look at the text as if from a distance and venture to ask their own questions, however simple they were.

More strategies that involved discussing the text appeared when reading in Polish. The subjects discussed the text information, explained to themselves what they understood; they also expressed their opinion, e.g., agreement or disagreement with the text information and extrapolated on the basis of the information provided in the text. Below, a few examples are presented.

> *well (...) the author is clever (...) really clever. He can see issues which reflect our reality (...) I think only very few people can notice such obvious things.*

> *The reason is that both emotional and physical pains are not always pathological states. (reading aloud the text) Who claims that it's pathological? I think it is not pathological at all.*

> *children know that the brain is useful in the process of thinking but they don't associate, no, this brain with emotions or like here exactly sadness or love. Don't they? Yes, exactly and here I associate again, yes we seem to associate that, don't we? Let's take love; we associate love with the heart but not with the brain, and in fact as if later we start to associate it with other things, for example everything is in our brain, not in our heart, but it is the brain. And it's how I understand it, link it and it makes me think, think.*

The reason why several students were more eager to discuss the ideas from the text while reading Polish may reflect their ability to focus not only on a construction of the textbase but also the situation model of the text.

The students **commented** more often **on their way of reading the text** while reading in English than in Polish (WAY). The students commented on the following aspects of their reading the English text:
- reading carefully, reading slowly, reading sentence by sentence, reading in a more global way, etc. (in many cases students explained why they were reading in a particular way);
- analyzing the text, comparing ideas from different paragraphs, inferring the meaning of certain concepts;
- reading and simultaneously translating sentences into Polish (students called this process "silent translation" or "translation in their mind," emphasizing that this action helped them to comprehend the English text);
- translating in their mind and visualizing ideas.

Additionally, many students discussed their style of learning and how it influences their reading, e.g., one said: "I am a visual learner so while reading I usually focus on pictures." Students also compared various ways of reading, i.e., reading in different situations, such as during English classes, tests and the think-aloud session.

As regards reading in Polish, in their comments most of the students focused on explaining the reasons why they understood or did not understand the text (5 comments), only one comment described a technical aspect of reading the text (omitting sentences in reading). By way of comparison, comments concerning reading in English in all the cases entailed commenting on the technical aspects of reading and were caused by problems the students experienced while understanding the text.

To sum up, the students commented more frequently on their own way of reading in English than in Polish. It seems that the students when reading in English were more sensitive to how they were reading the texts. The larger number of comments on reading the English text may be attributed to the higher level of metacognition, i.e., person knowledge (Flavell 1981; see Part I, Chapter 4, Section 4.3.1),which the students developed while encountering comprehension problems. More comments related to the technical aspects of reading in the reports on the English text may indicate that students while reading a foreign language still focused on so called lower-level skills of reading – skills which become automatized when readers develop fluency in comprehension.

In reading in English, more **rational/logical strategies** were found than in reading in Polish. By way of repetition, this category of strategies reflected students' attempts to manipulate the text, e.g., to compare or link different parts of the text in order to construct comprehension. The analysis (see Table III.3. and III.4.) shows that out of 7 strategies the following five were reported more frequently: predicting the development of ideas, speculations about the implications of the given text information (PRED), making backward inferences to explain current text information by drawing on previously given text information and identifying the main idea (IMI), summing up information to capture the essential information (main ideas) presented in the text with the reader's own words and drawing conclusions (SUM), focusing on certain parts of the text and emphasizing certain words (FOC) as well as identifying the purpose of parts of the text, e.g., as an introduction, the main idea, examples to support the main idea, a conclusion (IPUR). This finding implies that comprehending the text in English required more action on the part of the readers. In other words, when reading in the FL, the subjects needed more strategies to construct the propositional textbase, which is the network of ideas presented in the text.

More **rereading strategies** were observed in reading in English. In reading in the FL, the students reported the following factors that made them reread the text (in brackets the number of strategies are provided):

- difficulty and complexity of the text (2);
- lack of understanding of the content of the paragraphs (4);
- difficulty in understanding words (6);
- difficulty in identifying the main ideas of the paragraphs (5);
- looking for links with the earlier sentences in the paragraph to confirm understanding (7);
- lack of concentration (8).

The following factors seemed to contribute to a rereading of the Polish text:

- looking for confirmation of comprehension of the whole paragraph (4);
- looking for confirmation of predictions about the paragraph (1);
- difficulty in identifying the main ideas of the paragraphs (1);
- lack of concentration (1);
- other factors (1).

It is worth noting that while reading English, all the subjects reported rereading sentences or parts of sentences in the paragraphs that they talked about; in rereading the Polish text, half of the strategies involved rereading the whole paragraph. In conclusion, the results show that the main difference lies in the number of these strategies reported by the students, i.e., more strategies were reported in English (33) than in Polish (8). It seems that the strategy of rereading played different roles in coping with the two texts. In English, rereading helped students to deal with the difficulty of the text as well as to understand the ideas of the text and words that they did know (which indicated focus on both the lower- and higher-level subskills of reading). In reading Polish, the readers applied this strategy to find confirmation of their understanding and predictions (thereby concentrating on higher-level subskills of reading, those involving comprehension). In reading English, the subjects far more often resorted to rereading as a solution to losing concentration, which may imply that the process of reading the English text required more attention. Another difference is that while rereading in Polish the students operated on larger parts of the text, i.e., the whole paragraph; in English, they reread single sentences or their parts. This finding shows that in contrast to reading in their mother tongue, reading in the FL entailed manipulating within a more local co-text.

2.4. Conclusions

In conclusion, the analysis of strategies identified in the reports shows differences in certain aspects of students' reading in Polish and their reading in English. In reading in Polish, the subjects seemed to focus more on higher-level skills than on lower-level skills. They concentrated more on forming the propositional textbase and the situation model of the text than on developing the surface form of the text, which means processing the text in order to construct a network of semantic information and working on their own interpretations of the text. In reading in English, the students concentrated on both higher- and lower-level skills. They seemed to work on the surface form (which was demonstrated by students' attempts to understand unknown vocabulary) as well as the propositional textbase (which involved attempts to comprehend the text). In reading in Polish, the following actions indicate a development of the situation model of the text: more active personal involvement on the part of the reader, asking oneself questions concerning the ideas of the text, as if arguing with the text and its author, discussing the text content, expressing agreement or disagreement and extrapolating. Also the use of emotional strategies may be considered indicative of students' attempts to construct the situation model of the text. In reading in English, the subjects demonstrated a higher level of metacognition, i.e., they were aware of how they were reading. This can be attributed to the increased sensitivity to comprehension problems the students experienced while reading the English text. In Polish while rereading the text the students processed larger parts of the text, e.g., paragraphs; by contrast in English – smaller, which involved focusing on individual sentences. This difference may be explained by the students' tendency to use a narrow co-text in reading English and a wider co-text in reading Polish.

Additionally, this stage of analysis indicates differences between the individual students in their use of strategies. Some students reported more extensively in both Polish and English; the others were less verbose both in their mother tongue and the foreign language. This allows me to assume that there may be some similarities between how the individual students processed the texts in Polish and English. This assumption will be discussed in a further section of this part.

As regards the conceptualization of reading, at this stage of analysis, reading appears to be a list of actions. The actions, reflecting the students' reading, pointed to the prominent role that the text played in their readings. It became clear that it was necessary to account in more detail for the dialogue between reader and text. This led me to the next stage in the analysis.

3. Analysis of problems and solutions: Stage 2

3.1. Research questions

To explore the interaction between the reader and the text, a concept of reading as a problem-solving activity was accepted (after Olshavsky 1976/1977). The aim of the analysis was to see what the subjects identified as difficult in their reading and how they coped in such situations, i.e., what solutions they applied. Reading problems were defined as places in students' reports in which students paused in the text and commented on those moments. Very often students named such reading experiences "difficulties," e.g., by saying that they did not understand something or found something unclear or disappointing. In many cases, the readers asked themselves questions concerning their reading problems, e.g., "what does it mean?," "how does this word refer to that one?".

The following research questions were asked at this stage of the study:

- What problems did the students encounter in their reading of the Polish text and in their reading of the English text?
- What solutions did they apply to cope with the problems in reading in Polish and in reading in English?
- What do the results of the analysis of the students' problems and solutions indicate about the differences in reading in Polish and reading in English?

3.2. Procedures applied in the analysis

To identify students' problems and solutions, it was necessary to observe how the readers approached the text and to what text signals they reacted; in other words, to look at how the students, in taking advantage of the text, constructed their mental representations of the texts. The analysis looked at the mental structures (a set of ideas) that students used to build their models of the text (their comprehension of the texts).

It also became clear that it was necessary to prepare an analysis of the text and to relate it to how particular students coped with the text. To analyse the text, the expository text grammar model by Britton was used (see Part I, Chapter 3, Section 3.4.3.2.). By way of repetition, Britton (1994: 641 citing Gernsbacher 1990) claims that "expository texts are intended to build a structure in the readers' mind." It offers a set of sentences, and it is the reader's task to obtain the structure of ideas. Britton (1994: 644) concludes that "the mental structures that readers derive from a text often will be incomplete or incorrect, when compared to the structure intended by the author."

Thus, to infer how the students constructed their models of the texts (i.e., their comprehension), two steps were taken. First, both the Polish and the English text were "deconstructed" using Britton's grammar, which resulted in the identification of the main propositions of the texts as well as the interconnections among them. The results of the deconstruction of the two texts are given in the Appendices (see Appendix 1 and 2). Then, in each protocol the ideas the student constructed on the basis of the text were related to the ideas of the text and finally the problems and solutions of each student identified. The results of this analysis are presented below.

3.3. Results

3.3.1. Problems and solutions applied in reading in Polish and English – a comparison of comprehension processes

The comparison of how the subjects coped with the problems they encountered while reading the texts point to certain similarities as well as differences between reading in Polish and reading in English. A similar number of problems was identified in reading each text: 78 problems were found in reading the Polish text and 74 problems in reading the English text (Table III.7.). To see whether those differences were statistically significant, the Wilcoxon signed-rank test was applied. The results (see Table III.8. and Figure III.4.) show that no statistically significant differences were found between the number of problems noted in reading in Polish and the number of problems in reading in English.

Table III.7. Number of problems in reading in Polish and English by individual students

Subjects	A	B	C	D	E	F	G	H	I	J	Total
Number of problems in Polish	12	17	20	1	1	3	15	5	3	1	78
Number of problems in English	19	6	16	1	2	1	10	4	11	4	74

Source: own study.

Table III.8. Number of problems noted in reading in Polish and in English – a comparison

Language	Median	Lower quartile	Upper quartile	Wilcoxon test	
				S	p
Polish	4	1.5	14.25	24.5	.859
English	5	2.5	10.75		

Source: own study.

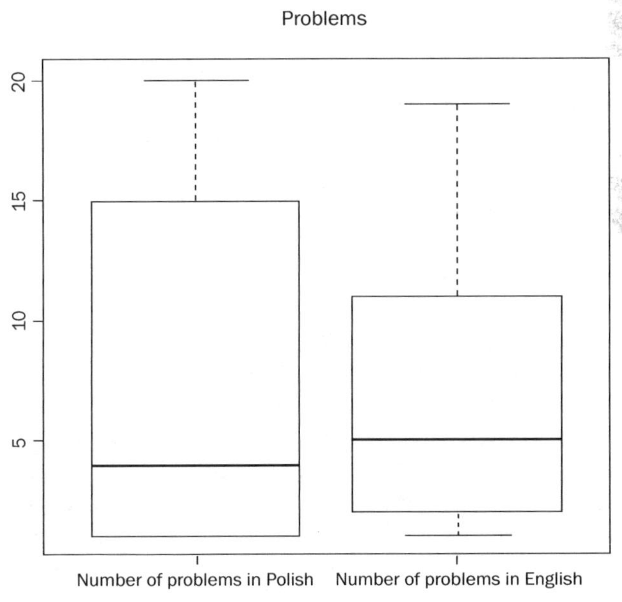

Figure III.4. Median ranks for the number of problems in reading in Polish and in English

Source: own study.

Table III.9. Problems and solutions in reading in Polish and English – comparison

The Polish text	The English text
Problems	**Problems**
Not understanding the text information	Not understanding the text information and not understanding vocabulary
Strategies involved in solving problems	**Strategies involved in solving problems**
Paying attention to the title and subtitle	Paying attention to the title and subtitle
Paying attention to the picture	Paying attention to the picture
Paying attention to the first and last sentences in paragraphs	Paying attention to the first and last sentences in paragraphs
Referring to earlier parts of the text	Referring to earlier parts of the text
Drawing on prior knowledge	X
Dialoging with the text ideas	X
Summing up the information	Summing up the information
X*	Translation
Attributing comprehension problems to the text and the author	Attributing comprehension problems to one's language competence (not knowing vocabulary)

* the sign X indicates that a given strategy did not appear in the students' protocols

Source: own study.

A qualitative comparison (Table III.9.) shows that the main difference concerns the source of problems. In reading the Polish text, the students reported difficulties in comprehending ideas; while in reading the English text, the protocols reflected problems in both comprehending ideas and understanding vocabulary. The analysis revealed that the subjects used the same types of strategies to solve problems in reading both texts. The following actions were applied in reading in English and in Polish: paying attention to the title and subtitle, paying attention to the picture, paying attention to the first and last sentence in paragraphs, referring to earlier parts of the text, summing up the information. The following strategies were used only in reading in Polish: drawing on prior knowledge and dialoguing with the text ideas. For obvious reasons, translation was used only in reading in English. Another difference is that while reading the Polish text, the learners attributed their comprehension problems to the text and the author; in contrast, while reading in English, they attributed their comprehension problems to their language competence (usually not knowing vocabulary). The most common processes involved in solving problems in reading the texts are discussed in detail below.

Referring to earlier parts of the text

In this strategy applied in reading in Polish and in English, the students drew on the previously given text information in order to make backward inferences and explain the current text information. The readers also used this strategy to work on the ideas that they did not comprehend while reading the previous parts of the text. This helped the students to modify and correct the outcome of their earlier comprehension. While reading the English text, they also referred to vocabulary items that they had not managed to understand in the earlier parts of the text. It is important to emphasize that returning to the unanswered questions concerning understanding text ideas and vocabulary was a popular approach; the readers were very persistent in raising the questions that they had not answered earlier. It was interesting to observe that such "gaps" in the students' models sometimes hindered comprehension of the current text information.

Drawing on prior knowledge

This strategy was observed only in reading in Polish. Two different functions that this approach played were identified: facilitative and debilitative. In the first case, the strategy helped the subjects to make backward inferences to explain the current text information. In the latter case, the readers encountered in the text an idea that he/she recognized as familiar and by elaborating on this idea they developed a false impression that their comprehension was successful. For example, the readers drew on their prior knowledge (e.g., what they know about the body/soul dualism) to confirm the way they understood the text, ignoring, however, text clues that directed them to a different understanding.

Dialoguing with the text ideas

It is the next strategy that was observed only in reading in Polish. Sometimes the students experienced problems with accepting text information. In such situations, they commented on text ideas and often expressed disappointment or surprise. They were "faithful" to their own beliefs, which sometimes did not agree with the arguments presented in the text. In many cases, this behaviour distracted the readers from following instructions left by the author in the text.

Summing up the information

As a remedy action, this strategy was applied more frequently in reading in Polish than in reading in English. Another difference was that in reading in Polish the subjects summed up larger parts of the text, i.e., a few paragraphs or the whole article. In reading in English, in most cases, summing up involved parts of paragraphs; summing up the whole article was applied in reading the last paragraph only by very few students. The students summed up the text they had read for a number of reasons: to organize the propositions in their model, to see how the text develops particular ideas, to evaluate their comprehension (e.g., after forming a new idea). In some cases, this action helped the subjects to realize that their comprehension was incorrect.

Translation

Translation (from English into Polish) was applied by all the students. It facilitated their attempts to infer the meaning of unknown words; the students looked for Polish equivalents of English words that they considered important in constructing their comprehension. Additionally, translation was done to solve problems connected with understanding ideas. It seems that in some cases managing to translate difficult parts of the text absolved the students from a necessity to monitor and evaluate their comprehension. This means that the readers seemed to feel satisfied with their translation; they were not aware of their incomplete or incorrect comprehension. This situation can be partly explained by the nature of the think-aloud method. Since the study was conducted in Polish, for some readers introspective reporting took the form of a direct, literal translation of the text they read. It may be assumed that the ability to read and at the same translate the text "distracted" the students from a more conscious and more effective development of the process of comprehension.

Identifying the source of comprehension problems

While reading the Polish text, the students blamed the text and the author for their comprehension problems. They complained about the complexity of the text and its poor coherence. The author was blamed for raising theses and not supporting them with sufficient arguments. In reading in English, the readers ascribed their problems to their foreign language competence; in most cases, they complained about not remembering the meaning of the words. It is worth noting that several students prided themselves on knowing the words in the text that they considered crucial for their comprehension, emphasising thereby the importance of vocabulary in their reading.

3.3.2. How did the students cope with vocabulary problems in reading the English text?

The protocols demonstrated the vocabulary difficulties the students encountered when constructing their models. The students reported their failure to understand the following words: "obsolete," "affluence," "abundance," "capacity." Sometimes the subjects named these words "the key words" in their understanding of the article. All the students who reported a concrete lack of a vocabulary item made an attempt to guess the meaning of the words.

As regards understanding "obsolete" (which appears in the title), the reports indicate that the most frequent strategies the students applied were continuing to read and translation. Unfortunately, neither strategy proved effective. The translation attempts indicated that the students did not manage to infer the meaning of the word. Those who decided to read on (i.e., to start reading the next part of the text) did not return to this word in their further reading. The most frequent strategy the students applied while working on the meaning of the other words was to continue reading and use a wider local context around the text, i.e., reading more carefully the sentence before and after the difficult word. It was surprising to observe that the students did not continue working on the meaning of the unknown words, unless the word appeared in the text again. Very rarely did they make an attempt to restart their work while reading a paragraph in which the words did not occur.

To understand how the students worked out the meaning of the words, let us look at the analysis of the English text (see Appendix 2). "Abundance" occurs in the first paragraph and is followed by words that can be treated as examples of abundance , i.e., "more labour-saving machines, more comforts." Further, it is paraphrased as "a rich life for everyone." It is worth noting that the word "abundance" is presented as a superordinate term, i.e., one at a higher level of generality than "labour-saving machines," "comforts" and "choices." Moreover, the word is defined by "more." It seems that the context around the word (lexical cohesion of this part of the text) provides readers with sufficient data so that they can understand the paragraph without knowing the exact meaning of the word. Surprisingly, only one student (Student I) reported noticing the superordinate function of the word; however, he was not able to infer its exact meaning.

The word "affluence" appears in the second paragraph. The meaning of the word is enhanced by lexical cohesion of the text, i.e., "lavish" and "luxuries" in the sentences surrounding "affluence." Both "abundance" and "affluence" reoccur in paragraph 7. The students noticed the words and tried to work out their meaning again. They referred to the earlier paragraphs and translated the whole sentences in which the words appear, however leaving the difficult words untranslated. This means that their attempts were not effective. For example, Student C referred to paragraph 2 in the following way:

> S: *Now the last paragraph. (..) I've stopped at the first sentence and I'm going back to the sentence with "affluence" in the second paragraph. Because I claim that this sentence is VERY (the student emphasises this word] important.*
> T: *Which one?*
> S: *Well, this first in this paragraph. It's what I think. So I'm thinking [laughter] I'm going back to this paragraph, in which this word has appeared and I'm going to read it again to infer the meaning. (..) uhm Now I'm thinking about looking it up in a dictionary.*

One may wonder why the readers paid attention to these two words throughout their work and attempted to guess their meaning again. It seems that they simply needed the words to understand the text. Britton's (1994) text grammar offers the following explanation: an unknown word creates a kind of empty node in the reader's model, an incomplete place that calls for instantiating, i.e., filling with meaning. When the position of this word becomes fixed in the reader's model, deciding on or confirming the meaning of this word is needed in the process of evaluating and revising the structure of the reader's model.

To sum up, the analysis of the protocols indicates that encountering new vocabulary items resulted in attempts to infer their meaning. Failures to apply successful strategies resulted in: losing an opportunity to form a new proposition in one's comprehension (as was the case with "obsolete"), incomplete understanding of a paragraph or very general comprehension of a paragraph (e.g., Student I's conclusion about the author's attitude to progress despite his lack of understanding of "abundance" in the first paragraph).

3.3.3. How did the students cope with difficulties in understanding concepts?

The protocols show that the readers were sensitive to the main **paralinguistic devices** of the text, such as the title and subtitle. In this way, the subjects identified the overall subject of the text, which they developed in their further reading. The students also reacted to the picture, which, I would say, they treated as part of the text. The title, subtitle and picture helped the readers to make predictions about the content and type of the text and thereby construct the first propositions in their comprehension. The subjects referred to the picture also in their further work. It seems that the picture helped them to develop nodes in their comprehension that had been initiated by the text earlier. It also facilitated evaluation of the interconnectedness of nodes within the models the readers had developed. This seems to illustrate Gernsbacher's (1991) claim that both reading comprehension and picture-story comprehension may be underpinned by the same cognitive mechanisms (see Part I, Chapter 3, Section 3.4.3.1.).

The reports indicated that the readers constructed their models around the **key words**, i.e., the words that serve the function of key concepts in their comprehension. It is clear that the students first identified the main topic of the text, i.e., progress in the English text and the body/soul dualism in the Polish text. Then, the readers kept attaching subordinate parts of the model, e.g., advantages and limits of progress in the English text, and various opinions concerning the body/soul dualism in the Polish text. Although the subjects read the text paragraph by paragraph, they often shifted their attention to earlier places in the text, e.g., in order to "refresh" those nodes in their comprehension that they considered important for their current state of understanding. All the readers developed their models in a top-down direction. They began from the main topic and then added new material. It is worth emphasising that this is the hierarchy provided by the texts; in each text both the title and the first paragraph forward the main topic of the text.

The most direct text signals noticed by the students seem to be **overlaps of content words** between paragraphs, not only the adjacent ones. Content words directed the students to build mental structures and link paragraphs. The readers referred to earlier paragraphs in order to develop nodes already present in their models, but which needed further development. The reports showed how the subjects reacted to the incompleteness of their nodes and how persistent they were in the attachment of incoming information. As an example of this behaviour, let us follow how the subjects searched for the development of the concept of limits in the English text.

The word "limits" appears in the last sentence of the first paragraph. All the students paid attention to this sentence; however, at this stage they did not report any comprehension problems. They looked for more information about the concept of limits while reading the next two paragraphs, although these sections did not contain the word "limits." Some students were very disappointed that they could not develop their understanding of this concept. They asked the following questions: "Why is there nothing about limits here." One subject, while reading the third paragraph, attempted to predict what "limits" may refer to, wondering whether "limits" are disadvantages of progress. She said:

> *I'm still wondering where the limits from the uhm first paragraph are; I'm wondering if this really really matters uhm if this is important here, if this will (..) as if it seems (...) because the whole article, I think, is about progress, that although it has disadvantages people expect changes.*

The same student said the following while reading the fifth paragraph:

Now I'm going to read the fifth paragraph and I'm still going to wonder if the text will be about those negative sides of progress if progress is a good thing uhm and now something has come to my mind uhm about the first paragraph, about those limits. I simply think that those limits can be, can be, that the limits of progress can be its negative sides.

Drawing on Britton's grammar, it becomes clear that by doing this, the student worked on the incomplete node referring to "limits" in her model of the text before filling it with the information finally available in the text. The analysis of the article (see Appendix 2) shows that the third paragraph is a move-up to the concept of limits from the first paragraph. It also overlaps with the information expressed in the second paragraph. The students reported linking this paragraph with either the last sentence in the first paragraph (which says that "progress may have limits after all") or with the second paragraph (which describes advantages of progress). In the first case, the students saw paragraph 3 as a continuation of "limits" from paragraph 1; in the latter case, they noticed a contrast between the good sides of progress (from paragraph 2) and the limits enumerated and explained in paragraph 3. The protocols show that both solutions proved effective and the readers were satisfied with their comprehension.

It is important to underline the role of the **first** and the **last sentences** of paragraphs in the students' construction of comprehension. The first sentences in paragraphs often provide material for new nodes in readers' comprehension or they enlarge on the information mentioned before (see Appendix 2). For example, the first sentence in the sixth paragraph in the English text "The global distribution of wealth raises the same question in a more urgent form." contains both the old and new information. The last sentences in the text paragraphs are often conclusions of the paragraphs; they unitize the information that has been developed throughout the paragraph. For example, "Progress is an offer we have been unable to refuse." (the last sentence in the fourth paragraph in the English text) is an example of a sentence which summarizes the message of the whole paragraph. The last sentence in a paragraph may also signal new information that will be developed in the next paragraph. An example of the given-new structure is the last sentence in the first paragraph in the English text: "Or so we used to believe, until recent events began to suggest that progress may have limits after all."

The think-aloud reports show that in reading both texts the subjects spent more time on reading the first and last sentences (which was demonstrated by the larger amount of reporting). Several students commented on the specificity of the first and last sentences in the paragraphs. Below, several examples are provided.

Student I about the sixth paragraph of the Polish text:

I'm reading the first sentence of the next paragraph. It just came to my mind that the author sort of knows how to write texts. The first sentence in each paragraph is always so nice, it introduces, in a nice way says what the whole paragraph will be about. (..) It stirs my curiosity, invites me to read on.

Student D about the first sentences in paragraphs in the English text:

Uhm well I first went through the whole paragraphs, then I decided to focus only on the first sentences of the consecutive paragraphs and sometimes halfway in the paragraph, where the main idea was developed, I returned to the first sentence to examine these ideas again, yes, they helped me a bit.

Student C about the last sentence in the second paragraph in the Polish text:

Well, and again the last sentence, I don't know, do all the readers do this? They pay attention to the last sentence (laughter). Yes, it really shows, it explains.

Student A about the last sentence in the first paragraph:

Uhm, ours, uhm, now I go back, back to the last sentence in the first paragraph; to see more precisely I go back to the last sentence I read once again the last sentence (...) and in the last sentence it is mentioned that progress.

Another linguistic feature to which the readers reacted was the conjunction "yet" in paragraph 4 in the English text. The subjects reported sensitivity to an adversative relation signalled by the word; in a visible way, it seemed to influence the students' comprehension. For example, Student E, while reading this paragraph, said: "Uhm, it is a short paragraph, but at this point it changes the way of reasoning of the person reading this text." Alike, Student G explained: "Oh I can see a change, the author does not elaborate on the negative aspects of our civilization anymore." It is surprising that the readers did not report noticing the word "ale" (Eng. "yet"), playing the same linguistic function in the Polish text, in paragraphs 1 and 3. In both texts, the words serve as signals that direct readers to stop developing the comprehension initiated by the preceding text and to confront their model of the text with the information that follows the conjunction. By way of repetition, Britton (1994, see Part I, Chapter 3, Section 3.4.3.2.) says that the process of following such text signals to construct one's comprehension is highly automatic and therefore may not appear in the readers' introspection. The difference between treating the conjunctions in Polish and English may suggest that while reading in a foreign language the readers were more focused on the surface structure of the text; in other words, they paid more attention to the individual words of the text.

3.4. Conclusions about the students' comprehension of the text

The analysis provides valuable information about how the students constructed their models of the text. In reading both texts, they began their work from the title and subtitle. They focused on the information that they found familiar – the idea of progress in the English text and the idea of soul in the Polish text, ignoring what seemed new and unfamiliar – the idea about progress being obsolete and exclusive (later developed as the idea of democracy) and the idea about rejecting dogmas. It often happened that when reading a particular paragraph the students focused first on the propositions that they had formed earlier, sometimes ignoring the text instructions offered in the particular paragraph.

The analysis of the reports reflecting reading in Polish and English suggests that reading comprehension of the text is a long process; propositions after their initial formation need strengthening so that they can be accepted and incorporated into the reader's model. The protocols show how persistent the subjects were in strengthening "underdeveloped" nodes in their representations, which sometimes resulted in the overlooking of new information in the text (cf. Part I, Chapter 3, Section 3.4.3.3. for Britton's explanation of activating mental structures in the reader's representation of the text). The analysis points to a number of strategies the subjects applied to solve their problems. Summing up played an important role in this process; enumerating the ideas which the readers had managed to form earlier strengthened the current nodes and their links with other nodes in the readers' representations. Summing up was very helpful at the end of reading the article; the readers collected the propositions they had constructed earlier, following a bottom-up direction (i.e., from less to more general ideas) – encompassing in this way the whole model that they had formed while reading the text.

It is important to note that there were protocols in which students reported very few situations that I classified as problems. Two subjects did not seem to experience much difficulty while reading; they simply paraphrased the text message formulating thereby propositions in their model. One student (Student D), on the other hand, focused on only the first sentences in the paragraphs and due to her "superficial" fast reading style she did not identify many situations as problems. This finding demonstrates individual differences among the subjects of the study.

As regards differences between reading in Polish and reading in English, the following conclusions can be drawn:

- No differences were found between the number of problems in reading in English and the number of problems in reading in Polish.
- Most of the strategies applied in copying with reading difficulties occurred in both reading in Polish and in reading in English, which implies that the two processes share certain similarities.
- Differences in the reports concerning the source of students' reading difficulties and differences concerning the main focus of students' comments seem to indicate a more significant role of higher-level skills (focus on understanding the text idea) in reading in Polish and lower-level skills (focus on vocabulary) in reading in English.
- While reading the Polish text, the students summed up larger parts of the text; when reading the English text, they summed up smaller parts of the text. This indicates the students' tendency to use a narrow co-text in reading in English and a wider co-text in reading in Polish.

- In reading in English, the students ascribed their problems to their insufficient FL competence; in reading in Polish, they complained about the complexity of the text and the way the author of the text develops ideas.

The above-mentioned results confirm the findings concerning differences between reading in Polish and reading in English obtained at the previous stage of the study (see Chapter 2 in this part).

It is important to note that there was an undeniable advantage of applying a text grammar model to this analysis. It allowed me to look at the process of students' comprehension as a process of constructing a model of text. This model-based theory of comprehension facilitated the exploration of two factors intertwined in the process of reading: text and reader. It helped to combine an analysis of the text with an investigation of how students read this text.

The analysis showed how each of the subjects made attempts to cope with the difficulties he/she had encountered, suggesting that each reader had his/her own "idiosyncratic" way of reading. The results of the analysis implied that to obtain a more comprehensive picture of how individual subjects read the text, more concern should be devoted to the content of comprehension, i.e., students' models of the texts. This led to the analysis of ideas (propositions) that the students formed while constructing their models of the text.

4. Analysis of propositions: Stage 3

4.1. Research questions

Also at this stage of the study, Britton's grammar was applied to analyze students' protocols and the texts. For each reader, the results of two analyses, that of the protocol and that of the text, were compared. This helped to show how each reader constructed his/her model of the text (i.e., what propositions he/she developed in his/her comprehension), drawing on the text clues. It was assumed that "[i]n the comprehension process, meaningful text units are transferred into propositions" (Louwerse and Graesser 2006: 427; see Part I, Chapter 3, Section 3.1.). In students' comprehension, after Britton (1994), propositions were viewed as nodes – units of meaning that constitute the network of ideas developed by readers during the reading of the text. It is important to stress that at this stage of the study the term "proposition" is used both in the analysis of the text and the analysis of students' protocols. It refers to text units (in the text analysis) and the ideas the students constructed on the basis of the text (in the analysis of TA protocols).

The main aim of this stage of analysis were to answer the following questions:

- How did the readers construct the models of each text?
- What propositions can be identified in the students' representations of the texts?

This stage did not aim to find differences between students' reading in Polish and their reading in English. It meant to enrich the results obtained in the problem/solution analysis and to explore the content of the representations of the texts, i.e., identify and analyze propositions that the subjects constructed while reading the texts.

4.2. Results

4.2.1. Identifying different types of propositions

Different types of propositions were identified in the students' protocols. Below, a few examples of the propositions identified in protocols (Table III.10.) are provided. The first is a protocol of how Student C read the introductory part and the first paragraph of the Polish text; this is placed in the right column of the table. In the left column is listed a list of propositions formed during reading. This is followed by a description of how the reader developed her model of these parts of the text.

Table III.10. Student C reading the introductory part and the first paragraph of the Polish text – an extract from a protocol. Both the text and the TA report have been translated into English.

Section in the text	Propositions formed during reading	Think-aloud reports
The introductory part	– A soulless egghead, he has the brain in his grasp and doesn't believe in the soul? – Why is he holding the brain? – The material of the spirit. – Neurobiology.	*S: First I'm looking at the picture, I'm ignoring the text. I'm looking at the picture and reading (the caption below the picture) "A soulless egghead " uhm, it's intriguing, "he has the brain in his grasp and doesn't believe in the soul." Why? And why is he holding the brain in his hand?* *T: Is he?* *S: Yes, he is. And the brain in this (..) Oh, my God! This is so interesting for me! (laughter) "The material of the spirit", yes. Uhm, well and right away I associate it with (..), when I looked at this text, I looked, yes, at "The material of the spirit", at the picture, at the caption and at "neurobiology." (.) And that's all. And now I'm reading.*

The 1st paragraph	– The material of the spirit? – Neurobiology? – We treat the brain as the pocket-size PC of our soul? – According to Descartes our body is controlled by the spirit. – Brain is made of material substance and soul of non-material substance. – The brain influences the soul? The soul guides the body? – The brain is guided by the soul? (prediction). – The brain is our PC? – The brain is a pocket computer? – Body and soul can cooperate? – How is the connection between body and soul investigated by neurobiology? (prediction).	*T: What are you reading?* *S: Well, so "The material of the spirit" and this subtitle "neurobiology." (..) Right, well (…) I found it very interesting xx this statement of this Steven uhm about the brain (.) But how can we treat the brain as a PC of our soul? I understand a PC is a computer, but (.) I don't know but I don't treat the brain as a PC of our soul. It's so strange for me, I can't agree with this. (.) And it's also interesting, yes, it's interesting, the beginning of the article is interesting. Now I continue reading.* *T: What did you pay attention to when you were reading?* *S: Right, it caught my attention earlier, that the Cartesian myth, which means that we have separate, that is the body is directed by the spirit, which functions, yes I understand it OK, and this is so eh (… ..) I think that the article is about, about the role of the soul and what is the soul and what, eh, how we define the brain. And here they say that the soul directs our body and the brain is made of substance, and the soul is immaterial, which means that a distinction between these two things which are different. (…) And now it seems to me that the next paragraph will be about, uhm e.g., how the brain influences the soul, if it's possible, and how the soul, yes how the soul directs our body so that the brain listens to it, obeys it. And I'm wondering why this brain is a PC of our soul, it's a computer – what does it mean? Xx a computer and now I'm thinking (.) Why here, why is there the word "a computer," I don't understand this phrase, how can it be the pocket computer of our soul? so what does it mean? Does it mean that in this computer we can find everything? and it is the question that I'm wondering about. (..) And what xx in our soul and now I have such strange thoughts, and then it goes: "which in the name of its 'spiritual user' processes and manages information." So does it mean that the brain and the soul sort of cooperate with each other. And I'm wondering how it will develop, what is the connection between the brain and the soul from the point of view of neurobiology. I know from the subtitle that "Neurobiology has learnt how to examine what we call the soul" and this is interesting. And now I go on reading.*

Source: own study.

Student C begins constructing her comprehension by paying attention to the picture and asking a question concerning the caption below the picture: "Why is the man holding the brain?." The propositions related to the picture, title and subtitle take the form of questions, single words and phrases, which I assume may indicate uncertainty, incompleteness and a general character of understanding. Propositions reflecting her comprehension of paragraph 1 are constructed gradually. She starts reporting from what she finds the most surprising, i.e., the comparison of the brain to the pocket PC. She dialogues with the text ideas; she does not agree with the statement that "we treat the brain as the pocket-size PC of our soul." In the list of propositions constructed by the reader (in the left column), this proposition is indicated as an interrogative sentence. Then, the reader forms the next propositions which concern Descartes' myth. She begins by quoting from the text, but finally she is able to explain the text information in her own words. She says that she understands the message. It seems that she accepts the propositions in her comprehension. In the analysis, these propositions are written as affirmative statements. Then, the student predicts that the text will discuss the relationship among the brain, the soul and the body. In the protocol, these predictions are marked as interrogative statements. At this point of her report, she returns to her discussion about the brain as a PC. She asks questions and attempts to explain to herself what this comparison may mean. The propositions reflecting this part of comprehension are also indicated as interrogative statements. The student finishes reading this paragraph with an assumption that the body and the soul cooperate. It seems that the reader's comprehension is guided by the prediction that the text will provide an explanation of how the brain influences the soul. The reader links this prediction with the subtitle. Referring to the subtitle convinces her that her earlier prediction is worth following; she says that she is curious in what way neurobiology can explain the relationship between the body and the soul. In the analysis, the proposition is marked as an interrogative statement. In the report, the reader used the word "tak jakby" (which in English means "sort of"), which I have interpreted as a sign of uncertainty in comprehension.

The example reveals a few types of propositions that the reader constructed while reading the text. It elucidates two types of propositions, in this discussion named: **partial** propositions (marked as interrogative statements) and **final** propositions (marked as affirmative statements). **Partial propositions** are propositions that the students formulated very often at the beginning of the construction of their models and which reflect the reader's tentativeness or uncertainty concerning their comprehension. Quite often partial propositions were the results of students' predictions. The analysis of the subjects' protocols demonstrates that the students developed their partial propositions in an active manner by a number of techniques, such as paraphrasing their content, discussing, asking questions and linking them with other propositions. It may be assumed that these mechanisms allowed the readers to modify their propositions while reading the text and finally to accept them as important parts of their representation by incorporating them into the final version of their models. **Final propositions** are propositions about which the subjects did not report doubts. It was observed that also final propositions underwent changes. The students applied all the techniques mentioned above; in many cases they elaborated on the propositions, i.e., they added new propositions to them, thereby constructing more complex nodes.

While classifying propositions into partial and final, a few questions arose. One question referred to how to treat propositions that took the form of sentences quoted directly from the text. It was decided that such propositions would be viewed as partial or final, depending on the function of the proposition. It was observed that repeating verbatim parts of the text served two functions. It was a technique that the subjects used to confirm their comprehension of the parts of text they had read before. In other words, they read aloud the text to accept the propositions they had formed earlier by means of, e.g., paraphrasing or discussing the text. In this situation, quoting from the text was treated as a final proposition. The other function is connected with the initial stage of constructing propositions. The subjects read aloud the text to focus on the parts of the text that they wished to understand. In this case, the proposition was classified as partial. Another important question that occurred in the process of analysis was how to classify the propositions which the students formulated and about which they expressed a lack of understanding. In several cases, the subjects verbalized doubts about the meaning of the propositions they had constructed; they also reported difficulty in linking them with other propositions. Such propositions were classified as partial ones.

It is important to emphasise that each type of proposition, partial or final, can take the form of a single word or phrase. Such propositions may mean that the reader has managed to identify ideas of a general character, called macropropositions.

To sum up, two main types of proposition were identified in the protocols: partial and final. Partial propositions are those about which the reader demonstrates doubts, i.e., he/she is not sure about their "correctness" and treats them as plausible products of his/her understanding; partial propositions are also the ones constructed on the basis of the reader's predictions. Final propositions are those that the reader forms and accepts as "correct" and "stable" elements of his/her representation. It is crucial to state that this taxonomy of propositions will be necessary in the evaluation of students' comprehension, which will be discussed at Stage 5 in Chapter 6 (in this part).

4.2.2. The role of predictions in understanding the text

Below, the role of predictions and pictures in developing comprehension is discussed. The example (Table III.11.) shows how Student A read the introductory part, the first and the second paragraph of the English text.

Table III.11. Student A reading the introductory part, the first and the second paragraph of the English text – an extract from a protocol

Section in the text	Propositions formed during reading	Think-aloud reports
The introductory part	– Obsolete? – Dream has become too broad?	*S: First I'm looking at the title* *T: Uhm* *S: I'm looking at the title, reading the title, uhm (...) and right away reading the subtitle, because I can't understand the second word* *T: Which one?* *S: The second, the third, I mean "obsolete"* *T: Uhm* *S: So I'm reading the subtitle to understand (... ...) in the title, so I'm reading the subtitle (...) So here in the subtitle they mention some man, a historian I suppose, and I'm thinking about it, about, I mean uhm so I understand it more or less what the subtitle means and I'm trying to understand this metaphor, the meaning of this subtitle, so I'm thinking what it can mean. It may mean (..) it is compared, it is written about a dream, which is which became as if as if too much (the student is looking at the teacher)* *T: I cannot help you, sorry*
The 1st paragraph	– The globe. – Progress gives a more comfortable life but it may also have limits.	*S: So I'm still thinking about it, and I go to the first paragraph and now I'm reading the first paragraph, I'm still looking, I first looked at the picture, which is as if in the centre and attracts attention and I'm beginning to think a bit (...) because in the picture there is a globe and something sticking out of the globe so I'm wondering how it's connected with the text so I'm reading the first paragraph and thinking if it will interest me. I always read texts in this way. So now I begin to read the first paragraph. (...) I've read the first paragraph and (...) in the first paragraph it looks as if, if I were to summarise it, the whole paragraph is devoted to the concept of progress uhm what this progress, what we understand by progress, what progress means and what our ours (...) were uhm Now I'm going back to the last sentence in the first paragraph to to report more precisely, I'm reading the last sentence (...) and in the last sentence it's mentioned that progress although it that it sort of means more, it was said earlier "more" uhm more comfort (...) it can have some limits too. And now uhm I'm wondering what the second paragraph is about. I assume that the second paragraph will be somehow connected with the last sentence of the first paragraph. So I think it will be uhm it will be something about these limits (...) how they are connected with the concept of progress.*

Section in the text	Propositions formed during reading	Think-aloud reports
The 2nd paragraph	– Industrial countries live a rich life. – Goods which were luxuries in the past are available to everyone today. – Medicine reduces infant mortality and increases longevity. – Limits of progress?	*S: So now I'm reading the second paragraph (..).* *T: Please, don't forget to report the way you read this part.* *S: OK. First I'm reading in a normal way (…). Now as I've read the second paragraph more slowly so that I can summarize it I'm looking for the information which I can use for this summary. Now I'm reading each paragraph, I treat each paragraph as a complete part uhm and now uhm I'm going back to the second paragraph more less in this order uhm once more I begin from the very beginning (..) and I compare it with the first one, I compare I'm wondering how it's connected with the first paragraph, if it confirms what I thought earlier, my predictions about the second paragraph. I'm reading once again this first sentence (…) The first sentence is here uhm generally speaking uhm about more industrial uhm more industrial countries which like or it seems xxx more perhaps it's not about standard of living but it's about being rich uhm it seems hm here we have enumerated: first it's about rich people, who and now summarizing I'm reading all the time, reading about these rich people I can imagine this this uhm uhm this part of the text all the time uhm so uhm it means not rich people, yes right but this richness, which was created or generated by by xxx is uhm so I'm continuing to read this in order to translate that which is earlier (…) so once again I would say I'm reading from "affluence" till the bottom to get the whole (…) After reading this one more time uhm I'm trying to get the idea of this progress which is uhm here enumerated, that for example the examples that material goods that were luxurious but now they are normal things. For example, medicine has reduced mortality among infants and now is eradicating diseases that were difficult to wipe out in the past uhm and there is an increase I mean people don't die so young, an increase in this what you call it uhm we live longer. Later the second paragraph ends in this way but I find it very surprising because it's all the time about this progress and there is nothing about limits imposed as if by uhm (…) yes the point is that I expected to find in the first paragraph information about these limits which which sort of accompany progress uhm but however so far there's been the comparison of former times uhm with present times. This means what was in the past, how it has changed, about progress uhm and now after reading this uhm I'm thinking about what the next paragraph will be about, I'm wondering that perhaps there will be something more about these limits or it will be devoted to progress as a concept. So I'm beginning to read.*

Source: own study.

In this analysis, let us look at the role of predictions in constructing comprehension. While reading the first paragraph, the reader predicts that the next paragraph will develop the issue of limits of progress. In the second paragraph, she compares the two paragraphs, hoping to find confirmation for her earlier expectations. She realizes, however, that her predictions are not confirmed and expects that the idea of limits will be developed in the further part of the text. It seems that in this example predicting directed the reader in her comprehension; it also helped the subject to evaluate the interconnectedness of the ideas in her representation. The analysis implies that predictions play an important role in developing an understanding of the text; they seem to be units of information (in the protocol they are viewed as partial propositions, thus marked as interrogative statements) to which readers return and develop while constructing their models of the text. Propositions initiated by predictions often undergo a process of modification – they may be confirmed or rejected; sometimes, enlarged and strengthened, they may "end up" as propositions that the reader accepts in the final network of his representation (i.e., as final propositions).

4.2.3. The role of pictures in understanding the text

Both examples discussed above elucidate the role of pictures in the process of understanding the text. In both analyses, the representations that the subjects constructed on the basis of pictures are indicated in the same way as the propositions that the students formed while reading the text (in Table III.10. it is *Why is he holding the brain?* and Table III.11. *The globe.*) The reports indicate that in the readers' comprehension pictures played the same role as the text does; both provided the readers with material which they could use to construct the representations of the text (see Part I, Chapter 1, Section 3.4.3.1. for Gernsbacher's view on picture comprehension).

Below, one more example taken from the report of Student C (see Table III.10. for the protocol concerning the beginning of the text) is presented. It shows how the reader took advantage of the photo. At the end of reading the text, the student decided to encompass all the paragraphs and link them with the photo. This helped her to state the purpose of the text and its main topic concerning the role of the brain and the soul in human emotional life.

> *What I'm wondering about are the emotional states described here, but I think it's not so clear. I don't know. Does it all hang together? (.) Well. What am I thinking about now? (..) I'm thinking about what I've just read, about all these paragraphs and this picture with the caption "Bezduszny mózgowiec" (Eng. "a soulless egghead"). (.) I mean that the whole text is, aims to explain that all those emotional states, in general emotions and feelings are not connected with the soul. That it is the brain that is responsible for this.*

Also Student A used the picture in developing her representation of the text. Below, her report of reading the fourth paragraph is presented. The reader continues her attempts to find information concerning the limits of progress (to enlarge the propositions in her representation she had formed in the first paragraph; see Table III.11.). She refers to the picture of the globe, which she noticed at the beginning of reading the text (in the analysis the proposition corresponding to the picture is indicated as "the globe"). The reader decides that the picture illustrates the results of her understanding of progress, i.e., both its positive and negative aspects. This facilitates her comprehension of the main topic of the text.

I'm still wondering about those limits from the uhm the first paragraph (...) because the whole text, I've just reached the fourth paragraph, I think the text is about progress, that people want it although it has some disadvantages. (...) I think the whole text will talk about it. And now I'm looking at the picture, I'm going back to the picture uhm. In fact I can link it with what I've read, this globe which has the sort of things that can make our life easier, some springs, some technical things that pop out of the globe, is it so? Progress as, technical aspects as a symbol of progress, as uhm very important features of progress. Yes and here xx but it's clear that something does not work here in the picture so here in the picture there are negative sides of this progress, well it seems so. So there is progress, its technical aspects and all this but still it doesn't work. And this refers to the paragraphs I've just read. So after the fourth paragraph I go back to this picture and I decide to go on uhm reading. Now I'm going to read paragraph 5 and I'm wondering if it will develop those negative aspects (...) and now limits from the first paragraph came to my mind and (...) I thought that limits of progress can be its negative aspects. Limits can slow down progress.

4.2.4. Strategies the students used to evaluate their comprehension

The analysis of propositions provided additional information concerning strategies used by the students, the issue investigated at the earlier stage of the study. New insight was gained into how the students evaluated their comprehension. The following strategies applied to check the correctness of comprehension were identified:

- shift of focus, i.e., referring to earlier parts of the text to check the cohesion of one's model of the text (Strategy A);
- paraphrasing propositions which the reader considers tentative (partial propositions) to strengthen their plausibility in the model (Strategy B);
- summing up the propositions in one's representation to check its content and the interconnectedness of its nodes (Strategy C);
- drawing on background knowledge to check the "correctness" of propositions formed on the basis of text information (Strategy D).

Below, two examples taken from the protocol of Student C are provided.

I come back to this "Descartes' baby," to this Bloom. Uhm because here there was, right (.) yes, this sentence here "and although they know that the brain is used in the thought process, they do not accept that," yes those children and someone else doesn't accept, yes that's right. Yes, the text is about this, about brain functions xx activities. Well and now I look again at this text in bold "Contemporary neurobiology has shown that the soul does not exist." I come back to this statement that this is in essence brain activity, it seems that the whole article xx that the soul does not exist. For me it is sheer abstraction, to be honest. But, it's supported by the arguments here, yes, it really is.

(Student C reading the Polish text)

> *Now uhm I'm thinking how to put it together and answer the question that is put in the title. Because there are facts given here uhm because progress that influences us, medicine and all those advantages. But on the other hand there are some disadvantages of progress. Living standards, yes, I think that living standards are nowadays for us things that in the past were ee something unusual. So now I'm wondering about how to answer this question. I mean not what I think about it, my opinion is not important but what this article says.*
>
> (Student C reading the English text)

The first extract demonstrates the last stage of reading the Polish text. Having finished reading the last paragraph, the reader decided to return to the earlier paragraphs and the propositions in her representation she had constructed on the basis of those parts of the text (Strategy A). This led her to confirm the conclusion she had drawn before (the process of drawing this conclusion is not shown here). The reader said that the whole article illustrates the argument that there is no soul and that the soul is in fact an activity performed by the brain. It is interesting to observe how she evaluated the product of her comprehension. She accepted her conclusion, emphasizing that it is supported by arguments from the text. At the same time she claimed that she found it totally abstract, probably drawing on her background knowledge (Strategy D). This means that she was able to see the difference between the text ideas and her opinions. The reader was able to distance herself from the ideas that she had constructed on the basis of the text – which indicates her ability to approach the text in a critical way, i.e., to process the text at a propositional level as well as to be ready to develop a situation model of the text (see Part I, Chapter 3, Section 3.1.2.).

Student C applied similar techniques to evaluate her comprehension while reading the English text. She decided to link the ideas she had comprehended and attempted to link them with the title, which is the question *Is progress obsolete?* (Strategy C). It is important to point out that also in reading the English text, she was aware of the aim of her reading. It seems that she distinguished constructing comprehension on the basis of the text (i.e., constructing the propositional textbase) from interpreting the text to present her own evaluation of the text (constructing the situation model).

4.3. Conclusions

In summary, this stage of the study allowed me to identify different types of propositions the subjects constructed in their reading, i.e., partial and final propositions. This distinction will be used in the evaluation of students' comprehension at the next stage of the study. Additionally, the analysis of students' protocols in terms of propositions enriched the results obtained at the earlier stages of the study, i.e., the analysis of strategies and the problem/solution analysis. More insight was gained into how the readers had evaluated their comprehension as well as the role that predictions had in developing understanding. The analysis also enabled me to look more closely at the role of the pictures that accompany the texts in the subjects' reading.

5. Students' idiosyncratic patterns of constructing comprehension: Stage 4

5.1. Research questions

The findings of the previous stages of the study demonstrated differences between the subjects, e.g., in the amount of reporting and the manner of processing the texts. Therefore, the main aim of this stage of the study was to answer the following questions:

– Are there any idiosyncratic patterns that the readers followed while reading in Polish and in English?
– Are there any differences in the patterns the students used in reading the English text and reading the Polish text?

The aim of this section is to analyze the students' protocols in terms of their individual patterns of developing comprehension. It was hypothesized that readers may approach texts in their mother tongue and in a foreign language in a similar manner, which would indicate a possibility of a transfer of strategies from one language to the other.

5.2. Results and conclusions

The protocols were inspected to identify strategies that are the most frequent for the readers in each language. Also characteristic features of reporting were taken into consideration. Below (Table III.12.), the results of the analysis are presented.

Table III.12. The students' individual patterns of developing comprehension

Reader	Most common strategies and characteristics of reporting the English text	Most common strategies and characteristics of reporting the Polish text
Student A	a very verbose report, a variety of strategies reported, consistent in pursing her initial predictions, summing up as a technique to evaluate the final state of comprehension	a very verbose report, consistent in pursing her initial predictions, a variety of strategies reported, summing up as a technique to evaluate the final state of comprehension
Student B	a very verbose report, frequent predictions, consistent in pursing her predictions, frequent reference to her background knowledge, a variety of strategies reported, able to evaluate the product of comprehension	a very verbose report, consistent in pursing her initial predictions, frequent reference to her background knowledge (focusing on the information she found interesting), a variety of strategies reported, aware of her comprehension failures

Reader	Most common strategies and characteristics of reporting the English text	Most common strategies and characteristics of reporting the Polish text
Student C	a very verbose report, consistent in pursing her predictions, a variety of strategies reported, asking questions, summing up as a technique to evaluate the final state of her comprehension, a critical approach to the product of comprehension	a very verbose report, consistent in pursing her initial predictions, a variety of strategies reported, dialoguing with the text (asking questions, agreeing/disagreeing with the text information), summing up as a technique to evaluate the final state of her comprehension, a critical approach to the product of comprehension
Student D	a very brief report, a very haphazard style of reading (focusing only on the first sentences, "jumping" from paragraph to paragraph), as a result constructing a very simple model of the text (a network of very general ideas drawn from paragraphs), satisfied with her comprehension; no attempts to evaluate the final state of comprehension	a very brief report, a very haphazard style of reading (focusing only on the first sentences, "jumping" from paragraph to paragraph), aware of comprehension failures, an attempt to evaluate the state of comprehension when problems occur
Student E	a very brief report, reading with ease, very few problems reported	a very brief report, reading with ease most of the article, when problems occur evaluating the state of his comprehension
Student F	a verbose report, reading with ease, identifying main ideas as the most frequent strategy	a verbose report, reading with ease, identifying main ideas as the most frequent strategy
Student G	a verbose report, a variety of strategies reported, discussing the text information, reacting emotionally, active in solving problems	a verbose report, a variety of strategies reported, discussing the text information, reacting emotionally, active in solving problems
Student H	a verbose report, reading with ease, very few problems reported, paraphrasing as the most frequent strategy	a verbose report, apart from vocabulary difficulties very few problems reported, paraphrasing as the most frequent strategy
Student I	a verbose report, a variety of strategies reported, very frequent strategy of making associations, many problems reported, many comprehension failures, lack of concentration, aware of his problems	a verbose report, a variety of strategies reported, a very frequent strategy of making associations, many problems reported, many comprehension failures, difficulty in encompassing the whole text, aware of his problems
Student J	a verbose report, reading with ease, identifying main ideas as the most frequent strategy, discussing the text information, very few problems reported, a very logical approach to the text	a verbose report, reading with ease, identifying main ideas as the most frequent strategy, discussing the text information, very few problems reported, a very logical approach to the text

Source: own study.

The comparison indicates that all the subjects reported in a similar way while reading in Polish and in English. They were verbose to a similar extent in both reports. The same strategies were observed in both reports. Below, a few reports are presented.

For example, Student I kept making associations in both reports. When reading the Polish text, he made digressions about his roommate. The English text made him think about two Polish political parties: PO (Platforma Obywatelska) and PiS (Prawo i Sprawiedliwość).

Here it's more about prozac. When I see the word "Prozac," I see in my mind all those American films where there is always a blond female heroine who has to eat it (Prozac) (... ... ..) Reading on I come across antidepressants and all the time I can see my roommate who has depression and is now undergoing medical treatment (...) uhm (..). I'm still reading the fourth paragraph which is about depression and tranquillizers. All the time when I'm reading it I see my neighbour (...) this sentence is very interesting "Many spouses in not understanding what their partner is experiencing ask: why don't you just get a grip?" And it's exactly what I keep saying to my roommate – why don't you simply get up? The alarm clock keeps ringing for half an hour, but my roommate is still in bed; first I didn't understand that he was sick, I thought he was lazy. I feel sorry for him but I often laugh at him.

(the Polish text)

It's about progress (....) "It means a rich life for everyone," yes and now I associate this sentence with PO – "so that everyone can live a better life." And the next sentence "not for the privileged classes alone" with PiS, and they make each other's life difficult, and I can see Jarek's face when he is speaking in the parliament; (...) saying it I forgot what the main idea of the paragraph is, I drifted away too much.

(the English text)

Student D read both texts in a "erratic" way.

S: In the next paragraph which I began to read uhm it's about the price that we have to pay for progress and now I've jumped to the next paragraph to see what the text consists of, that's why I decided not to read the whole paragraph but to go on to the next uhm one.
T: You mean the one beginning with "yet none?"
S: uhm no. I didn't even notice it, I jumped right away to "real question."
T: I see. So what are you doing now?
S: Now, I'm reading. (...) And now I've jumped to the next one.

(the English text)

I've read the first sentence which says that uhm which refers to uhm Descartes, who claims that our body is controlled by the spirit uhm and biological conditions have no impact on us. And now I've decided to stop reading this paragraph but instead uhm to focus on the sentences in bold uhm the text in bold. (..) uhm here it's clearly said that contemporary neurobiology has show that the soul does not exist, so I expect to find some arguments on how scientists reached this conclusion and I've decided to jump to the next sentence in bold (..)

(the Polish text)

This analysis illustrates similarities in reporting while reading in both languages. It is difficult to conclude whether the similarities in reporting reflect similarities in reading and whether we can assume any transfer between the languages, probably from the mother tongue to a foreign language. This issue will be investigated further in the analysis of the interview with the subjects concerning their reading in both languages (see Chapter 7).

6. Evaluating the readers' comprehension – how well the subjects understood the texts: Stage 5

6.1. Research focus and analysis of results

The main aim of this stage of the study was to evaluate the students' comprehension of each text and to compare the reading comprehension results in relation to the English text and to the Polish text. It is important to explain that this analysis is based on the taxonomy of propositions identified at Stage 3.

In order to evaluate reading comprehension, an ability to identify the main idea of each paragraph was measured. Students' reports were analyzed to see how well the subjects understood the texts. The propositions that the subjects constructed were evaluated in relation to each paragraph. The readers' performance while reading each paragraph was compared with the answers presented below (see model answers) and scored from 1 to 4 points. The following scoring criteria were accepted to evaluate the students' comprehension of each paragraph:

Very good (4 points) – the protocol indicates complete understanding of the main idea of the paragraph; only paraphrasing the text, i.e., talking about it in one's own words, is accepted for this score;

Good (3 points) – the protocol indicates partial comprehension of the main ideas, the reader ignores some important parts of the main message; only paraphrasing the text, i.e., talking about it in one's own words, is accepted for this score;

Fair (2 points) – the report indicates superficial comprehension, i.e., the student understands pieces of text information but is not able to find links among them and to draw conclusions concerning the main idea of the paragraph; only paraphrasing the text, i.e., talking about it in one's own words, is accepted for this score;

Poor (1 point) – miscomprehension, missing the main idea; instead of paraphrasing the text only reading aloud the text is identified, in the case of the English text translating the text is observed;

0 point – the protocol related to reading a particular paragraph was not found.

It is important to emphasize that only final propositions are taken into account, i.e., evaluated in this analysis; partial propositions are ignored – those about which the subjects expressed doubts (see Stage 3 of the study, presented in Chapter 4 in this part). In the case when comprehension of a particular paragraph is developed in the further (consecutive) paragraph (thereby partial propositions change into final propositions), points are added to the score of this particular paragraph.

Model answers for the Polish text:

Par. 1. People accept Descartes' theory, which claims that the immaterial spirit and the material body are two distinct things.

Par. 2. There is no soul; neurobiological research shows that the soul is in fact an aspect of the brain processing. Example: new methods of observing the brain (magnetic resonance imaging) indicate that every emotion and thought is reflected in the brain functioning.
Par. 3. The idea that there is no soul has not been accepted by people's common knowledge. Example: people are not ready to accept the finding that meditation and education change our mind (i.e., the brain).
Par. 4. Paul Bloom in his book *Descartes' Baby* claims that people are natural-born dualists, which means that we accept in a natural way that body and mind are distinct entities. Example: children who perceive the world in this manner.
Par. 5. We may experience further illusions if we do not modify our opinions concerning the role of the brain in our life, i.e., if we do not accept the truth that the brain plays such an important role in our life. Example of such misunderstandings: the use of Prozac.
Par. 6. Although emotional pain (just like physical pain) is a normal reaction to various stimuli that we encounter in life and may even facilitate our abilities to analyze our life, we should not suffer more than necessary – so the use of Prozac is justified.

Model answers for the English text:
Par. 1. Progress involves democracy. It means a better life for everyone, not only for those privileged. But it seems that progress may have limits.
Par. 2. When compared with life in the past, nowadays industrial countries lead a better, richer life. Examples: better general living standards, more advanced medicine, longevity.
Par. 3. We pay a price for progress. Examples: consumption results in producing garbage, living longer entails spending more money on the health-care system, changes involve more stress.
Par. 4. We are aware of the problems that progress causes but we agree to accept the consequences that the problems lead to.
Par. 5. Our general opinion about progress has changed. Although reports of a negative influence on the earth (examples: global warming) are controversial, we face the question whether endless progress is possible.
Par. 6. The question as to whether endless progress is possible concerns also a democratic distribution of wealth. An equal distribution of wealth, also among poor populous countries such as India or China, would result in breaking the limits of the earth.
Par. 7. Progress does not make sense if it does not mean a just distribution of wealth. In the past it was assumed that progress would be available to everyone. (All people would demand more, which would result in more advanced machinery.) Demand for a better life would create a constant economic development.

Table III.13. Reading comprehension scores – the Polish text

Subjects and scores Polish	A	B	C	D	E	F	G	H	I	J	**Total**
p. 1	4	3	4	3	4	4	2	4	2	4	34
p. 2	4	4	4	2	4	4	3	4	2	4	35
p. 3	2	3	2	1	1	1	2	3	1	4	20
p. 4	4	1	4	2	4	1	3	4	1	4	28
p. 5	3	2	4	1	2	1	2	3	1	4	23
p. 6	2	2	1	1	2	1	1	1	1	2	14
Total: in points and percents	**19** **79**	**15** **63**	**19** **79**	**10** **42**	**17** **71**	**12** **50**	**13** **54**	**19** **79**	**8** **33**	**22** **92**	**154** **100** Mean **15.4** **64%**

Source: own study.

Table III.14. Reading comprehension scores – the English text

Subjects and scores English	A	B	C	D	E	F	G	H	I	J	**Total**
p. 1	3	1	2	3	4	4	3	4	2	4	30
p. 2	4	2	4	3	4	4	4	4	4	4	37
p. 3	4	3	4	0	4	4	4	4	4	4	35
p. 4	4	4	3	0	4	1	4	4	4	4	32
p. 5	2	1	2	1	4	4	3	4	4	4	29
p. 6	2	2	2	2	3	3	2	3	3	4	26
p. 7	2	1	2	1	3	2	3	4	1	4	23
Total: in points and percents	**21** **75**	**14** **50**	**19** **68**	**10** **36**	**26** **93**	**22** **79**	**23** **82**	**27** **96**	**22** **79**	**28** **100**	**212** **100** Mean **21.2** **75%**

Source: own study.

The scores for all the students are presented in Table III.13. and III.14. The comparison of the scores for each text is done in Table III.15. below. The mean scores for each text show that the readers performed better while reading the English text. The analysis also revealed which paragraphs were the most difficult. In the Polish text, it was paragraphs 3, 5 and 6; in the English text – paragraphs 6 and 7. To compare how the subjects performed while reading each text, the following grades were defined.

80% – 100% very good (5)
79% – 65% good (4)
64% – 50 % satisfactory (3)
49 and less – poor (2)

The analysis indicates that half of the subjects demonstrated the same level of reading comprehension in reading in both languages. Two students scored slightly better while reading in English (a one-level difference). The other three students scored much better while reading the English text (a two-level difference). The reasons why the three students performed so poorly while reading the Polish text will be discussed in the section which analyzes the interviews with the readers about their reading style. Similar scores in reading in Polish and in English were obtained by 70% of the subjects.

Table III.15. Reading comprehension scores in Polish and in English (presented as percentages and grades) – comparison

Subjects and scores	A	B	C	D	E	F	G	H	I	J
Total English	75 (5)	50 (3)	68 (4)	36 (2)	93 (5)	79 (5)	82 (5)	96 (5)	79 (4)	100 (5)
Total Polish	79 (5)	63 (3)	79 (4)	42 (2)	71 (4)	50 (3)	54 (3)	79 (4)	33 (2)	92 (5)

Source: own study.

To see whether those differences are statistically significant, the Wilcoxon signed-rank test was applied (Table III.16.). P values that are lower than .05 indicate differences that are statistically significant. Thus, the results show that there are no differences between reading comprehension scores in Polish and reading comprehension in English. Also Figure III.5. illustrates this finding.

Table III.16. Reading comprehension scores for the Polish and English text

Language	**Median**	**Lower quartile**	**Upper quartile**	**Wilcoxon test**	
				S	**p**
Polish	67	51	79	12	.131
English	79	69.75	90.25		

Source: own study.

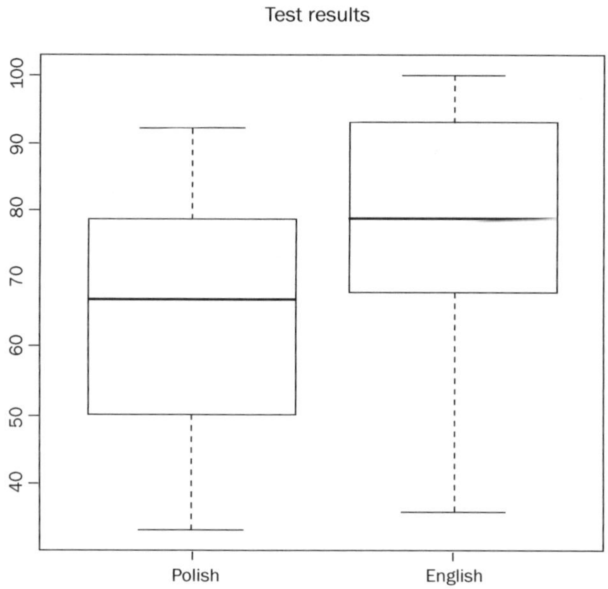

Figure III.5. Reading comprehension scores for the Polish and English text presented as median ranks

Source: own study.

6.2. Conclusions

Statistical analyses indicate that the students' reading comprehension scores related to the Polish text did not differ from those related to the English text. Their ability to understand the main ideas of text paragraphs was as good in reading in Polish as in reading in English. This provides an important argument in the discussion about the possibility of transfer of reading ability between the two languages. It may be assumed that the same level of reading ability demonstrated by the students in the study can facilitate transfer of reading ability, probably between Polish and English.

Additionally, the inspection of the students' reports provided information concerning parts of the texts that the subjects found particularly difficult. As regards the English text, what proved the most difficult to understand was the concept of democracy. The first paragraph introduces two concepts: progress and democracy; 5 out of 10 students reported paying attention to the word "democracy" and developing the concept of democracy in their reading. Two students noticed this concept; however, they did not discuss it, e.g., what it may mean and how it may develop in the further parts of the text. Three subjects did not report noticing the concept of democracy in relation to progress. Consequently, most of the readers did not understand the concept of the democratisation of affluence in paragraph 7, which, as indicated in Table III.12., was the most difficult paragraph for the subjects. It seems that the students did not take advantage of numerous overlaps of ideas between concepts in paragraph 7 and the earlier parts (see Appendix 2). This resulted in an incomplete, partial understanding of the text. This means that the representation of the text the subjects developed does not reflect the message intended by the author of the article.

As regards the Polish text, the most difficult paragraphs were paragraph 3, 5 and the last one. The last paragraph, probably because of its digressive character (see Appendix 2), turned out to be only partially comprehended even by the best readers, e.g., Subject J (see Table III.13.). Paragraph 3 and 5 draw on the concept of dogmas, which is introduced in the subtitle. Out of 10 students only one reader reported paying attention to this proposition and developing it in her further comprehension.

7. The interview with the students: Stage 6

7.1. Research focus

The interview was conducted after the think-aloud session. The subjects were asked to comment on their general reading styles in Polish and in English, not only those manifested during the think-aloud session. Additionally, the readers were asked to comment on the think-aloud technique. In this chapter, we focus only on the results concerning students' reading styles.

7.2. Results

7.2.1. Students' individual styles of reading in relation to the Polish and the English text

The interviews encouraged the subjects to describe their styles of reading each text. Additional data was obtained about the students' idiosyncratic styles of reading in relation to L1 reading and FL reading (see Stage 4). Furthermore, the analysis helped to account for the results of the quantitative evaluation of the students' comprehension presented above (see Stage 5). The results also highlighted factors that could have contributed to the students' reading performance. The most important findings concerning some of the students are discussed in Appendix 3. Conclusions concerning all the subjects are presented below.

All the subjects were able to enumerate and describe aspects which they considered the most important in how they read each text. In most cases, the students saw differences between how they read the Polish text and how they read the English text (in the summary below marked as "d"). Several students were able to identify the style of reading that they use in both reading in Polish and reading in English, indicating thereby the style that is common in their reading in the two languages (in the summary marked as "c"). There were students who were able to identify the style typical of their reading in English and in Polish and at the same time noticed differences between how they read the two texts during the TA task (marked as "c and d"). The information about the subjects may be summarized in the following way:

Student A (d) – translating difficult words in reading in English;

Student B (c, d) – in both languages making frequent predictions and following them when reading, asking questions about the text and searching for answers, drawing on her personal beliefs and background knowledge; due to unfulfilled predictions and poor text organization she was not satisfied with her comprehension of the Polish text;

Student C (d) – translating difficult words and reading aloud in reading in English;

Student D (c, d) – in both languages a fast reader, focusing on topic sentences, constructing the main topic of the text and combining it with her opinions about the topic of the text;

Student E (c, d) – in both languages viewing his style of reading as a process of reconstructing the author's message on the basis of the text clues, aware of the role of his convictions in reading;

Student F (d) – considered his way of reading the English text different from his way of reading the Polish text, in reading in English he was more careful and more attentive to the text;

Student G (c, d) – in both languages a reader critically approaching text ideas; because of the topic she did not read the Polish text very carefully;

Student H (c) – in both languages a slow careful reader;

Student I (c, d) – in both languages a restless reader, when reading making frequent digressions and drawing on his interests and background knowledge, controlling his carelessness in reading the English text;

Student J (c) – in both languages a logical reader, carefully and strategically analyzing texts.

In conclusion, as regards the subjects' idiosyncratic patterns of constructing comprehension, the information obtained from the interview seems to enrich the conclusions drawn at the previous stage of the study (see Stage 4). The following features of the students' individual styles of reading identified at Stage 4 were confirmed (Table III.17.):

Table III.17. The students' individual styles of reading – the results from the interview with students

Reader	Most common strategies and characteristics of reporting the English text	Most common strategies and characteristics of reporting the Polish text
Student B	frequent predictions, consistent in pursing her predictions, frequent reference to her background knowledge	consistent in pursing her initial predictions, frequent reference to her background knowledge (focusing on the information she found interesting), aware of her comprehension failures
Student D	a very haphazard style of reading (focusing only on the first sentences, "jumping" from paragraph to paragraph)	a very haphazard style of reading (focusing only on the first sentences, "jumping" from paragraph to paragraph)
Student I	a very frequent strategy of making associations	a very frequent strategy of making associations, many comprehension failures, aware of his problems
Student J	a very logical approach to the text	a very logical approach to the text
Student G	discussing the text information	discussing the text information

Source: own study.

The analysis shows that all the subjects were able to identify and describe their individual way of reading and the strategies that they used in reading each text. This provides clear evidence of both person and strategy knowledge, important aspects of metacognition (see Part I, Chapter 4, Section 4.3.1.). The subjects were also able to talk about and analyze their reading difficulties, which demonstrates their awareness of the demands of the reading tasks – task knowledge, which is another aspect of metacognition (see Part I, Chapter 4, Section 4.3.1.). Furthermore, the results revealed factors that could have influenced the subjects' reading comprehension, evaluated quantitatively at Stage 5. It helped to understand the nature of the problems that the individual students encountered in reading.

7.2.2. Differences between reading in Polish and reading in English

Most of the students saw considerable differences between their reading in Polish and reading in English. The main difference lies in the fluency and speed of reading; they evaluated their reading in Polish as more fluent and faster. They explained that in their mother tongue, "they focus on every third word." In English, they try to read carefully every single sentence so that they will not miss important information. They said that in reading English, they pay special attention to vocabulary to make sure that they understand all the words. For example, Student B explained the following:

> *I paid attention to the vocabulary that I know and I was happy that I could understand it because this text is authentic. And when I can understand words from an authentic text, I'm glad. (...) And I think that when texts are written in a newspaper, the language is in most cases up to date. That's why I was so happy that I managed to understand the words in the text. I think such words may come in handy in real life. Sometimes it seems to me that we learn vocabulary that is a bit out of use, so I'm really glad when such real life words appear in texts we read in class.*

Several readers underlined the role of translation in inferring the meaning of unknown words. One student reported translating in her mind the text when reading in English. Rereading was considered a more frequent strategy in reading in a foreign language; the students used this strategy to monitor and evaluate their comprehension.

The students reported feeling more confident when reading Polish texts, which involved experiencing more satisfaction with the product of their comprehension. Several students reported feeling uncomfortable when reading in English regardless of the difficulty of the text; they added that even translating all the unknown words does not release the feeling of stress. In general, the subjects emphasized the need to concentrate on the text while reading in English, justifying this approach by feeling respect for the foreign language. The following example taken from Student I's report illustrates the fact that the Polish and English texts were treated in two different ways.

> *T: How would you characterize yourself as a reader of newspaper texts in Polish and in English?*
> *S: When I read in Polish, I try to read very quickly, I jump every three, four words. And I understand the idea. When it comes to reading in English, uhm how should I put it – I simply don't knock off work like that.*
> *T: Why is that so?*
> *S: I don't know, I can't say (...) probably because it's not my native language and all the time I realise that I must concentrate a little if I want to understand what's written here. I suppose it can be due to my respect that it is not my native language. And in Polish, in Polish I read fairly quickly, I'm really fluent.*

Two students expressed very unique opinions, different from the other students. Student F is the only subject in this study who finds reading English texts easier than reading Polish texts. He prefers English texts because "they are written in a better, more natural way" (see Part I, Chapter 3, Section 3.5.5. for similar results obtained by Eggington 1987). He adds that he "has always preferred English texts because they are more concrete and easier to read and interpret." It is difficult to say what he means by this but it seems that he finds the rhetoric of English texts more convincing (see Appendix 3 for more examples taken from this student's protocol). When talking about his reading in the two languages, he emphasized that he reads English texts faster and can understand them easier. He added, like the other students in the study, that in reading in English he pays more attention to the vocabulary and ideas expressed in the text. He explained that the main reason why he finds reading in English easier is the training that he was given during his English lessons. He appreciated advice concerning analysing the text information and coping with difficult vocabulary, complaining that the Polish education system did not provide him with this kind of help (see Part I, Chapter 4, Section 4.3.6. for a discussion about the role of FL instruction in developing metacognition). When asked whether it would be possible to implement when reading Polish the strategies he had been taught during English lessons, he answered that reading in Polish is completely different from reading in English and that the transfer of reading strategies is almost impossible. He explained that the main difference lies in the constant attention given to vocabulary in an English text and the conscious attempts to understand the text information. To illustrate how he views this difference, he said that reading an English text is like "developing a theory about this text," which may mean the reader's awareness about the strategies he applies to construct his representation of the text.

Student G reported using the strategy of "mental reading aloud" in processing both languages. In the following extract from the interview, she describes this strategy:

> *S: When I read in English, I'm afraid one shouldn't do it, but when I read I sort of read and say in my mind, as if I was reading aloud, as if I was to read aloud the text to someone else. While reading in English I sort of read the text aloud. (...) I think others read faster.*
> *T: And what about reading in Polish? Do you read in the same way?*
> *S: In Polish I also do the same, with intonation of course, as if I was to read the text for someone else, I mean to read correctly so that someone could understand it.*
> *T: Why do you think it's not a good habit?*
> *S: It's not good when one has to read the text quickly; reading aloud slows you down.*

It seems that the student reported the process of subvocalisation manifested by what she called reading aloud. As numerous studies indicate (see Part I, Chapter 2, Section 2.2.1.), subvocalisation is a natural aspect of reading. Readers become aware of the phonological aspect of the reading process (described by them as the stream of words being pronounced in their mind) when they read carefully, which was the type of reading the TA task elicited. It may be assumed that subvocalisation played a different role when the student read in English and when she read in Polish. It seems that in reading English, she subvocalizes individual words, which may reflect her need to cope with foreign language words (which were not yet raudatimized, as Carver's rauding theory explains; cf. Part I, Chapter 2, Section 2.2.2.). As regards her reading in Polish, the action of reading aloud with proper intonation can be a strategy that facilitates the development of her understanding of the text (probably by constructing a situation model, i.e., her own interpretation of the text information). Unfortunately, the data obtained in the interview does not provide sufficient evidence to account for her behaviour in more detail.

7.3. Conclusions

In summary, the students were aware of how they read in Polish and in English. They view reading Polish texts and reading English texts as different processes. They commented on the fluency and ease of processing Polish texts. In reading English texts they emphasized a focus on vocabulary – unknown and difficult vocabulary as well as words that they understand but which seem particularly valuable in their learning English as a foreign language. There were students who apply translation and reading aloud as strategies facilitating reading in English; translation helps them to reduce stress connected with understanding vocabulary. These two strategies underline the importance of lower-level skills in FL reading. Additionally, it seems that the subjects showed different attitudes to Polish and English texts. They read Polish texts to understand information; English texts are viewed as material the subjects read for information and which can also help them to improve their English competence.

The analysis complements the information concerning the students' idiosyncratic styles of reading obtained at Stage 4. Both studies underline the importance of individual differences in reading, raising the questions about the relationship between one's styles of reading in L1 and his/her styles of reading in FL as well as the relationship between styles of reading and reading comprehension. The use of translation points to the role of L1 in FL reading. It stimulates a discussion about the nature of FL reading and inspires an exploration of the similarities and differences between FL and L1 reading as well as the possibility of transfer between the two abilities.

8. Evaluation of the study

8.1. General comments on the design of the study

In this section, I present general comments on the overall design of the study. I draw on the opinions of several research experts who discuss how to design and develop research. This will help me to describe the endeavours undertaken in my study.

The first comment comes from Brannen (1992: 3–4, cited in McDonough and McDonough 1997: 223), who observes that "the practice of research is a messy and untidy business which rarely conforms to the models set down in methodology textbooks … The cart often comes before the horse … Researchers are often required to conduct balancing acts between a number of pragmatic considerations." It seems that these words rightly describe my study. Having completed the study, it became clear that in my study I had not followed a traditional chain of stages including: "hypothesis/idea → choice of materials → investigation → results" (McDonough and McDonough 1997: 80). I had not been "able to follow such a neat and logical set of stages" due to "dead-ends, new data, data that [did] not seem to 'fit'" (McDonough and McDonough 1997: 80). However, when preparing the report of the study, I decided to follow Wilczyńska and Michońska-Stadnik's (2010) advice and focus on the final product of my intellectual research efforts, without bothering the potential reader with the starting points and dead-ends encountered during the process of conducting the study.

In the evaluation of my study, two other opinions of research specialists seem pertinent. Köckeis-Stangl (1980: 341, cited in Grotjahn 1987: 64) describes the relationship between the research problem and the research method, claiming that "there is wide unanimity that the research problem should first be established and that only then an appropriate research method should be chosen (or developed)." The author warns that

> [t]he traditional canonical methodology ... becomes an obstacle, if not a straitjacket, particularly since ... its application provides us with by no means especially secure results, but does cause many researchers to fancy themselves secure, to pay attention only to observing rules established in advance, and not to undertake an independent critical examination of their method themselves.

The other quotation I wish to present concerns a development of a qualitative study. McDonough and McDonough (1997: 53) claim that "it is typical for qualitative data collection choices to evolve, as in the action research spiral ..., as insights and tentative conclusions by the researcher indicate the need for other confirmation." The above-quoted opinions reflect the process that I went through when initiating, designing and conducting my study. I began the study with a very general question as to whether there was any aspect of reading in which Polish students of EFL show more skill in their L1 and which learners could improve upon in the process of reading in English. This question, which arose from my research interests, my earlier studies (e.g., Kusiak 2007) as well as my teaching experience, was a starting point to be tested out in the investigation. I made a decision to apply an on-line method since I believed that the think-aloud analysis would provide a good opportunity to observe how students approach texts in both languages and to compare students' reading in the two languages. The general question evolved, which resulted in six stages of the study. New insights and tentative conclusions – the results of the consecutive analyses – required further confirmation. As a result, reading, the main object of the study, underwent the process of (re)conceptualisation. This process is discussed below in Section 8.3.

8.2. Evaluation of the reliability and validity of the study

In the exploratory-interpretative paradigm, the criteria of reliability and validity are evaluated in a different way than in the analytical-nomological one (Grotjahn 1987). Below, I present the evaluation criteria for exploratory-interpretative studies suggested by Ericsson (1986, cited in McDonough and McDonough 1997), Grotjahn (1987) and Wilczyńska and Michońska-Stadnik (2010). The criteria are used to discuss the reliability and validity of the study described in this book.

Grotjahn (1987) claims that in exploratory-interpretative studies, the main aim of researchers should be to ensure validity. He suggests two prerequisites for obtaining valid data: openness and communication. The criterion of **openness** means avoiding "a theoretical structuring of the object of research ... until it is structured by the informants [i.e., subjects] themselves" (Grotjahn 1987: 65). This criterion may even imply refraining from literature research and the formation of research hypotheses prior to conducting a study. In my opinion, it can be rather difficult for researchers to follow this suggestion. Prior to the study they usually familiarise themselves with the studies concerning the object of their research and can easily state general questions they wish to investigate. As regards my study, I think I met the criterion of openness by staying sensitive to the findings the study was bringing at its particular stages, which resulted in the reconceptualisation of the main object of the study. This criterion was also observed during the TA session. The questions asked to foster students' reporting had not been prepared in advance; instead they were adjusted to the learners' reporting styles and the current difficulties the subjects were experiencing. Similarly, to achieve the same purpose, the questions given during the retrospective interview conducted after the think-aloud session were of the same non-intrusive nature.

The criterion of **communication** is connected with the criterion of openness. It redefines the role of the researcher and the subject in the study. In the analytical-nomological methodology, the subject is treated as the object of research, and communication between the researcher and his/her subjects is considered a threat to the validity and reliability of the study. In the exploratory-interpretative paradigm, by contrast, the subject is regarded as an informant "whose subjective theories are of central importance for the process of theory construction" (Grotjahn 1987: 65) and ensuring an equal relationship between the researcher and subjects – as a condition for obtaining valid data. In my study, communication between me and the subjects was enhanced due to the simple fact that, as a person conducting the think-aloud study, I was also the subjects' (i.e., the informants') teacher. I assume this could have contributed to the subjects' feeling comfortable when reporting their thoughts. Another factor which seems important in securing the criterion of communication is that all the informants volunteered to participate in the study and even expressed interest in its results.

In the analytical-nomological paradigm, the concern for quality of data is ensured by pre-testing research instruments for validity and reliability. In interpretative research, this can be realised by the analysis of "disconfirming evidence" and "discrepant cases" (McDonough and McDonough 1997; Wilczyńska and Michońska-Stadnik 2010), which can serve "as a powerful antidote to looking only for evidence to support the researcher's conclusion" (McDonough and McDonough 1997: 54). In my study, examples of such "disconfirming" findings seem to be the data which revealed differences in how the learners approached the texts. This observation led me to examine students' idiosyncratic reading styles, which in turn enabled me to obtain a more complete picture of how students read in their L1 and FL.

Another factor which can contribute to the quality of interpretative research is providing a complete and detailed analysis of the data (Wilczyńska and Michońska-Stadnik 2010), in which the researcher justifies and explains the procedures applied in the study, thereby underlining the reliability of his/her efforts. As regards my study, I have attempted to secure the criterion of reliability by providing careful presentation of the development of the study and illustrating my discussions with relevant examples obtained in the analyses. Also the material included in the Appendices aimed to serve this purpose.

Another powerful procedure that I applied in my exploratory-interpretative study to increase its research quality is triangulation. This is discussed in the next section.

8.3. Triangulation

The present study was conducted within the exploratory-interpretative paradigm (as defined by Grotjahn 1987; Pressley and Afflerbach 1995). Data analysis was carried out by means of interpretative procedures, such as qualitative content analysis, as well as statistical analysis. To gain more confidence in the findings and to obtain a less-biased picture of the research object, several types of triangulation (cf. Denzin 1970, as cited by van Lier 1994: 13) were employed: **theoretical triangulation**, which involved interpreting the same set of data from several different perspectives; **data triangulation**, which means making use of a variety of data sources to study the same issue and **methodological triangulation**, which entails making use of multiple research methods to investigate the same issue.

Let us look at Table III.18. All the stages in the study were embedded in the psycholinguistic view of the reading process, which conceptualises reading as a cognitive intrapersonal process (Bernhardt 1991). However, within this view, two theoretical orientations were distinguished: **strategic**, which views reading as a strategic problem-solving process during which the reader applies strategies to cope with difficulties he/she encounters when reading texts, and **constructivist**, which underlines reading as "a reader's direct engagement with text ideas rather than engagement filtered through specific strategies" (Kucan and Beck 1997: 284), thus highlighting the reader's constructing the model (representation) of the text. Stage 1 and 2 in the study draw on the strategic view of reading; whereas stages 3, 4 and 5 – on the constructivist view of reading. Data in the study was obtained from two sources: students' thinking aloud and interviews, which enabled me to study students' individual styles of reading in relation to the Polish and English text as well as the differences between reading in Polish and reading in English. As regards methodology, two research methods were applied: think-aloud methodology and interviews. Both methods provided insight into how students read in their L1 and FL as well as information about students' individual reading styles.

Apart from the three types of triangulation discussed above, one more type of triangulation was employed. It involved **using different procedures to analyse the same set of data** (i.e., the think-aloud data), which allowed me to focus on different aspects of the object of the study, reading in L1 and FL, at different stages of the study (see Table III.18.).

Table III.18. The different types of triangulation employed in the study

Analysis procedure (stage of the study)	Source of data	Theoretical orientations within a psycholinguistic view
Analysis of reading strategies (Stage 1)	TA protocols	reading as a strategic problem-solving process
Analysis of problems and solutions (Stage 2)	TA protocols	reading as a strategic problem-solving process
Analysis of propositions (Stage 3)	TA protocols	reading as a process of constructing the model of the text

Analysis procedure (stage of the study)	Source of data	Theoretical orientations within a psycholinguistic view
Analysis of idiosyncratic patterns of constructing comprehension (Stage 4)	TA protocols	reading as a process of constructing the model of the text
Evaluation of students' comprehension (Stage 5)	TA protocols	reading as a process of constructing the model of the text
Interviews with students (Stage 6)	interviews conducted with each student by the author of the study	--------------------- (not applicable)

Source: own study.

This combination of theoretical orientations, research methods, data types and analysis procedures, referred to by Denzin (1970, cited in van Lier 1994: 13) as **multiple triangulation**, has several advantages. Theoretical triangulation aided the validity of the study, allowing me to conceptualise the object of the research (i.e., reading in L1 and FL) in several different ways. The following aspects of reading were investigated: reading strategies (Stage 1), the problems readers encountered and the solutions they applied (Stage 2), the propositions students constructed when reading (Stage 3), students' idiosyncratic patterns of constructing comprehension (Stage 4) and students' ability to identify the main ideas in the texts (Stage 5). It is important to underline that the study looked at both the process of reading (Stages 1, 2, 3, 4) and the product of reading (Stage 5). The advantage of methodological triangulation was that it provided an opportunity to study the same problem by means of two research methods. Students' individual styles of reading in relation to the Polish and English text, and the differences between reading in Polish and reading in English were investigated by think-aloud protocols (which elicited simultaneous and immediately consecutive reporting) and direct retrospective interviews. This allowed me to compare the results of the two analyses and to gain more insight into the issues under investigation.

As stated above, triangulation allowed me to ask the same questions several times and thus enriched the findings obtained at the earlier stages. Below, all the stages of the study are discussed; the results that were enriched and confirmed are underlined.

Stage 1 (the analysis of strategies) resulted in the identification of four strategy categories: technical, emotional, rational/logical and evaluating/critical. At this stage, the following findings concerning differences between reading in Polish and reading in English were obtained:

- In reading in Polish, the subjects seemed to focus more on higher-level skills than on lower-level skills.
- In reading in English, the students concentrated on both higher and lower level skills.
- In reading in Polish, actions that indicate a development of the situation model of the text were identified, such as more active personal involvement on the part of the reader and extrapolating. The use of emotional strategies was also considered indicative of students' attempts to construct the situation model of the text.

- In reading in English, the subjects demonstrated a higher level of metacognition, i.e., awareness of how they were reading.
- While rereading the Polish text, the students processed larger parts of the text, e.g., paragraphs; in English they focussed on smaller parts, e.g., individual sentences.

At **Stage 2** (the analysis of problems and solutions) additional information was obtained about the following strategies identified at Stage 1: referring to earlier parts of the text, drawing on prior knowledge, dialoguing with the text ideas, summing up the information and translation. The following conclusions regarding differences between reading in Polish and reading in English, suggested at the earlier stage, were confirmed:

- the more significant role of higher-level skills (focus on understanding the text idea) in reading in Polish and lower-level skills (focus on vocabulary) in reading in English;
- students' tendency to use a narrow co-text in reading in English and a wider co-text in reading in Polish.

Stage 3 (the analysis of propositions) brought more insight into several strategies identified at Stage 1, namely the strategy of predicting the development of ideas and evaluating/critical strategies. A focus on the propositions students constructed when reading the texts created an opportunity to observe the role of predictions in constructing comprehension of the text. It was also possible to observe how the students evaluated the products of their comprehension, thereby to understand better the nature of the evaluating strategies applied by the learners.

Stage 4 identified students' idiosyncratic patterns of constructing comprehension. The interviews with the students (Stage 6) provided further information about students' individual styles of reading in relation to the Polish and the English text.

Stage 5 measured readers' comprehension of the texts, viewed as an ability to identify the main ideas of the texts. The results pointed to certain differences among the students in reading both texts, e.g., to the very poor performance of some students. It was possible to explain those differences by analysing the data obtained in the interview at Stage 6.

Further, the retrospective interviews (**Stage 6**) confirmed the findings from Stage 1 concerning the students attitudes' towards L1 and FL texts, especially those pointing to the students' emotional engagement when reading. The learners' comments also provided explanation as to why the subjects regarded the strategies of translation, reading aloud and rereading so important in reading in English. This finding underlined the importance of lower level skills in reading in English (thereby supporting the observation from the earlier stages of the study).

To sum up, I do hope that the different types of triangulation I employed in the study have increased the trustworthiness of my research and improved the validity and reliability of the evaluation of its findings.

8.4. Limitations of the study

Despite all the attempts taken to secure the validity and reliability of the research, I regard the findings of the study to be limited. It is impossible to say whether they are transferable to other bilingual readers or other text types. The following factors could have influenced the generalisability of the results:

- the think-aloud methodology applied in the study;
- the size of the sample;
- the choice of texts;
- my role as researcher in the study.

Think-aloud research has undeniable advantages, such as providing direct evidence about reading processes and promoting exploration. However, the basic question every researcher conducting a TA study has to face is whether the method itself does not change the object of research, which can influence the validity of the study. To answer this question in relation to my study, I suggest looking at the opinions the students expressed during the interview that took place after the TA session.

All the students said that the TA technique had changed their way of reading the texts. This means that they would have approached the texts in a different way, had they not been told to talk aloud about their reading. The subjects' comments vary. Several students reported that thinking aloud had disturbed their understanding, complaining about having to spend additional energy on talking about the product of her reading. There were also subjects who had benefited from this technique. They reported that the TA technique had slowed down their reading, which resulted in a better monitoring and evaluating of what they read.

One reader explained how the TA technique had helped her to approach the texts more carefully and had prepared her to discuss them. She said:

> *When it comes to an academic text, first I have to analyse the text, to explain it to myself to be able to talk about it. The same took place here; it's a scientific text and I had to think to paraphrase its content so that it sounds, so that it could reflect what I think, so that it would be clear what I say about the text.*

In summary, all the students claimed that the TA method had had a certain impact on how they had approached the texts. As to the effect of the technique on understanding, the opinions were divided. There were students who said that reading and talking about how they read had disturbed their comprehension as well as subjects who said that it had encouraged them to approach the texts in a more careful manner.

Another factor that can make think-aloud research problematic when used with FL learners is the **language** used by subjects in thinking aloud. In my study, the students were asked to report in Polish (their native language), which I considered to be the most natural. However, in the case of thinking aloud about the English text, this decision raises the question of the interaction between the two languages, i.e., the language of the text (English) and the language of reporting (Polish). In the following comment, one of the students discusses disadvantages of the use of Polish in talking about the English text. The student said:

Perhaps it would have been different if I had used English when talking about the English text. Yes, it would have been different. Because I had to switch [into English] when reading the English text, and when talking about the text, I had to switch into Polish, and that's why I used English words "progress", I said "paragraph" and this confused me. But, uhm, I read for general ideas, I read in English but I tried to express them by means of Polish words; and this was difficult. When I was reading the text, I was thinking how I was going to talk about the text in Polish, so my attention was divided between those two mental processes. And if I could have reported in English, I would have had more time and even energy to focus on the text, to summarise its paragraphs and talk about them.

It is possible that some students could have underreported their thinking because of the use of Polish as the language of reporting. This issue seems important and would definitely require further investigation.

Another factor worth raising in this discussion is the **task** the informants were asked to perform. The subjects were directed to read each text paragraph by paragraph. This imposed on the learners a certain way of approaching the texts, e.g., reading the text paragraph by paragraph and making pauses. It seems that for some students this was an artificial way of reading the texts. Several students claimed that the TA technique had imposed on them the way of reading which was not their normal style of reading. They would have preferred to skim the text (i.e., to read it quickly for general understanding) before reading it more carefully.

The protocols show that several students chose to read the texts aloud during the TA session. One of them (Student G) said that reading aloud had helped her to talk about her understanding of the text. She explained her decision in the following way:

It was like this: either I was reading in silence and I forgot what I wanted to say, or I was reading the text aloud and I didn't comprehend much (...) so I realized that reading aloud was not much different than silent reading, it cost me no more effort, but it helped me to remember to think aloud about the text. I know that if I had begun to read in silence, I would have said nothing here to record. Either I focus on one [silent reading] or the other [thinking aloud]. I wouldn't have been able to switch from one to the other.

This example seems to imply that despite the instructions provided before the TA session, there were subjects who interpreted the TA task in their own way. This could have influenced the results of the study.

Another major concern in this discussion is the **size of the sample**. Ten students constitute a relatively large sample for a think-aloud study. However, an increase in the number of subjects would permit the use of parametric statistics, which could have revealed statistically significant differences in the cases where only general tendencies were identified. For example, the analysis of strategies at Stage 1 (see Chapter 2 in this part) showed that the following three critical strategies were more frequent in reading in Polish: asking questions about the text information (QUEST) and discussing the text information and extrapolating (DISCUS). It also indicates that in reading in English the students applied more rereading (RR) than when reading in Polish. None of these differences, however, proved statistically significant. A larger number of students could have demonstrated statistically significant differences.

The **choice of texts** is another important factor that could have influenced the results of the study. The aim of the study was to compare how students read in their native language and in a foreign language. Therefore, attempts were made to select texts that could be regarded as comparable. Both texts were authentic news magazine articles; I evaluated the topics of the texts to be ones of general interest. I assumed that the subjects would find the texts of comparable difficulty and interesting enough to continue reading.

The analysis of the propositions of the texts conducted at Stage 2 (see Chapter 3 in this part and Appendix 2) revealed certain differences between the texts. The differences show that the Polish text has a more "dense" network of ideas, which can make it more reader-responsible, thus more difficult for the reader. I think that the texts may reflect two different ways of organising expository written texts, ones typical of Polish and English respectively (see Part I, Chapter 3, Section 3.5., which discusses contrastive rhetoric). This assumption raises the question as to whether it would be possible to select or construct texts in the two languages that would be of equal "propositional" and rhetorical value.

Another factor determining whether a text is difficult or easy is the readers' prior knowledge about the information presented in the text (cf. Ericsson 1988). Unfortunately, no questionnaire to measure the subjects' background knowledge related to the ideas presented in the texts was administered. Thus, it is not possible to say whether the two texts used in the study demonstrated a similar level of difficulty in this respect.

The results of the interview conducted with the students at Stage 6 helped me to answer the question as to whether the texts seemed of a comparable nature to the students of the study. In their comments, the students compared the two texts that they were asked to read. Both texts were viewed as challenging. Two students thought that the texts demonstrated the same level of difficulty. Two other subjects considered the Polish text easier to read; they said that the text was more "reader-friendly" and "digestible" because of its topic and development of ideas. They did not like the English text because of its more scientific topic (connected with the world economy and politics) and the more dense network of ideas presented on in the text. However, most of the students (the other six) found the English text easier to read. They liked the text because of the more "homogenous" topic (here they meant developing the same topic throughout the text) and the clear organization of arguments (those presenting the advantages and disadvantages of progress); they criticized the Polish text for a lack of coherence, i.e., presenting a variety of themes without developing them. It is crucial to underline here that the students' intuitive evaluation of the cohesion of each text agrees with the results of the text propositions analysis (see Appendix 2).

To sum up, it seems that the texts selected for the study could have influenced the findings. It may be assumed that using another type of text (not expository) and different topics would have produced different results.

It is needless to say that the **researcher** plays a crucial role in securing the reliability and validity of the study. Let me start this section with a digression concerning differences between analytical-nomological and exploratory-interpretative methodology, which will lead me to a discussion of my role as researcher in the study. Grotjahn (1987: 66) claims that:

> Whereas analytical-nomological methodology stresses *explanation* in terms of relating facts to each other by means of theory-based assumptions of regularities, exploratory-interpretative methodology strives for *understanding* ... in terms of a reconstruction of how the informant relates facts to each other by means of his own assumptions of regularity. The aim is the interpretative reconstruction of structures of sense, of the view of the world and of self, as well as of everyday knowledge.

Therefore, "the researcher himself becomes a research instrument by virtue of his role as interpreter" (Grotjahn 1987: 66).

In my study, I was the only researcher responsible for coding and interpreting the data. Although simple steps were taken to secure reliability (see Part III, Chapter 1, Section 1.7.), to increase the reliability of the coding process cooperation with other researchers would have been needed. This collective interpretation would undoubtedly increase the reliability of understanding what reading in L1 and reading in FL are like.

It is important to discuss my role as a researcher in the think-aloud session. As explained earlier, I attempted to stay in the background and limit my role to fostering the students' verbal reporting. I intended to intervene only when the students had been silent for particularly long. However, the analysis of the data revealed some other forms of intervention. The most frequent were reacting to what the students were saying, e.g., by inserting "uhm" and asking the subjects (usually those less verbose in reporting) to elaborate on what they had said earlier. It seems that both ways of intervention could have influenced the subjects' performance during the session. The former type of reaction points to an interactional character of the think-aloud session. It demonstrates the think-aloud task as an "act of communication" (Smagorinsky 1998: 166), not as an experimental situation in a "nonreactive setting" (Ericsson and Simon 1998: 179). The question arises whether it would have been possible to organize a sterile environment in which "social interaction is not intended, and the experimenter is seated behind the subject and hence is not visible" (Ericsson and Simon 1993: xiv). As regards the latter type of intervention, i.e., urging the subjects to develop their report, I think it illustrates my attempts to obtain a comparable amount of report from all the subjects, also those not willing to verbalise extensive amounts of thought. The result of this intervention technique was eliciting immediately consecutive reporting, verbalization that occurred immediately after reading a part of the text, not only concurrent one as it had been assumed before the study.

In conclusion, it is worth reiterating that despite the unquestionable advantages of TA methodology, in an evaluation of the validity and usefulness of the study, it is important to consider the influence of who is thinking aloud (subjects of the study), the researcher and task type. In this section, I have aimed to discuss all the three factors. I suggest that the limitations of the study discussed above can be addressed in future investigations.

9. Implications of the findings

9.1. Implications for further research

The patterns depicted in the study can be regarded as research questions to be investigated in future think-aloud studies. It might be useful to continue Stage 3 of the study (see Chapter 4 in this part). Drawing on Britton's (1994) grammar, this stage explored the content of the representations of the texts and resulted in identifying various types of propositions that the subjects constructed while reading the texts. The analysis did not aim to find differences between students' reading in Polish and their reading in English. It could be interesting to follow this question by means of the research techniques applied at this stage. For example, one could look at the number of final and partial propositions in reading in L1 and FL.

The study (Stage 1) allowed me to gain some insight into how the students constructed comprehension on the basis of the text and how they interpreted and evaluated the texts. This showed how the learners developed the propositional textbase and how they constructed the situation model in relation to the text they were reading. More think-aloud research is needed to explore the two ways of approaching the text in relation to both L1 and FL.

The results (Stage 1 and 2) indicated the more significant role of higher-level skills (demonstrated as a focus on understanding text ideas) in reading in Polish and lower-level skills (demonstrated as a focus on vocabulary) in reading in English. In future comparative think-aloud studies, it could be useful to extend the conceptualisation of higher-level and lower-level skills, which would mean investigating other aspects of reading than those identified in my study.

The analysis of strategies conducted at Stage 1 identified a group of emotional strategies, which reflect readers' emotional reactions and involvement in relation to the text. The results indicate that affective response to texts was observed in both reading in Polish and reading in English. More emotional strategies were found in reading the Polish text than the English text. I believe more attention should be devoted to affective aspects of reader reactions to the text. Such studies could be conducted within, e.g., Reader Response Theory (Rosenblat 2004) or Dual Coding Theory (Sadoski and Paivio 1994), as suggested by Sadoski and Paivio (2007). Proposition-based theories of reading, such as those on which I drew in my study, i.e., van Dijk and Kintsch (1993) and Gernsbacher (1991), do not address mental imagery or emotional reaction – which are also crucial aspects of reading comprehension.

The results of the study point to the importance of illustrations in reading comprehension (see Section 4.2.3. in this part). Unfortunately, the theoretical perspectives applied in the study did not allow me to investigate this issue. As Gyselinck and Tardieu (1999: 215) suggest, "research using concurrent methodology tasks could prove very useful to a more precise understanding of how pictures and texts are integrated in working memory."

It is important to note that the main focus of the verbal reports investigating reading has been cognition. However, as underlined by Afflerbach (2000: 174), "readers are more than cognitive in their reading." It seems that "thinking aloud has assumed new functions in reading research. These new functions involve investigating not only individual cognitive processing but also the cognitive processing that transpires in a social context and is influenced by that context." To obtain a more complete picture of foreign language reading, future research should explore both the cognitive and socio-cognitive factors influencing reading. This can mean, for example, investigating the interaction between readers' psychological processing and the cultural and social backgrounds of the subjects, e.g., the literacy practices that their specific cultures "impose" on them (as advised by Bernhardt 1991 and Smagorinsky 2001). It can also involve exploring the social and cultural context in which thinking aloud takes place, e.g., how the relationship between the subjects and the researcher influences the information reported (as investigated by Sasaki 2008).

This shift from the individual constructivist perspective to the social constructivist perspective (the names of perspectives are suggested by Kucan and Beck 1997) encourages researchers to explore how learners make sense of the text in collaborative discussions. (In fact, it has been the aim of my more recent study – Kusiak 2012). Learners can be asked to talk to themselves and other students about the text they are trying to comprehend or they can be interviewed after the lesson about their efforts. This would mean recording students' private speech or the comments they share with their peers as well as analysing their responses to interviews. Such self-report data can provide valuable information about students' perceptions of classroom activities and their collaborative attempts to construct the meaning of a text. In fact, using the TA technique in pair discussions about texts is exactly what one of the subjects of my study suggested. This is what she said:

> *S: If I had someone to talk to, I could read and we could exchange what we understood, because now I don't know if my comprehension is correct. (...)*
> *T: How could the other person help you?*
> *S: Well, I would be able to see how this person is doing it and I could compare it with how (..) with my way of reading. How I view the text is my business, but if I understood the text, what is written here and if I added something, yes? to the text. It seems to me that it would be good if I had another person to talk to, or if you could say something but I know you cannot participate (laughter). But, well, it could be a good idea; one could feel more confident in terms of his comprehension. Uhm, because now I'm not sure about mine.*

In this quotation, the student underlines the advantages of the think-aloud session conducted in pairs. She would have benefited from cooperating with another reader, which would have helped her to evaluate her comprehension. The example clearly demonstrates the dynamic cooperative character of reading, emphasising the interplay between individual and collective comprehension. It also shows the relationship between developing the propositional textbase (reflected in the words "I understood the text, what is written here") and the situation model of the text (demonstrated in the comment "I added something"). It seems that cooperative thinking aloud may be an effective reading technique for advanced FL learners, who in their reading construct both types of text representation.

In sum, think-aloud methodology lends itself to investigating many aspects of reading comprehension within various theoretical orientations. Think-aloud protocols help one to detect processes that are invisible to other research methods. I hope that the study described in this book and the suggestions presented above have elucidated the potential of the method and will encourage researchers to initiate their own reading research.

9.2. Teaching implications

As has been emphasised earlier, think-aloud methodology offers a window into learners' understanding of texts. Kucan and Beck (1997: 292) explain that "[i]n general terms, the potential to reveal, which is the power of thinking aloud as a method of research, is also an aspect of its potential as a method of instruction." TA protocols can reveal to teachers reading processes that are not visible in a traditional classroom situation. While reading aloud, students reveal their unstructured responses to the text; whereas in the classroom learners' answers are usually prompted by teacher questions. Thinking aloud has proved effective in reading comprehension instruction. Thinking aloud was first employed by teachers, who made overt to their students the strategies they were using in reading FL texts. Later, approaches were developed to engage learners themselves in thinking aloud. Reciprocal Teaching, Collaborative Strategy Instruction and Questioning the Author are examples of the latter mode of classroom instruction (Kucan and Beck 1997). In **Reciprocal Teaching**, students take turns in reading the text and talking in public about how they understand what they are reading. They also seek feedback from the class and provide clarification of any difficulties they encounter while reading the text. Cotterall (1991) and Akkakoson (2011) showed that Reciprocal Teaching can successfully raise FL adult learners' awareness of their reading strategies. The interactive dialogue among the learners allowed students to observe their reading strategies and compare them with those of other readers.

Collaborative Strategy Instruction, developed by V. A. Anderson and Roit (1993), draws on the principles of Reciprocal Teaching but has "a decidedly [more] conversational tone, with both teachers and students asking general kinds of questions that people might ask in discussing books or articles" (Kucan and Beck 1997: 286). Its focus on engaging students in classroom discussions encourages learners to describe not only how they read the text but also what they think about the text.

Also **Questioning the Author** reflects a movement from teacher-dominated tasks to learner-led discussions. It demonstrates "a kind of shared thinking aloud within a social context", as Trabasso and Magliano (1996: 25, cited by Kucan and

Beck 1997: 287) call it. Learners ask a variety of questions concerning the message communicated in the text as well their interpretations of the text ideas. Thus, in verbalising and exchanging their thoughts they practice critical reading skills.

It is important to emphasise that both Collaborative Strategy Instruction and Questioning the Author proved effective in teaching reading to American school students. V. A. Anderson and Roit (1993), who compared interactive and traditional reading classes of students aged 11–16, observed a better performance in the collaborative instruction group, i.e., gains in reading comprehension scores as well as significant changes in teacher and student interaction during discussions about texts. Studies that focused on Questioning the Author (e.g., Beck *et al.* 1996) brought similar results, confirming the facilitative effects of thinking aloud in a classroom context. It seems, however, that more research concerning the use of the above-mentioned techniques in a FL education is needed.

Although the study presented in this book did not use thinking aloud as a method of instruction, the results of the study offer some teaching implications. The following implications for classroom practice are worth pointing out. As mentioned earlier, TA protocols provide the teacher with an opportunity to observe the reading strategies their students use as well as to identify factors that influence their students' reading. This leads to a better understanding of the reading that the students attempt to master and raises awareness of how the students under investigation read and what problems they encounter. In the present study, the following factors seem to have influenced the students' construction of comprehension: background knowledge (the protocols underlined both its facilitative and debilitative effects), students' personal convictions concerning the topic discussed in the text and their individual reading styles. As regards strategies, the most revealing finding for me was the students' frequent use of translation when reading in English. I think that if I were to design a reading course for the subjects of the study, the information collected in the TA session would undoubtedly help me to prepare a more effective, better individualised form of instruction (see Kusiak 2007 for a report of the action research that drew on the TA method).

Thinking aloud can be a useful technique in learning from texts (see Alexander and Jetton 2000 and Chodkiewicz 2009 for more information about this kind of reading). A facilitative role of this technique in learning from a text was emphasized by several students in the interview. For example, one of the students explained:

> *Well, reading and thinking aloud takes more time than silent reading. But on the other hand, it can be beneficial, for example, in studying the text. I would for sure remember the information better, if I were to learn from this text.*

It seems that thinking aloud can enhance the studying of academic expository texts, which are examples of the sort of authentic texts advanced FL learners often read (cf. *Common European Framework*, Coste *et al.* 2003). It can increase readers' reflection about the content they attempt to study and the language that is the medium of presenting this content.

Thinking aloud appears to be an alternative technique of assessing students' reading comprehension (see Stage 5). Instead of submitting standardised tests, teachers can ask students to read texts and think aloud. It would allow teachers to assess not only the product of reading (which is assessed by traditional reading comprehension tests), but also the process of reading. It is worth emphasising that an application of TA-based assessment would require from the teacher special care in securing the reliability, validity and authenticity of the testing technique (see Alderson 2001).

TA-based teaching can take various forms. Apart from the collaborative teaching techniques discussed above, an interesting idea could be to instruct the students to listen to (or read) their TA protocols after the TA session. This would raise learners' awareness of factors that shape their reading in a FL and their individual reading styles. In this way, both teachers and learners can benefit from the TA method.

In summary, the TA technique seems to be a useful technique in teaching and assessing FL reading. Engaging FL learners in thinking aloud can result in increasing both teachers' and students' awareness of the nature of this skill, presenting reading as both product and process. Recent attempts to involve students in collaborative discussions seem to indicate new directions for thinking aloud as a method of instruction, ones in which both cognitive and socio-cultural aspects assume an increased importance.

CONCLUDING SUMMARY

The research project presented in this book has been inspired by several factors. Firstly, it was my experience as a teacher in a foreign language teacher training college, which stimulated me to reflect on the role of a native language in foreign language learning, the issue which I had investigated in one of my earlier studies (Kusiak 2009). This has contributed to the formation of a general question which initiated the study, namely whether there was any aspect of reading in which students show more skill in Polish and which students could improve upon in the process of reading in English. In other words, I wished to find out whether students who can be considered proficient readers of Polish (L1) and advanced readers of English (FL) read expository texts in a similar manner. The reason for selecting this type of text was that expository text, because of its potential to present new information, is the genre of textbooks and other reading materials that college students read for their study purposes.

Another factor motivating me to undertake this study was my research interest in reading in a foreign language, whose various aspects I had investigated in my previous studies. The results of the present study has contributed to my better understanding of FL reading, particularly in relation to L1 reading. The findings of the present study have shed light on, e.g., the role of strategies in FL reading (investigated in Kusiak 2000), the nature of metacognition (explored in Kusiak 2001) and the role of L1 in EFL learning (tackled in Kusiak 2009). Finally, an increasing number of cross-linguistic studies and the relatively few studies into reading conducted in the Polish context encouraged me to embark on my own research project as a contribution to the already existing body of research.

Throughout the book, I have attempted to explain the complexity of the dual-language involvement of FL/L2 reading, i.e., to show how L1 and FL/L2 factors interplay in FL/L2 reading. The first part of the book has been intended as a general introduction. It examines the most essential components of reading comprehension, starting from so-called lower-level language processing, related to phonology, vocabulary and sentence; further focussing on higher-level processing components, which involve discourse level and text structure knowledge. This is followed by the analysis of the role of background knowledge, metacognition and metalinguistic knowledge in reading. In the case of each component, the discussion first concentrated on the role of a given factor in L1 reading, then on its role in FL/L2 reading and finally on cross-linguistic studies, which investigate the interaction of L1 and FL/L2 aspects in bilingual reading. In this part, I have also discussed various theoretical perspectives and models within which each component has been investigated, introducing at the same time the main principles of the van Dijk and Kintsch (1983) model and Britton's (1994) theory, which have contributed to the conceptualisation of reading comprehension explored in the empirical project described in Part Three.

Part Two focuses on the think-aloud methodology and protocol analysis research into reading comprehension. Its main aim is to establish the framework for the empirical study conducted for the present book. First, the theoretical and practical aspects of think-aloud methodology are discussed; later are presented the results of selected think-aloud studies which explore various aspects of the reading comprehension process. This discussion has been organised as that in Part One, i.e., the studies were divided into three groups: focussing on L1 reading, FL/L2 reading and cross-linguistic influences in FL/L2 reading.

Finally, Part Three presents and discusses the results of the think-aloud study which explored how Polish learners read expository texts in their L1 (Polish) and a foreign language (English). The study aimed to provide information on a general question: what are the similarities and differences between the students' performance in Polish and in English. I believed that the study would contribute to a more exact description of advanced readers of EFL (often students of Polish universities and colleges) and could offer some important teaching implications.

The project consisted of six stages, which explore reading strategies, problems in reading and solutions, the way the subjects constructed their representations of the texts, the students' individual patterns of developing comprehension and effectiveness in identifying the main ideas. The results of the interview conducted with the students after the think-aloud session provided additional information about the issues investigated in the think-aloud task. The findings revealed both differences and similarities between the subjects' reading in Polish and their reading in English. Verbal reports indicated several **differences.** In reading in Polish, more focus on higher-level skills than on lower-level skills was observed; whereas in reading in English, the subjects concentrated on both higher- and lower-level abilities (see Stage 1 and 2 of the study). In reading in English, the actions which helped the learners to work on unknown vocabulary were more visible. In reading in Polish, the following strategies indicated the subjects' development of comprehension: the active personal involvement of the readers, discussing the text content, extrapolating as well as the use of emotional strategies. This demonstrates that in the FL the students worked on the development of the surface form and the propositional textbase, while in their L1 mostly on the propositional textbase and the situation model. Moreover, reading the English text was accompanied by a higher level of metacognition. More focus on lower-level skills in English can be explained by the fact that the subjects' reading in EFL had not become automatised yet, which could hinder students' ability to evaluate texts more critically and develop their own interpretations. These findings corroborate the findings of several previous studies, e.g., those of Jenkin *et al.* (1993), Davis and Bistodeau (1993), Pritchard and O'Hara (2008). The above-mentioned results were confirmed by the data obtained from the students during the interviews (Stage 6). The subjects themselves emphasised the differences between how they read in the two languages. They reported faster and more fluent reading in Polish and more problematic reading in English, mainly due to attention devoted to vocabulary. In terms of comprehension, they underlined a "carefree" style in reading the Polish text and certain amount of respect for a foreign language text, which in the case of several students was reflected in the scores the students received for their understanding (Stage 5).

In reading in Polish, the learners worked on a wider co-text; whereas in English – on a more narrow co-text. This was observed in the subjects' strategy of rereading the text (Stage 1) and summing up the text (Stage 2). This finding echoes the results of cross-linguistic studies which looked at coherence development (e.g., those by Horiba, van den Broek and Fletcher 1993). It seems that also this result may indicate more focus on lower-level skills in reading the English text and more focus on higher-level skills in reading in Polish, confirming thereby the conclusion presented above.

In reading in English, the students ascribed their problems to their insufficient FL competence; in reading in Polish, they complained about the complexity of the text and the way the author of the text develops ideas – which was also observed by Davis and Bistodeau (1993). This result emphasises the role of language competence in the subjects' FL reading. Probably, insufficient FL competence, particularly that related to vocabulary knowledge, did not allow the learners to focus on the ideational content of the text to the same extent as in reading in their L1.

The findings of the present project indicate that the learners' reading in English and reading in Polish shared certain **similarities**. No difference was found between the number of problems the students reported in reading in Polish and those identified in reading in English. Most of the strategies the learners applied were identified in both reading the Polish text and reading the English text. This was also observed by Block (1986). Additionally, the students' effectiveness to comprehend the main ideas of the Polish text did not differ from the same ability in relation to the English text. The analysis of the learners' idiosyncratic patterns of constructing comprehension and the data obtained from the interviews indicated that the readers reported in a similar manner when reading in Polish and reading in English, which implies that the students demonstrated the same reading style in the two languages. This finding echoes the result of Cavalcanti's (1987) think-aloud study. The analysis of students' individual styles pointed to another interesting observation – the uniqueness of students' reading styles, which they demonstrated in reading regardless of the language of the text. A similar phenomenon was found by Sarig (1987).

The discussion concerning similarities between reading in L1 and reading in FL raises the question of a transfer of certain aspects of reading competence between the two languages. The results I obtained in the present project have encouraged me to venture the opinion that there is a possibility that such a transfer occurred in the subjects' reading, most probably in the area of reading strategies. More investigation could help to further specify the nature of the transfer and its contribution to both FL and L1 reading.

The think-aloud project discussed in this book offers some didactic implications for FL instruction. I believe that the think-aloud methodology can be also applied as a useful instruction technique. It can increase both the teacher's and the learners' awareness of the specificity of FL reading. It can help advanced learners to learn from texts, e.g., in Content and Language Integrated Learning. Protocol analyses can also serve as an alternative technique in assessing learners' reading comprehension. The study has underlined the importance of Polish in EFL reading, which was reflected in the facilitative role of translation in FL reading comprehension. This may encourage educators to revise their convictions concerning the use of L1 in a FL classroom, also in the teaching of advanced learners (see Gabryś-Barker 2005 for a thorough study-based discussion about the role of L1 in FL teaching). Another conclusion that can be derived from the study is that vocabulary knowledge seems an essential component of FL reading, even for advanced learners. The students' attempts to cope with unknown words have demonstrated that the use of FL texts can facilitate vocabulary learning. The role of the written context in EFL vocabulary instruction has been emphasised in FL research, e.g., by Chodkiewicz (2000).

I believe the project described in this book will contribute to a better understanding of FL reading, particularly its inter-linguistic character. I also hope that this work will inspire further research into this aspect of foreign language competence.

APPENDICES

APPENDIX 1.

Below, it is explained how Britton's grammar model (see Part I, Chapter 3, Section 3.4.3.2.) has been used in the analysis of the texts used in the study. As an example, paragraph 3 from the English is analysed.

> *To be sure, we pay a price for progress. Constant change gives rise to widespread nervousness and anxiety. In solving old problems, we often create new ones in their place. Improvements in life expectancy make possible an aging population that puts a growing strain on the health-care system. Private cars give us unprecedented mobility but swell the volume of traffic to the point of gridlock. In the course of enjoying the delights of consumption, we generate so much garbage that we are running out of places to dump it.*

Figure 1 shows a representation of the structure intended for the reader in the form of a set of nodes and links connecting them.

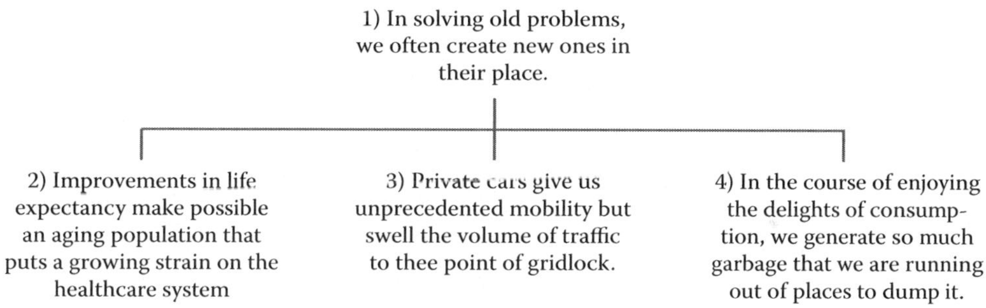

Figure 1: Hypothetical mental structure for paragraph 3 of the English text

Source: own study.

It is clear to notice the relation of coordination between the nodes expressed in the sentences numbered (2), (3) and (4), and the relation of subordination between node (1) and the other three nodes, i.e., (2), (3) and (4).

Let us now look at other clues that can guide the reader in following the exposition, apart from the grammar of exposition discussed above. They are: overlap of content words, syntactic clues, the given-new structure, and explicit signal words and phrases. As for the first clue, the reader may notice an overlap between units of the text, e.g., a sentence may contain a content word from an earlier sentence, which informs the reader to enlarge on the overlapped node, i.e., to attach the new information to that node. In the text below, we can see an overlap between the following two parts of text: "not whether endless progress is desirable but whether it is even possible, as we have known it in the past" (from the first sentence) and "the same question" (from the latter one). The reader, having read sentence (2), can decide that the two parts of the text refer to the same idea.

(1) *For the first time we find ourselves asking not whether endless progress is desirable but whether it is even possible, as we have known it in the past.*
(2) *The global distribution of wealth raises the same question in a more urgent form.*

Syntax can also provide the reader with structure building instructions. In (3) below, the three noun clauses placed after the colon have a prominent position syntactically. They refer the reader to "abundance" as well as inform him/her that the idea of abundance is likely to be enlarged on in the next part of the text. If the reader follows such instructions, he/she finds in sentence (4) that his/her predictions were correct.

(3) *Progress means abundance: more labor-saving machines, more comforts, more choices.*
(4) *It means a rich life for everyone, not for the privileged classes alone.*

In a similar way, on syntactic grounds, the reader is guided in understanding sentence (5). An initial position of "To be sure" underlines the importance of the next clause of the sentence and encourages the reader to assume that it is the to-be-enlarged-on node. Sentences (6) and (7) support this assumption.

(5) *To be sure, we pay a price for progress.*
(6) *Constant change gives rise to widespread nervousness and anxiety.*
(7) *In solving old problems, we often create new ones in their place.*

Another class of text features that can instruct the reader in constructing structures is the given-new structure. In a sentence, there is some information from the sentence before and some new information which moves the discourse forward. The new information to be enlarged on is typically near the end of the sentence. In (8), the last phrase, "a lavish standard of living," is the new information that is developed in (9). The canonical given-new rule is followed again in (9) and (10).

(8) *Compared with the rest of the world, industrial nations enjoy a lavish standard of living.*
(9) *The affluence generated by industrialism looks even more impressive when compared with living standards that prevailed throughout most of the millennium now drawing to a close.*
(10) *Goods that would once have been considered luxuries have become staples of everyday consumption.*

Other clues that can help the reader to follow the exposition are signal words and phrases that specify the nature of the intended links. In (11), the signal word "Yet" instructs the reader to establish an adversative relation between (12) and the text before. In other words, the reader is to build a new node (corresponding to "our faith in progress") and put it in contrast to a hypothetical negative opinion about progress that the disadvantages of progress enumerated above could give rise to.

(11) In the course of enjoying the delights of consumption, we generate so much garbage that we are running out of places to dump it.
(12) Yet none of this destroys our faith in progress.

APPENDIX 2.

This appendix consists of three sections: 1) the analysis of the English text; 2) the analysis of the Polish text and 3) the comparison of the two texts.

1. The analysis of the English text

First the text is presented, then the analysis.

IS PROGRESS OBSOLETE?
A NOTED HISTORIAN ARGUES THAT THE DREAM HAS BECOME FAR TOO EXCLUSIVE

1) Progress and democracy, we assume, go hand in hand. Progress means abundance: more labor-saving machines, more comforts, more choices. It means a rich life for everyone, not for the privileged classes alone. Or so we used to believe, until recent events began to suggest that progress may have limits after all.

2) Compared with the rest of the world, industrial nations enjoy a lavish standard of living. The affluence generated by industrialism looks even more impressive when compared with living standards that prevailed throughout most of the millennium now drawing to a close. Goods that would once have been considered luxuries have become staples of everyday consumption. Medicine has reduced infant mortality and conquered many of the diseases that formerly struck down people in their prime. A vast increase in life expectancy dramatizes the contrast between our world and that of our ancestors in the distant past.

3) To be sure, we pay a price for progress. Constant change gives rise to widespread nervousness and anxiety. In solving old problems, we often create new ones in their place. Improvements in life expectancy make possible an aging population that puts a growing strain on the health-care system. Private cars give us unprecedented mobility but swell the volume of traffic to the point of gridlock. In the course of enjoying the delights of consumption, we generate so much garbage that we are running out of places to dump it.

4) Yet none of this destroys our faith in progress. The benefits, we think, outweigh the costs. As long as the question of progress is posed in this way, the question answers itself. The price may be high, but few would seriously choose not to pay it. Progress is an offer we have been unable to refuse.

5) The real question today is whether progress has built-in limits. Environmentalists argue that the earth will not support indefinite economic expansion along the old lines. Reports of global warming, damage to the ozone layer and long-term atmospheric shifts caused by deforestation raise further doubts about unlimited growth. Even though much of this evidence remains controversial, it has already transformed the debate about progress. For the first time we find ourselves asking not whether endless progress is desirable but whether it is even possible, as we have known it in the past.

6) The global distribution of wealth raises the same question in a more urgent form. If we consider the effect of extending Western patterns of consumption to the rest of the

world, the potential impact on the earth is truly staggering. Imagine the populations of India and China equipped with two cars to a family, air conditioning in private homes and appliances galore, participating fully in a consumer economy that already makes heavy demands on the world's environment even when it is confined to a mere fraction of the world's population. It is obvious that the wasteful, heedless life now enjoyed by the West cannot be made available to everyone without stretching the energy resources of the earth, as well as its adaptive capacity, beyond the breaking point.
7) The idea of progress loses all meaning if progress no longer implies the democratization of affluence. It was the prospect of universal abundance that made progress a morally compelling ideology in the past. According to the old way of thinking, the productive forces unleashed by industrialism generated a steadily rising level of demand. Even humble men and women could now see the possibility of bettering their condition. The desire for a full life, formerly restricted to the rich, would spread to the masses. The expansion of desire – the motor of progress – would assure the expansion of the economic machinery necessary to satisfy it. Economic development would thus continue indefinitely in a self-generating upward spiral, without any foreseeable end or limit.

The article starts with the title "Is Progress Obsolete?" printed in big letters and the subtitle, which is placed below. The title is the topmost injunction of exposition to be expanded in the text. The subtitle introduces the idea of the dream that has become too exclusive. There is an idea overlap between the ideas expressed in the title and the subtitle, i.e., the idea of the dream refers to the idea of progress. However, there are no direct clues so the reader may not notice this link.

The first paragraph (see the table below) develops the idea of progress. By the use of "we," the author invites the reader to draw on his/her common knowledge shared with the writer. The paragraph introduces the concept of democracy, extending thereby the concept of progress. This means that the reader is directed to construct two nodes corresponding to the two concepts that "go hand in hand:" the idea of progress and the idea of democracy. Further, the text defines progress, enumerating its advantages, e.g., abundance. The phrase "a rich life for everyone, not for the privileged classes alone" signals a contrast between "everyone" and "the privileged;" this part of the sentence moves up the reader to "democracy" and "exclusive." The last sentence introduces the idea of limits of progress, thus extending the idea of progress.

The second paragraph (see the table below) continues the idea of a rich life from the first paragraph. It develops the contrast between "the rest of the world" and "industrial nations" (introduced earlier), thus encouraging the reader to enrich his/her node related to democracy. To emphasise this contrast, the author introduces the idea of the gap between "our world" and "that of our ancestors" and provides examples of this difference.

The third paragraph (see the table below) introduces the idea of a price we pay for progress, indirectly referring the reader to the idea of limits from the first paragraph. The author illustrates the idea of price with a few examples. The antonyms: "old," "new," "delights," "garbage" and a signal word "but" help the reader to see the idea of the contrast between the old problems that people have and the solutions to these problems, which create new problems.

The fourth paragraph is a conclusion of the ideas presented earlier; it unitises the information concerning the advantages and limits of progress. The conjunction "yet" instructs the reader to establish an adversative relation to a hypothetical negative opinion about progress that the limits enumerated above can give rise to. It introduces the idea of our faith in progress. The last sentence sums up our attitude to the two contrasting aspects of progress.

The fifth paragraph moves up the reader to "the question of progress" and the idea of limits discussed in the previous paragraphs. A new idea of the real question is introduced. Similarly, a new type of limits, built-in limits, is presented. Both ideas are developed on the basis of examples concerning damage done to the environment. The last sentence serves as a conclusion in the debate about progress, explaining the idea of both "the question of progress" and its built-in limits.

The sixth paragraph continues the idea of built-in limits, discussed in paragraph 5, this time by raising the issue of democracy, which was introduced in the first paragraph. "The global distribution of wealth" is placed in the initial position in the sentence and discussed throughout the paragraph. The last sentence is a conclusion drawn from the arguments presented in the text.

The last paragraph elaborates on the development of democracy. Past forms of verbs, e.g., "was," "made," "generated" make it clear for the reader that the ideas expressed refer to "the old way of thinking" about progress. The verb form "would" specifies a hypothetical version of how progress may develop. There is a cascade of synonymous words: "the expansion of desire," "the motor of progress," "the expansion of the economic machinery," "economic development," serving as move-down signals that resembles "a self-generating upward spiral". They move the reader directly to the picture, which accompanies the text.

Table 1. The analysis of paragraphs 1, 2 and 3 of the English text used in the study

Moves	Fragments of the text	Clues in the text for the reader
EXPAND	*Is progress obsolete?*	– Introducing the idea of progress and the idea of progress being obsolete.
ENLARGE ON	*A NOTED HISTORIAN ARGUES THAT THE DREAM HAS BECOME FAR TOO EXCLUSIVE*	– The idea overlap between the idea of dream and the idea of progress; alternatively it may be perceived as the introduction of a new idea of the dream, which the reader may expect the writer to clarify further; – Introducing new information about the dream, i.e., that it is exclusive, which indicates lack of sharing, excluding someone.
ENLARGE ON **Move down** ("exclusive") **Move up** the title ("progress")	*Progress and democracy, we assume, go hand in hand.*	– Adding new information about progress, i.e., introducing the idea of democracy; – Adding new information about the dream being exclusive; – The use of "we" invites the reader to share the author's view; it also directs the reader to common knowledge shared by many people.

Moves	Fragments of the text	Clues in the text for the reader
Move down ("progress")	*Progress means abundance: more labor-saving machines, more comforts, more choices.*	– Adding new info about progress about its advantages.
Move down ("progress") **Move up** ("democracy")	*It means a rich life for everyone, not for the privileged classes alone.*	– Adding new info about progress, i.e., its advantages; – Introducing a contrast between two ideas: the idea of everyone and the idea of privileged classes, thereby extending the idea of democracy.
Move down (the previous sentence)	*Or so we used to believe, until recent events began to suggest that progress may have limits after all.*	– Introducing a new idea of limits, thus extending the idea of progress.
Move up ("abundance")	*Compared with the rest of the world, industrial nations enjoy a lavish standard of living.*	– Extending the idea of abundance and rich life; – Stressing a contrast between "the rest of the world" and "industrial nations," thus extending the idea of democracy.
Move down ("a lavish standard of living", "industrial nations")	*The affluence generated by industrialism looks even more impressive when compared with living standards that prevailed throughout most of the millennium now drawing to a close.*	– Emphasizing the link between "affluence" and "industrial nations."
Move down (the idea of living standards in the past)	*Goods that would once have been considered luxuries have become staples of everyday consumption. Medicine has reduced infant mortality and conquered many of the diseases that formerly struck down people in their prime. A vast increase in life expectancy dramatizes the contrast between our world and that of our ancestors in the distant past.*	– Introducing the idea of the gap between our world and that of our ancestors; – Providing examples of this difference.
Move up ("limits" from par. 1)	*To be sure, we pay a price for progress.*	– Referring to the idea of limits.
Move down ("a price for progress") **Move up** ("life expectancy" from par. 2)	*Constant change gives rise to widespread nervousness and anxiety. In solving old problems, we often create new ones in their place. Improvements in life expectancy make possible an aging population that puts a growing strain on the health-care system. Private cars give us unprecedented mobility but swell the volume of traffic to the point of gridlock. In the course of enjoying the delights of consumption, we generate so much garbage that we are running out of places to dump it.*	– Extending the idea of limits; – Giving examples of limits; – Overlap between the idea of limits and the idea of problems; – Reference to the idea of life expectancy from paragraph 2; – A signal word "but" and the antonyms: "old" – "new," "delights" – "garbage" stress the idea of contrast between changes and new problems.

Source: own study.

2. The analysis of the Polish text

First the text in its original version, then an exact translation of the Polish text are presented. This is followed by the analysis.

MATERIA DUCHA

NEUROBIOLOGIA NAUCZYŁA SIĘ BADAĆ TO, CO NAZYWAMY DUSZĄ. TRZEBA ODRZUCIĆ DOGMATY I SKORZYSTAĆ Z TEJ SZANSY.

STEVEN PINKER

1) W sposób naturalny wierzymy w mit kartezjański, wedle którego naszym ciałem kieruje duch, dokonujący wyborów niezależnie od uwarunkowań biologicznych. Przyjmujemy za pewnik: mózg jest z materii, a duch z pierwiastka niematerialnego. Zgadzamy się oczywiście, że mózg bierze udział w życiu umysłowym, ale wciąż traktujemy go jak kieszonkowego peceta naszej duszy, który w imieniu „duchowego użytkownika" przetwarza i zarządza informacjami.
2) **Współczesna neurobiologia wykazała, że dusza nie istnieje**. To w istocie aktywność mózgu, która służy przetwarzaniu informacji. Nowe techniki obrazowania wiążą każdą myśl i emocję z aktywnością neuronów. Każda zmiana funkcjonowania mózgu – na skutek wylewu, działania leków, czynników elektrycznych czy zabiegu chirurgicznego – zmienia też nasz umysł.
3) Ale odkrycie to nie znalazło jeszcze odbicia w wiedzy potocznej. Mówimy ludziom, by „używali swojego mózgu," snujemy rozważania na temat jego transplantacji, co w gruncie rzeczy winno nazywać się przeszczepem ciała. Zaskakuje nas fakt, iż medytacja, edukacja i psychoterapia rzeczywiście zmieniają mózg.
4) Paul Bloom, profesor psychologii na Uniwersytecie Yale, dowodzi w swojej książce „Dziecko Kartezjusza," iż podział na ciało i umysł wpisany jest w sam nasz sposób myślenia. Dzieci łatwo przyjmują opowieści, w których żaba przemienia się w księżniczkę czy dusza opuszcza ciało, by przeżyć doświadczenia inaczej dla niej niedostępne. I chociaż wiedzą, że mózg jest użyteczny w procesie myślenia, to zaprzeczają, by to on właśnie decydował o przeżywaniu smutku lub miłości.
5) Brak związku między zdrowym rozsądkiem a nauką nie jest jedynie osobliwością akademicką. Osiągnięcia neurobiologii stawiają nas samych w kłopotliwym – nieznanym dotąd – położeniu. Jeśli będziemy wciąż upierać się, iż jesteśmy tylko kimś, kto w bliżej nieokreślony sposób używa mózgu, czekają nas dalsze niepotrzebne złudzenia. Rewolucja, jakiej dokonał prozac, jest tu dobrym przykładem. Dziś, gdy leki antydepresyjne i środki uspokajające są stosowane powszechnie, krytycy zaczynają się zastanawiać, czy nie tracimy zdolności pokonywania problemów zwykłą siłą woli. Wielu małżonków nierozumiejących tego, co przeżywa partner, pyta: „Czemu po prostu nie weźmiesz się w garść?". Problem w tym, że człowiek w depresji wcale nie jest leniwy. Po prostu te fragmenty jego mózgu, które mogłyby spowodować „wzięcie się w garść," nie funkcjonują prawidłowo. W tym stanie „czarna przyszłość" jest dosłownie rzeczywistością obiektywną. Chory nie oczekuje niczego. „Podrasowanie" mózgu za pomocą leków może być czasem najlepszym sposobem ożywienia maszynerii, którą nazywamy wolą.
6) Przyczyna leży w tym, że ból emocjonalny, tak jak fizyczny, nie zawsze jest stanem patologicznym. Lęk dostarcza nam impulsu, uczula na niewidoczne zagrożenia. Obniżony nastrój po katastrofalnych przeżyciach pomaga poddać ponownej ocenie nasze per-

spektywy na przyszłość. Ale tak, jak chirurg robi wszystko, by pacjent nie cierpiał katuszy, tak nie powinno się zmuszać człowieka, by przy analizowaniu sytuacji, w jakiej się znajduje, przeżywał więcej lęku czy stanów depresyjnych niż to konieczne.

THE MATERIAL OF THE SPIRIT

NEUROBIOLOGY HAS LEARNT HOW TO EXAMINE WHAT WE CALL THE SOUL. DOGMAS NEED TO BE REJECTED AND THE OPPORTUNITY TAKEN.

Steven Pinker

1) We believe in the Cartesian myth in a natural way, according to which our body is controlled by the spirit, undertaking choices independent of biological conditions. We take as certain that the brain is of matter while the spirit of a non-material element. We agree of course that the brain takes part in mental life, yet we continually treat it as the pocket-size PC of our soul, which in the name of "the spiritual user" processes and manages information.
2) **Contemporary neurobiology has shown that the soul does not exist**. This is in essence brain activity which serves in the processing of information. New techniques for imaging connect each and every thought and emotion with neuron activity. Each change in brain functioning – as a result of a stroke, the action of drugs, electrical factors or an operational procedure – also alters our mind.
3) Yet this discovery has still to find reflection within common knowledge. We tell people "to use their brain," we dream up solutions concerning its transplantation, something that in point of fact should be called body transplantation. We are startled that meditation, education and psychotherapy do actually change the brain.
4) Paul Bloom, a professor of psychology at Yale University, proves in his book "Descartes' Baby" that the division into body and mind is encoded into our very way of thinking. Children easily accept stories in which a frog changes into a princess or where the soul leaves the body in order to experience something otherwise inaccessible to it. And although they know that the brain is used in the thought process they do not accept that it decides on experiences of sorrow or love.
5) The lack of a link between common sense and science is not merely an academic peculiarity. The achievements of neurobiology place us in a difficult – hitherto unknown – situation. If we are to continue to stick by the conviction that we are only somebody who uses their brain in a clearly indeterminate way then further unnecessary illusions await us. The revolution undertaken by Prozac is, here, a good example. Today when antidepressants and tranquillisers are widely used critics have started to ask whether we are not losing the ability to overcome problems by simple will power alone. Many spouses in not understanding what their partner is experiencing ask: "Why don't you just get a grip?" The problem lies in the fact that a depressed person is not a lazy one. Simply those fragments of his brain which could result "in getting a grip" do not function properly. In this state "the black future" is literally an objective reality. The patient expects nothing. "Souping up" the brain by means of drugs may sometimes be the best way to revive the machinery we call will power.
6) The cause lies in the fact that emotional pain just like the physical is not always a pathological state. Fear provides us with an impulse, makes us sensitive to invisible dangers. Low spirits after catastrophic experiences help us to reevaluate our perspec-

tives for the future. And yet in the way that a surgeon does everything for a patient not to suffer agony so one should not force a patient in analysing the situation he finds himself in to experience more fear or depressive states than are necessary.

The caption below the photo of Steven Pinker, the author of the text, is as follows: "A soulless egghead Steven Pinker, the author of the text, has the brain in his grasp, he doesn't believe in the soul." The caption was not included in the analysis. The main reason is that the subjects of the study were not instructed at what stage of their reading they should talk about this element of the article.

The text starts with the title "Materia ducha" ("The material of the spirit") printed in big letters and the subtitle placed below. The title introduces a topic that the reader may associate with psychology, philosophy or religion. The subtitle narrows the reader's doubts, introducing the idea of neurobiology and its research into what we used to call – soul. Additionally, the subtitle raises the idea of taking the opportunity to reject dogmas. Unfortunately, the text does not provide any clues about what dogmas the author means. The reader may ignore this vague idea and leave it unconnected to his/her background knowledge or other ideas that he/she will construct while reading. The reader may also find it difficult to see the overlap of ideas between the concepts evoked by the words "duch" ("spirit") and "dusza" ("soul") and may consequently fail to build a structure that links the two ideas.

The first paragraph extends the idea of spirit (introduced in the title and the subtitle). It introduces the idea that people accept Descartes' theory, which claims that the non-material spirit and the material body are two distinct things. The use of the verb "przyjmujemy" ("we take as certain") emphasizes the idea that the principles of this theory are shared by most people, including the reader. In an implicit way, the reader is directed to the idea of dogmas, presented in the subtitle. The conjunction "ale" ("yet") presents the idea of contradiction in these views: although we accept the principles about body/spirit dualism, we still underestimate the role of the brain (which is part of the body), e.g., in mental processes and tend to treat it as part of the spirit.

The second paragraph starts with the sentence in bold, signalling that the information will be important. The sentence moves the reader up to the idea of neurobiology introduced in the subtitle. It introduces the idea that there is no soul and explains that neurobiological research shows that the soul is in fact an aspect of the brain processing. To understand this idea, the reader should construct a link between "myśl i emocję" ("thought and emotion"), which are aspects of the spirit, and "aktywnością neuronów" ("neuron activity"), which is part of the brain. The last sentence in this paragraph moves up the reader to "życiu umysłowym" ("mental life"), mentioned in the previous paragraph. It introduces the idea of how changes in the brain processing influence the mind. However, the last sentence may be confusing for the reader; even if he/she constructs a mental structure corresponding to the mind, it may be still unclear how to attach this idea to his/her representation of the whole text.

The third paragraph (see the table below for a detailed analysis) starts with the conjunction "ale" ("yet"), which establishes an adversative relation between this sentence and the previous paragraph. It introduces the idea of common knowledge, i.e., popular opinions held by people. The conjunction emphasizes a contrast between what neurobiology has discovered about the spirit and the soul and what we think about this issue. The further part of the paragraph provides examples of such opinions. In an implicit way, the idea of common knowledge and the examples of popular beliefs presented in this paragraph refer the reader to the "dogmaty" ("dogmas") mentioned in the subtitle.

The fourth paragraph (see the table below for a detailed analysis) develops the idea related to Descartes' theory. It introduces Paul Bloom's book *Descartes' Baby* and his thesis that people are natural-born dualists, which means that they accept in a natural way that body and mind are distinct entities. The next part of the paragraph presents an example about children who perceive the world in this manner. This part of the text is important for the reader; it helps him/her to construct a link between the node representing the mind and the node corresponding to the spirit, thus clarifying the main topic discussed in the text, i.e., body (brain) – mind (spirit/soul) dualism.

The fifth paragraph continues the idea that was first discussed in paragraph 3. It moves up the reader to the idea that the results of scientific research are not reflected in our popular beliefs. It introduces the idea of the unnecessary illusions that we are likely to experience if we do not modify our opinions concerning the role of the brain in our life. To illustrate this argument, the author presents an example of a misunderstanding caused by the use of Prozac. To understand the role of this part of the text in the discussion concerning the brain, the reader should pay particular attention to the sentence "Po prostu te fragmenty jego mózgu, które mogłyby spowodować "wzięcie się w garść," nie funkcjonują prawidłowo." ("Simply those fragments of his brain which could result 'in getting a grip' do not function properly.") Another clue is a metaphorical use of the words "podrasowanie mózgu" ("Souping up the brain") and "maszyneria, którą nazywamy wolą" ("the machinery we call will power"). Both expressions emphasize the fact that the brain is part of the material body, not a non-material substance.

The last paragraph introduces the idea of pain. It starts with the word "przyczyna" ("cause"). However, the reader may not know to which of the words introduced earlier this word should be attached. The reader may fall back on his/her background knowledge about emotional pain. The last sentence in an indirect way develops the idea of depression; it links the idea of pain with depression and explains why the use of Prozac is justified.

Table 2. The analysis of paragraphs 3 and 4 of the Polish text used in the study

Moves	Fragments of the text	Clues in the text for the reader
Move down	*Ale odkrycie to nie znalazło jeszcze odbicia w wiedzy potocznej.* *Yet this discovery has still to find reflection within common knowledge.*	– "to odkrycie" ("this discovery") refers to the previous sentence, i.e., the results of neurobiological research; – Introducing the idea of common knowledge, i.e., knowledge shared by most people; – "ale" ("yet") establishes an adversative relation between this sentence and the previous paragraph.
Move down ("wiedza potoczna" – "common knowledge")	*Mówimy ludziom, by „używali swojego mózgu," snujemy rozważania na temat jego transplantacji, co w gruncie rzeczy winno nazywać się przeszczepem ciała.* *We tell people "to use their brain," we dream up solutions concerning its transplantation, something that in point of fact should be called body transplantation.*	– An example of common knowledge.
Move up ("wiedza potoczna" – "common knowledge") **Move up** ("dogmaty" – "dogmas" from the subtitle)	*Zaskakuje nas fakt, iż medytacja, edukacja i psychoterapia rzeczywiście zmieniają mózg.* *We are startled that meditation, education and psychotherapy do actually change the brain.*	– An example of common knowledge; – The use of "nas" ("we") stresses the idea of common knowledge; – In an implicit way, the idea of common knowledge and the examples of our popular beliefs presented in this paragraph refer the reader to "dogmaty" ("dogmas").
Move up ("mit kartezjański" – "the Cartesian myth" from paragraph 1)	*Paul Bloom, profesor psychologii na Uniwersytecie Yale, dowodzi w swojej książce „Dziecko Kartezjusza", iż podział na ciało i umysł wpisany jest w sam nasz sposób myślenia.* *Paul Bloom, a professor of psychology at Yale University, proves in his book "Descartes' Baby" that the division into body and mind is encoded into our very way of thinking.* *Dzieci łatwo przyjmują opowieści, w których żaba przemienia się w księżniczkę czy dusza opuszcza ciało, by przeżyć doświadczenia inaczej dla niej niedostępne. I chociaż wiedzą, że mózg jest użyteczny w procesie myślenia, to zaprzeczają, by to on właśnie decydował o przeżywaniu smutku lub miłości.* *Children easily accept stories in which a frog changes into a princess or where the soul leaves the body in order to experience something otherwise inaccessible to it. And although they know that the brain is used in the thought process they do not accept that it decides on experiences of sorrow or love.*	– Introducing the idea of professor Bloom and his book, which develops the idea of the Cartesian myth; – Reference to "mit kartezjański" (the Cartesian myth); – An example of the idea (introduced above) that body/soul dualism is a natural concept in our thinking; this example is subordinate to the idea from the previous sentence.

3. The comparison of the two texts

The comparison of the moves in the two texts looks as follows:

Type of move	Polish text	English text
Move down	12	17
Move up	12	22
Move out	1	1
Unitize	0	2

The comparison shows that the English text offers more move-down and move-up instructions than the Polish text. Another difference between the two texts concerns unitize moves; there are two such moves in the English text and no moves of this kind in the Polish text. There is no difference in a number of move-out moves. Additionally, in the Polish text 13 new ideas were introduced throughout the article; in the English text 7 new ideas were introduced (this is not indicated in the table above). The differences show that the Polish text has a more "dense" network of ideas, which can make it more reader-responsible, thus more difficult for the reader. The texts seem to reflect two different ways of developing arguments, characteristic of expository written texts produced in Polish and English respectively (see Part I, Chapter 3, Section 3.5. for more information about contrastive rhetoric).

APPENDIX 3.

Students' individual styles of reading revealed during the interview

The most important findings concerning three students are presented below.

Student B
Student B emphasized the role of predictions in reading both texts. She explained that in each case she had formed her expectations about the topic of the text on the basis of the picture that accompanied the text. While reading the texts, she asked herself questions and looked for information to answer these questions.

It seems that in reading in Polish she felt disappointed because her expectations were not fulfilled. She said:

> *S: umm, my expectations from the beginning of the article, I expected that having already seen the man really with the brain in his grasp, he doesn't believe in the soul, therefore he doesn't believe. Simply the questions I had asked myself before reading the texts failed to gain answers during the subsequent reading phases the stages of reading the article, I just did not find the answers to the questions which I had asked myself prior to reading and after an evaluation of the picture, the photo*
>
> *T: And what if questions hadn't been asked? Would that not have been better?*
> *S: But then it would be so superficial, for questions not to be asked. I'm also not sure if it doesn't depend on your personality, for example if I'm going to read something then I'm doing so with an aim in mind, if it's for pleasure that's ok. But one can only read such an article in order to become acquainted with some viewpoint, but I don't know that on xx this article for I thought that he'd convince one about this thesis, that he'd explain something to me, something would sway me*

The process of reading the English text, although also guided by the picture and her earlier predictions, looked slightly different. The student commented on reading the Polish text and reading the English text as follows:

> *Indeed that picture in the English text was sort of intriguing for me and as I didn't know exactly what it was about I was encouraged to read on. And I read, I read, to some degree I was somehow less critical in this text than the Polish one, but even the way of writing in English Lasch somehow better expressed things, more of my questions found answers, the facts were simply more discernible. Umm, every thesis had support in the text's subsequent development, while here were, in the Polish text, facts just thrown in, unjustified, in my opinion, sentences which had no factual support. And here really was an argument backed up by facts, that I liked in the English text and equally having only read that fragment of the article I was able to work out the picture, while here the picture imposed to a degree the content on me, the subject matter, imposed expectations, while in the English text there were in effect no expectations, the picture intrigued and expectations were fulfilled, while in the Polish text the picture didn't fully dictate expectations that the text was able to live up to. And I read and I read away but I didn't gain a lot about the spirit from that "Materia ducha."*

It seems that in reading the English text, her expectations were fulfilled. Unfulfilled expectations in reading the Polish text raised her sensitivity to the author's ideas. Student B stressed the role of personal convictions in her own reading. She claimed that because of her approach to the text she was much more critical in reading the Polish text; it was easier for her to accept the information from the English text ("I was much more humble/open to ideas in an English text," she said.) To what extent her personal beliefs influenced her reception of the text may be illustrated by the following quotation: "I believe in the soul, but I also believe in the mind. I think there is some link between the two. But to claim out of the blue that there is no soul is like to deprive us of soul. Yes, what is left is the brain but things do not work this way. Well, I don't know."

Student B also commented on the difference that she had noticed between the Polish and the English text. She explained that the difference lies in how the texts develop the main theses (i.e., a more logical and consistent organization in the English text) and in the role the picture played in reading each text (i.e., a more facilitative role in the English text).

To sum up, Student B is a reader who forms predictions at the beginning of reading and is consistent in her search for information that can fulfil her expectations. Although asking questions before and during reading the text can be an effective strategy, in her case it hindered her comprehension of each text. She did not find answers to her initial questions while reading both texts and consequently missed a lot of information that could have resulted in a more complete understanding. It seems that this behaviour may be one of the factors accounting for her comprehension scores; comprehension of each text was evaluated only as satisfactory (3 points). It is interesting to add that although she was satisfied with her comprehension of the English text, her understanding was evaluated only as satisfactory.

Student F

When asked to comment on his way of reading each text, Student F said:

S: I know it doesn't sound too good but I understood the English better; it's a difficult one for me to compare comprehension and that, as what I understood I understood but I can say that if asked I'd, I imagine, I'd have said the English text as it was exotic, in another language but that's only a question of how you look at things
T: And the Polish?
S: while the Polish text is simply forgotten, you read such a huge number of such texts that they're forgotten, while the English – I'm already left remembering the words, like "capacity" for instance, where they appear in the text, if someone said to me, I can point them out, but that's probably because I remember things by sight
T: So understanding you'd rank similarly, but if you were
S: yes, if I was some time later to be asked about the texts
T: then the English would be more important for you
S: certainly
T: while the Polish less so because of the subject matter or the language
S: the reading process; I know all the words on their own so not much attention's paid to the understanding, but when you start to read in English and analyse, subconsciously like,

I'm not even able to explain it.
T: and what did you analyse in the English text?
S: generally when I read some sentence or other I start to think about its whole meaning, let's say I read the whole sentence quickly, then I go back to the one before, "Progress and democracy go hand in hand," reading "Progress means abundance" I start to wonder about the meaning yet I try to arrange the whole thing backwards, so that it sounds good, while I don't do this in Polish, I simply read on, doesn't matter what I read earlier
T: so what do you arrange in the English text
S: I read one sentence, I read the next then I'm already returning in my thoughts to (...) the sentence and I do it like that for each sentence so as to know more or less what I've read about, next I look at some fragment and I already know what it's about xx
T: in other words going back and linking
S: yes, I also always, for instance, read a fragment of the text and on the basis of what I've read I come up with an idea about what's what so that if anyone was to ask what I'd read I'd be able to answer
T: so things were similar here
S: yes similar, but it's not that going back to the sentence before takes a minute or two because when I read I see it straight away

In short, Student F claimed that he could understand both texts. However, he could remember much more information from the English text. He explained that the main reason was that this text was "exotic," i.e., in a foreign language, which encouraged him to focus on new interesting words. The Polish text did not deserve such attention. Being aware of his reading, he could describe the strategies that he had applied in developing an understanding of the English text. In the quotation provided above, he reports in detail how he constructs the representation of the text when reading the text sentence by sentence. He describes predicting the text, combining the information that he understood and evaluating the product of his work. He says that his way of reading the Polish text differs from that of reading the English text. In reading in his mother tongue, he does not use the strategies that he uses in reading in English. He describes his way of reading in Polish as "simply reading on."

It seems that the difference in how the student approached the two texts could have been one of the factors influencing the difference in the scores that he obtained for his comprehension of both. His analytical and strategic approach to the English text resulted in a very good score; whereas a rather "careless" treatment of the Polish text only in a fair score.

Student J

Student J is one of the students who think that they read in both languages in the same way. He said:

I have the same way of reading, I read slow, I read slowly, oh! And I always read such texts, because they are popular scientific texts, umm, in a way whereby I read paragraph by paragraph. When I don't understand something then I read the given paragraph two or three times. Sometimes I'm reading an article in Polish and there's something I don't understand because it's not a logical statement for me so I try to stop and think over why we've got that sort of argumentation. But generally I read paragraph by paragraph, I never apply an approach of whizzing through the text any old how. If need be in looking through a newspaper I often when reading a headline pay a lot of attention to the illustration, the photos, I also read the captions under the photos because an article illustrated well with fitting captions often contains the most important points from the article itself.

Student J characterizes his reading style as a very logical process. He reads newspaper articles slowly, examining the text paragraph by paragraph. When problems appear, he rereads the text to understand the arguments presented in the paragraph. He can distinguish between the strategies he applies in the careful reading of a newspaper article and the quick browsing of a newspaper before selecting on what to read. His comprehension of each text was evaluated as very good. It seems that his logical slow way of reading was reflected in his performance during the TA tasks. It is crucial to note that one of the factors contributing to his success can be the nature of the TA task; eliciting reading paragraph by paragraph seemed to facilitate the student's natural way of reading.

BIBLIOGRAPHY

Aaronson, D. and S. Ferres (1983). Lexical categories and reading tasks. *Journal of Experimental Psychology: Human Perception and Performance* 9: 675–99.

Adams, M. J. and A. Collins (1979). A schema-theoretic view of reading. In: R. O. Freedle (ed.). *New Directions in Discourse Processing*, Vol. 2. Norwood, NJ: Ablex. 1–22.

Afflerbach, P. (1990). The influence of prior knowledge on expert readers' main idea construction strategies. *Reading Research Quarterly* 25: 31–46.

Afflerbach, P. (2000). Verbal reports and protocol analysis. In: M. L. Kamil, P. B. Mosenthal, P. D. Pearson and R. Barr (eds.). *Handbook of Reading Research*, Vol. 3. Mahwah, NJ: Lawrence Erlbaum Associates. 163–180.

Akkakoson, S. (2011). *Raising the Comprehension Skills of Thai Tertiary Readers of English Through Strategies-based Instruction.* Dissertation, University of Otago, Dunedin, New Zealand.

Alderson, J. C. (1984). Reading in a foreign Language: A reading problem or a language problem? In: C. Alderson and A. H. Urquhart (eds.). *Reading in a Foreign Language.* London: Longman. 1–24.

Alderson, J. C. (2001). *Assessing Reading.* Cambridge: Cambridge University Press.

Alderson, J. C. and A. H. Urquhart (1984). Postscript on Berman. In: C. Alderson and A. H. Urquhart (eds.). *Reading in a Foreign Language.* London: Longman. 157–9.

Alderson, J. C. and A. H. Urquhart (1985). This test is unfair: I'm not an economist. In: P. Haupman, R. LeBlack and M. B. Wesche (eds.). *Second Language Performance Testing.* Ottawa: University of Ottawa Press. 25–44.

Alexander, P. A. and T. L. Jetton (2000). Learning from text: A multidimensional and developmental perspective. In: M. L. Kamil, P. B. Mosenthal, P. D. Pearson and R. Barr (eds.). *Handbook of Reading Research*, Vol. 3. Mahwah, NJ: Lawrence Erlbaum Associates. 285–310.

Allen, E. D., E. B. Bernhardt, M. T. Berry and M. Demel (1988). Comprehension and text genre: analysis of secondary school foreign language readers. *Modern Language Journal* 72 (2): 163–72.

Amer, A. A. (1992). The effect of story grammar instruction on EFL students' comprehension of narrative text. *Reading in a Foreign Language* 8 (2): 711–20.

Anderson, A., S. C. Garrod and A. J. Sanford (1983). The accessibility of pronominal antecedents as a function of episode shifts in narrative text. *Quarterly Journal of Experimental Psychology* 35A: 427–40.

Anderson, R. C. and P. Freebody (1983). Reading comprehension assessment and the comprehension of knowledge. In: B. Hutton (ed.). *Advances in Reading Language Research: A Research Annual.* Greenwich, CT: JAI Press. 231–56.

Anderson, R. C. (1978). Schema-directed processes in language comprehension. In: A. M. Lesgold and J. W. Pellegrino, S. D. Fokkema and R. Glaser (eds.). *Cognitive Psychology and Instruction.* New York: Plenum Press. 66–78.

Anderson, R. C. and A. Davison (1986). *Conceptual and Empirical Bases of Readability Formulas.* Technical Report no 392. Urbana-Champaign: University of Illinois.

Anderson, R. C. and P. Pearson (1984). A schema-theoretic view of basic processes in reading. In: P. D. Pearson, R. Barr, M. L. Kamil and P. Mosenthal (eds.). *Handbook of Reading Research*, Vol. 1. New York: Longman. 225–91.

Anderson, R.C., R. E. Reynolds, D. L. Schallert and E. T. Goetz (1977). Frameworks for comprehending discourse. *American Educational Research Journal* 14: 367–82.

Anderson, V. A. and M. Roit (1993). Planning and implementing collaborative strategy instruction for delayed readers in Grades 6–10. *The Elementary School Journal* 94 (2): 121–37.

Arabski, J. (2002). Learning strategies of L1, L2 and L3 lexis. In: J. Arabski (ed.). *Time for Words: Studies in Foreign Language Vocabulary Acquisition.* Frankfurt am Main: Peter Lang. 209–15.

Asano, K. and M. Mochizuki Sudo (2006). An analysis of the factors reading rate, vocabulary ability, and speaking proficiency in relation to the test of English for international communication (TOEIC) scores of Japanese learners of English (A). *The Journal of the Acoustic Society of America* 120 (5) [online] questia.com [10.08.2010].

Baddley, A. (1999). *Essentials of Human Memory*. Hove, UK: Psychology Press.

Baddeley, A., M. Eldridge and V. Lewis (1981). The role of subvocalisation in reading. *The Quarterly Journal of Experimental Psychology* Section A, 33 (4): 439–54.

Baker, L. (1985). How do we know when we don't understand? Standards for evaluating text comprehension. In: D. L. Forrest-Pressley, G. E. MacKinnon and T. G. Waller (eds.). *Metacognition, Cognition, and Human Performance*, Vol. 1. New York: Academic Press. 155–206.

Baker, L. (1986). Standards for evaluating comprehension: Are some more critical than others? Paper presented at the meeting of the American Psychological Association, Washington, DC.

Baker, L. (1996). Social influences on metacognitive development in reading In: C. Cornoldi and J. Oakhill (eds.). *Reading Comprehension Difficulties: Processes and Intervention*. Mahwah, NJ: Lawrence Erlbaum Associates. 331–52.

Baker, L. and R. I. Anderson (1982). Effects of inconsistent information on text processing: evidence for comprehension monitoring. *Reading Research Quarterly* 17: 281–94.

Baker, L. and A. L. Brown (1984). Metacognitive skills and reading. In: P. D. Pearson, R. Barr, M. L. Kamil and P. Mosenthal (eds.). *Handbook of Reading Research*, Vol. 1. New York: Longman. 353–94.

Baron, J. and C. Strawson (1976). Use of orthographic and word-specific knowledge in reading words aloud. *Journal of Experimental Psychology: Human Perception and Performance* 2: 386–93.

Barnett, M. A. (1988). Reading through context: How real and perceived strategy use affects L2 comprehension. *The Modern Language Journal* 72 (2): 150–61.

Bates, E. and B. MacWhinney (1982). Functionalist approaches to grammar. In: E. Wanner and L. Gleitman (eds.). *Language Acquisition: The State of the Art*. New York: Cambridge University Press. 173–218.

Bates, E., S. McNew, B. MacWhinney, A. Devescovi and S. Smith (1982). Functional constraints on sentence processing: A cross-linguistic study. *Cognition* 11: 245–99.

Bazerman, C. (1985). Physicists reading physics: Schema-laden purposes and purpose-laden schema. *Written Communication* 2: 3–24.

Beck, I. L., M. G. McKeown, C. Sandora, L. Kucan and J. Worthy (1996). Quesitoning the author: A yearlong classroom implementation to engage students with text. *The Elementary School Journal* 96 (4): 385–414.

Beeman, M. and M. A. Gernsbacher (1994). *Structure Building And Coherence Inferencing During Comprehension*. Unpublished manuscript, University of Wisconsin.

Begg, I. and A. Paivio (1969). Concreteness and imagery in sentence meaning. *Journal of Verbal Learning and Verbal Behaviour* 8: 821–7.

Bereiter, C. and M. Bird (1985). Use of thinking aloud in identification and teaching of reading comprehension strategies. *Cognition and Instruction* 2: 131–56.

Berkemeyer, V. B. (1989). Qualitative analysis of immediate recall protocol data: Some classroom implications. *Die Unterrichtspraxis* 22: 131–7.

Berliner, D. (1986). In pursuit of the expert pedagogue. *Educational Researcher* 15 (7): 5–13.

Berman, R. (1984). Syntactic components of the foreign language reading process. In: J. C. Alderson and A. H. Urquhart (eds.). *Reading in a Foreign Language*. London: Longman. 139–56.

Bernhardt, E. B. (1991). *Reading Development in a Second Language: Theoretical, Empirical and Classroom Perspectives*. Norwood, NY: Ablex.

Bernhardt, E. B. and V. B. Berkemeyer (1988). Authentic texts and the high school German learner. *Die Unterrichtspraxis* 21 (1): 6–28.

Bernhardt, E. and M. Kamil (1995). Interpreting relationships between L1 and L2 readers: Consolidating the Linguistic Threshold and the Linguistic Interdependence Hypotheses. *Applied Linguistics* 16 (1): 15–34.

Bialystok, E. (2001). *Bilingualism in Development: Language, Literacy and Cognition*. Cambridge: Cambridge University Press.

Birch, B. M. (2002). *English L2 Reading: Getting to the Bottom*. Mahwah, NJ: Lawrence Erlbaum Associates. [online] www.questia.com [20.09.2011].

Black, J. B. (1985). An exposition on understanding expository text. In: B. K. Britton and J. B. Black (eds.). *Understanding Expository Text. A Theoretical and Practical Handbook for Analysing Explanatory Text*. London, Hillsdale: Lawrence Erlbaum Associates. 249–67.

Black, J. B., T. J. Turner and G. H. Bower (1979). Point of view in narrative comprehension, memory, and production. *Journal of Verbal Learning and Verbal Behaviour* 18: 187–98.

Block, E. (1986). The comprehension strategies of second language readers. *TESOL Quarterly* 20 (3): 463–94.

Bloom, A. H. (1981). *The Linguistic Shaping of Thought: A Study in the Impact of Language on Thinking in China and the West*. Hillsdale, NJ: Lawrence Erlbaum Associates.

Bobrow, R. and J. Brown. (1975). Syntheses, analysis, and contingent knowledge in specialized understanding systems. In: D. Bobrow and A. Collins (eds.). *Representation and Understanding: Studies in Cognitive Science*. New York: Acedemic Press. 103–29.

Bossers, B. (1992). *Reading in Two Languages*. Dissertation, Vrije Universiteit, Amsterdam.

Bradley, L. and P. E. Bryant (1979). The independence of reading and spelling in backward and normal readers. *Developmental Medicine and Child Neurology* 21: 504–14.

Brannen, J. (ed.) (1992). Combining qualitative and quantitative approaches: An overview. In: J. Brannen (ed.). *Mixing Methods: Qualitative and Quantitative Research*. Brookfield: Avebury. 3–37.

Bransford, J. and M. Johnson (1973). Consideration of some problems of comprehension. In: W. Chase (ed.). *Visual Information Processing*. New York: Academic Press. 383–438.

Breznitz, Z. and L. Berman (2003). The underlying factors of word reading rate. *Educational Psychology Review* 15 (3): 193–9.

Britton, B. (1994). Understanding expository text. In: M. A. Gernsbacher (ed.). *Handbook of Psycholinguistics*. San Diego: Academic Press. 641–74.

Britton, B. K. and S. Gülgöz (1991). Using Kintsch's model to improve instructional text: Effects of repairing inference calls on recall and cognitive structures. *Journal of Educational Psychology* 83: 329–45.

Brown, A. L. (1980). Metacognitive development and reading. In: R. J. Spiro, B. C. Bruce and W. F. Brewer (eds.). *Theoretical Issues in Reading Comprehension*. Hillsdale, N.J.: Lawrence Erlbaum. 453–82.

Brown, C. (2000). The interrelation between speech perception and phonological acquisition from infant to adult. In: J. Archibald (ed.). *Second Language Acquisition and Linguistic Theory*. Oxford: Blackwell. 4–63.

Bryant, P. E., L. Bradley, M. MacLean and J. Crossland (1989). Nursery rhymes, phonological skills and reading. *Journal of Child Language* 16: 407–28.

Butler, Y. G. (2002). Second language learners' theories on the use of English articles: An analysis of the metalinguistic knowledge used by Japanese students in acquiring the English article system. Studies in Second Language Acquisition 24 (3): 451–81.

Canney, G. and P. Winograd (1979). *Schemata For Reading And Reading Comprehension Performance*. Technical Report No. 120. Urbana: University of Illinois, Center for Study of Reading.

Carrell, P. (1982). Cohesion is not coherence. *TESOL Quarterly* 16: 479–88.

Carrell, P. L. (1983). Some issues in studying the role of schemata, or background knowledge, in second language comprehension. *Reading in a Foreign Language* 1 (2): 81–93.

Carrell, P. L. (1984). The effects of rhetorical organization on ESL readers. *TESOL Quarterly* 18: 441–69.

Carrell, P. L. (1987). Content and formal schemata in ESL reading. *TESOL Quarterly* 21 (3): 461–81.

Carrell, P. (1989). Metacognitive awareness and second language reading. *The Modern Language Journal* 73 (2): 121–34.

Carrell, P. (1991). Second language reading: Reading ability or language proficiency? *Applied Linguistics* 12 (2): 159–79.

Carrell, P. (2006). Introduction: Interactive approaches to second language reading. In: P. L. Carrell, J. Devine and D. E. Eskey (eds.). *Interactive Approaches to Second Language Reading.* New York: Cambridge University Press. 1–7.

Carrell, P. L., B. G. Pharis and J. C. Liberto (1989). Metacognitive strategy training for ESL reading. *TESOL Quarterly* 23 (4): 647–78.

Carver, R. P. (1977). Toward a theory of reading comprehension and rauding. *Reading Research Quarterly* 13: 8–63.

Carver, R. P. (1990). *Reading Rate: A Review of Research and Theory.* New York: Academic Press.

Carver, R. P. (1994). Percentage of unknown vocabulary words in text as a function of the relative difficulty of the text: Implications for instruction. *Journal of Reading Behaviour* 26: 413–37.

Carver, R. P. (2000). *The Causes of High and Low Reading Achievement.* Mahwah, NJ.: Lawrence Erlbaum Associates.

Cavalcanti, M. C. (1987). Investigating FL reading performance through pause protocols. In: C. Færch and G. Kasper (eds.). *Introspection in Second Language Research.* Clevedon: Multilingual Matters Ltd. 230–50.

Cazden, C. B. (1974). Play and metalinguistic awareness: One dimension of language experience. *The Urban Review* 7: 23–39.

Cazden, C. B. (1976). Play with language and metalinguistic awareness: One dimension of language experience. In: J. S. Bruner, A. Jolly and K. Sylva (eds.). *Play: Its Role in Development and Evolution.* Harmondsworth: Penguin.

Chan, C. K. K. and D. Y. K. Law (2003). Metacognitive beliefs and strategies in reading comprehension for Chinese children. In: C. McBride and H. C. Chen (eds.). *Reading Development in Chinese children.* Westport CT: Praeger. 171–82.

Chang, Y. and D. J. Watson (1988). Adaptation of prediction strategies and materials in a Chinese/English bilingual classroom. *Reading Teacher* 42: 36–44.

Chodkiewicz, H. (2000). *Vocabulary Acquisition from the Written Context. Inferring Word Meanings by Polish Learners of English.* Lublin: Maria Curie-Skłodowska University Press.

Chodkiewicz, H. (2009). Reading to learn and note-taking at academic level: Students' perceptions of strategies used. In: M. Wysocka (ed.). *On Language Structure, Acquisition and Teaching.* Katowice: Wydawnictwo Uniwersytetu Śląskiego. 114–27.

Cieślicka, A. (2000). The effect of language proficiency and L2 vocabulary learning strategies on patterns of bilingual lexical processing. *Poznań Studies in Contemporary Linguistics* 36: 27–53.

Clapham, C. (1996). *Studies in Language Testing 4: The Development of IELTS: A Study of the Effect of Background on Reading Comprehension.* Cambridge: Cambridge University Press.

Clark, H. (1975). Comprehension as an art. Paper read at the Psychology Symposium, Indiana University.

Clark, R. J. (1995). Developing critical reading practices. *Prospect* 10 (2): 65–75.

Clarke, M. (1980). The short circuit hypothesis of ESL reading: Or when language competence interferes with reading performance. *Modern Language Journal* 64: 203–9.

Clarke, M. (1993). The Short Circuit Hypothesis of ESL reading – or when language competence interferes with reading performance. In: P. Carrell, J. Devine and D. Eskey (eds.). *Interac-*

tive Approaches to Second Language Reading. Cambridge: Cambridge University Press. 114–24.

Clyne, M. G. (1987). Cultural differences in the organization of academic texts: English and German. *Journal of Pragmatics* 11: 211–47.

Coady, J. (1979). A psycholinguistic model of the ESL reader. In: R. Mackay, B. Barhman and R. R. Jordan (eds.). *Reading in a Second Language.* Rowley, Mass.: Newbury House. 5–12.

Cohen, A. (1986). Mentalistic measures in reading strategy research: Some recent findings. *English for Specific Purposes* 5 (2): 131–45.

Cohen, A. and C. Hosenfeld (1981). Some uses of mentalistic data in second language research. *Language Learning* 31 (2): 285–313.

Collins, A., I. Brown and K. Larkin (1980). Inferences in text understanding. In: R. J. Spiro, B. C. Bruce and W. F. Brewer (eds.). *Theoretical Issues in Reading Comprehension.* Hillsdale, NJ: Lawrence Erlbaum Associates. 385–407.

Coltheart, M., D. Besner, J. T. Jonassen and E. Davelaar (1979). Phonological encoding in the lexical decision task. *Quarterly Journal of Experimental Psychology* 31: 489–507.

Connor, U. (1996). *Contrastive Rhetoric. Cross-cultural Aspects of Second-language Writing.* Cambridge: Cambridge University Press.

Connor, U. (ed.). (2004). Intercultural rhetoric research: beyond texts. *Journal of English for Academic Purposes* 3 (4): 291–304.

Coste, D., B. North, J. Sheils and J. Trim (2003). *Common European Framework of Reference for Languages: Learning, Teaching, Assessment.* Council of Europe.

Cotterall, S. (1991). Meiko: case study of a successful language reader. *Reading in a Foreign Language* 8 (1): 611–30.

Cowan, J. R. (1976). Reading, perceptual strategies and contrastive analysis. *Language Learning* 26: 353–76.

Crismore, A., R. Markkanen and M. S. Steffensen (1993). Metadiscourse in persuasive writing: A study of texts written by American and Finnish university students. *Written Communication* 10 (1): 39–71.

Cummins, J. (1979a). Linguistic interdependence and educational development of bilingual children. *Review of Educational Research* 49: 222–51.

Cummins, J. (1979b). Cognitive/academic language proficiency, linguistic interdependence, the optimum age question and some other matters. *Working Papers on Bilingualism* 19: 197–205.

Cummins, J. (1980). The cross-linguistic dimensions of language proficiency: Implications for bilingual education and the optimal age issue. *TESOL Quarterly* 14: 175–87.

Cummins, J. (1986). Empowering minority students: A framework for intervention. *Harvard Educational Review* 56: 18–36.

Cummins, J. (1991). Interdependence of first- and second-langauge proficiency in bilingual children. In: E. Bialystok (ed.). *Language Processing in Bilingual Children.* New York: Cambridge University Press. 70–89.

Cziko, G. A. (1978). Differences in first and second language reading: The use of syntactic, semantic and discourse constraints. *Canadian Modern Language Review* 34: 473–89.

Čmejrková, S. (1994). Academic writing in Czech and English. Paper presented at the Conference on Academic Writing – Research and Applications, University of Helsinki, Finland.

Davies, A. (1984). Simple, simplified and simplification: What is authentic? In: C. Alderson and A. H. Urquhart (eds.). *Reading in a Foreign Language.* London: Longman. 181–95.

Davis, J. and L. Bistodeau (1993). How do L1 and L2 reading differ? Evidence from think-aloud protocols. *The Modern Language Journal* 77: 459–71.

Davison, A., P. Wilson and G. Hermon (1985). *Effects of Syntactic Connectives and Organizing Cues on Text Comprehension.* Champaign, IL: Center for the Study of Reading.

de Groot, A. (1965). *Thought and Choice in Chess.* The Hague, Netherlands: Mouton.
Denzin, N. K. (ed.) (1970). *Sociological Methods: A Source Book.* Chicago: Aldine.
Devine, J. (1988). A case study of two readers: Models of reading and reading performance. In: P. L. Carrell, J. Devine and D. E. Eskey (eds.). *Interactive Approaches to Second Language Reading.* Cambridge: Cambridge University Press. 127–39.
Devine, J. (1993). The relationship between general language competence and second language reading proficiency: Implications for teaching. In: P. Carrell, J. Devine and D. Eskey (eds.). *Interactive Approaches to Second Language Reading.* Cambridge: Cambridge University Press. 260–77.
Dijkstra, T. and W. J. B. van Heuven (1998). The BIA model and bilingual word recognition. In: J. Grainer and A. M. Jacobs (eds.). *Localist Connectionist Approaches to Human Cognition.* Mahwah, NJ: Erlbaum.
Dijkstra, T., H. van Jaarsveld and S. Ten Brinke (1998). Interlingual homograph recognition: Effects of task demands and language intermixing. *Bilingualism: Language and Cognition* 1: 51–66.
Dooley, C. and R. E. George (1988). A single case study illustrating the reduction in subvocalisation with electromyography. *Behavioural Psychotherapy* (16): 231–40.
Durkin, H. E. (1937). Trial-and-error, gradual analysis and sudden reorganisation: An experimental study of problem solving. *Archives of Psychology* 1937: 210.
Dussias, P. E. (2001). Sentence parsing in fluent Spanish-English bilinguals. In: J. Nicol (ed.). One Mind, Two Languages: Bilingual Language Processing. Cambridge: Blackwell. 159–76.
Duszak, A. (1994). Academic discourse and intellectual styles. *Journal of Pragmatics* 21: 291–313.
Duszak, A. (1997). Cross-cultural academic communication: a discourse-community view. In: A. Duszak (ed.). *Culture and styles of academic discourse.* Berlin: Mouton de Gruyter. 11–39.
Earthman, E. (1992). Creating the virtual work: Readers' processes in understanding literary texts. *Research in the Teaching of English* 26: 351–84.
Edfeldt Ake, W. (1960). *Silent Speech and Silent Reading.* Chicago: University of Chicago Press.
Eggington, W. G. (1987). Written academic discourse in Korean: Implications for effective communication. In: U. Connor and R. B. Kaplan (eds.). *Writing Across Languages: Analysis of L2 Text.* Reading, MA: Addison-Wesley. 153–68.
Ericsson, K. (1986). Qualitative methods in research on teaching. In: M.C. Wittrock (ed.). *A Handbook of Research on Teaching.* New York: Macmillan. 119–61.
Ericsson, K. (1988). Concurrent verbal reports on reading and text comprehension. *Text* 8 (4): 295–325.
Erickson, M. and J. Molloy (1983). ESP test development for engineering students. In: J. Oller (ed.). *Issues in Language Testing Research.* Rowley, MA: Newbury House. 280–8.
Ericsson, K. and H. Simon (1980). Verbal reports as data. *Psychological Review* 87: 215–53.
Ericsson, K. and H. Simon (1984). *Protocol Analysis: Verbal Reports as Data.* Cambridge, MA: Bradford Books / MIT Press.
Ericsson, K. and H. Simon (1987). Verbal reports on thinking. In: C. Færch and G. Kasper (eds.). *Introspection in Second Language Research.* Clevedon: Multilingual Matters Ltd. 25–53.
Ericsson, K. and H. Simon (1993). *Protocol Analysis: Verbal Reports as Data.* (Rev. ed.). Cambridge, MA: Bradford Books/MIT Press.
Ericsson, K. and H. Simon (1998). How to study thinking in everyday life: Contrasting think-aloud protocols with descriptions and explanations of thinking. *Mind, Culture and Activity* 5 (3): 178–86.
Eskey, D. (1993). Holding in the bottom: An interactive approach to the language problems of second language readers. In: P. Carrell, J. Devine and D. Eskey (eds.). *Interactive Approaches to Second Language Reading.* Cambridge, England: Cambridge University Press. 93–100.

Eysenck, M. and M. Keane (1995). *Cognitive Psychology: A Student's Handbook*. 3rd edition. Hove, UK: Psychology Press.
Fish, S. (1980). *Is There a Text in This Class?* Cambridge: Harvard University Press.
Fisiak, J. (ed.) (1984). *Contrastive Linguistics. Prospects and Problems*. Berlin – New York: Mouton de Gruyter.
Fisiak, J. (ed.) (1990). *Further Insights into Contrastive Analysis*. Amsterdam – Philadelphia: John Benjamins.
Fitzgerald, J. (2003). Multilingual reading theory. *Reading Research Quarterly* 38 (1): 118–22.
Flavell, J. H. (1978). Metacognitive development. In: J. M. Scandura and C. J. Brainerd (eds.). *Structural / Process Theories of Complex Human Behavior*. Alphen a.d. Rijn, The Netherlands: Sijthoff and Noordoff.
Flavell, J. H. (1981). Cognitive monitoring. In: W. P. Dickson (ed.). *Children's Oral Comunication Skills*. New York: Academic Press. 35–60.
Fletcher, C. R. and C. P. Bloom (1988). Causal reasoning in the comprehension of simple narrative texts. *Journal of Memory and Language* 27: 235–44.
Forrest, D. L. and T. G. Waller (1979). Cognitive and metacognitive aspects of reading. Paper presented at the meeting of the Society for Research in Child Development, San Francisco.
Frey, L. (2010). The nature of the suppression mechanism in reading: Insights from an L1–L2 comparison. Research project. Cambridge: Cambridge Centre and Applied Linguistics. http://www.psych.unito.it/csc/cogsci05/frame/poster/1/f885-frey.pdf [1.08.2012].
Frith, U. (1985). Beneath the surface of developmental dyslexia. In: K. Patterson, J. Marshall and M. Coltheart (eds.). *Surface Dyslexia, Neuropsychological and Cognitive Studies of Phonological Reading*. London: Erlbaum.
Frost, R., L. Katz and S. Bentin (1987). Strategies for visual word recognition and orthographic depth: A multilingual comparison. *Journal of Experimental Psychology: Human Perception and Performance* 13: 104–15.
Gabryś-Barker, D. (2005). *Aspects of Multilingual Storage, Processing and Retrieval*. Katowice: Wydawnictwo Uniwersytetu Śląskiego.
Gabryś-Barker, D. (2009). Turn on your TAP: memory in language processing. *Linguística. Revista de Estudos Linguísticos da Universidade do Porto* 4: 25–43.
Galtung, J. (1985). Struktur, Kultur und intellektueller Stil. Ein vergleichender Essay über sachsonische, teutonische, gallische und nipponische Wissenschaft. In: A. Wierlacher (ed). *Das Fremde und das Eigene*. München: Iudicium. 151–93.
Garner, R. and R. Reis (1981). Monitoring and resolving comprehension obstacles: An investigation of spontaneous text lookbacks among upper-grade good and poor comprehenders. *Reading Research Quarterly* 16: 569–82.
Garnham, A. (1981). *Mental Models as Representations of Discourse and Text*. Dissertation, Sussex University.
Gasparinatou, A. G. Tsaganou and M. Gridoriadou (2007). Effects of background knowledge and text coherence on learning from texts in informatics. In: Kinshuk, D. G. Sampson, J. M. Spector and P. Isaías (eds.). *Proceedings of IADIS International Conference and Exploratory Learning in Digital Age (CELDA 2007)*. Algarve, Portugal. 147–54.
Gass, S. M. (1983). Language transfer and universal grammatical relations. In: S. M. Gass and L. Selinker (eds.). *Language Transfer in Language Learning*. Rowley, MA: Newbury House. 69–82.
Gass, S. M. (1987). The resolution of conflicts among competing systems: A bidirectional perspective. *Applied Psycholinguistics* 8: 329–50.
Gernsbacher, M. A. (1989). Mechanisms that improve referential access. *Cognition* 32: 99–156.
Gernsbacher, M. A. (1990). *Language Comprehension as Structure Building*. Hillsdale, NJ: Erlbaum.

Gernsbacher, M. A. (1991). Cognitive processes and mechanisms in language comprehension: the Structure Building Framework. In: G. H. Bower (ed.). *The Psychology of Learning and Motivation*. New York: Academic Press. 217–63.

Gernsbacher, M. A. (1996). The structure-building framework: What it is, what it might also be, and why? In: B. K. Britton and A. C. Graesser (eds.). *Models of Understanding Text*. Mahwah NJ: Lawrence Erlbaum Associates. 289–311.

Gernsbacher, M. A. and M. E. Faust (1991). The mechanism of suppression: A component of general comprehension skill. *Journal of Experimental Psychology: Learning, Memory and Cognition* 17: 245–62.

Gernsbacher, M. A., D. Hargreaves and M. Beeman (1989). Building and accessing clausal representations: The advantage of first mention versus the advantage of clause recency. *Journal of Memory and Language* 28: 735–55.

Gernsbacher, M. A. and M. P. Kaschak (2003). Neuroimaging studies of language production and comprehension. *Annual Review of Psychology* 54: 91–114.

Gernsbacher, M. A. and R. R. W. Robertson (1994). The definite article "the" facilitates mapping in story comprehension. In: B. K. Britton and A. C. Graesser (eds.). *Models of Understanding Text*. Mahwah NJ: Lawrence Erlbaum Associates.

Gernsbacher, M. A. and R. R. W. Robertson (1995). Reading skill and suppression revisited. *Psychological Science* 6 (3): 165–9.

Gernsbacher, M. A., K. R. Varner and M. Faust (1990). Investigating differences in general comprehension skill. *Journal of Experimental Psychology: Learning, Memory, and Cognition* 16: 430–45.

Geva, E. (1992). The role of conjunctions in L2 text comprehension. *TESOL Quarterly* 26: 731–74.

Golebiowski, Z. (1998). Rhetorical approaches to scientific writing: An English – Polish contrastive study. *Text* 18 (1): 67–102.

Golebiowski, Z. (2005). Globalization of academic communities and the style of research reporting: The case of a sociology research article. *Transcultural Studies* 1: 57–72.

Goodman, K. S. (1971). Psycholinguistic universals in the reading process. In: P. Pimsleur and T. Quinn (eds.). *The Psychology of Second Language Learning*. Cambridge: Cambridge University Press. 135–42.

Gough, P. B. (1975). The structure of the language. In: D. D. Duane and M. B. Rawson (eds.). *Reading, Perception, and Language*. Baltimore: York Press.

Grabe, W. and F. Stoller. (2002). *Teaching and Researching Reading*. London: Pearson Education.

Graesser, A. and G. Bower. (1990). *Inferences and Text Comprehension*. San Diego, CA: Academic Press.

Graesser, A., J. M. Golding and D. L. Long (1991). Narrative representation and comprehension. In: R. Barr, M. L. Kamil, P. Mosenthal and P. D. Pearson (eds.). *Handbook of Reading Research*, Vol. 2. New York: Longman. 171–205.

Grotjahn, R. (1987). On the methodological basis of introspective methods. In: C. Færch and G. Kasper (eds.) *Introspection in Second Language Research*. Clevedon: Multilingual Matters Ltd. 54–81.

Gyselinck, V. and H. Tardieu (1999). The role of illustrations in text comprehension: what, when, for whom and why? In: H. van Oostendorp and S. R. Goldman (eds.). *The Construction of Mental Representations During Reading*. Mahwah NJ: Lawrence Erlbaum Associates. 195–218.

Haastrup, K. (1987). Using thinking aloud and retrospection to uncover learners' lexical inferencing procedures. In: C. Færch and G. Kasper (eds.). *Introspection in Second Language Research*. Clevedon: Multilingual Matters Ltd. 197–212.

Haberlaudt, K. (1984). Components of sentence and word reading times. In: D. E. Kieras and M. A. Just (eds.). *New Methods in Reading Comprehension Research*. Hillsdale, NJ: Lawrence Erlbaum Associates. 219–52.

Halliday, M. A. K. and R. Hasan (1976). *Cohesion in English*. London: Longman.

Hardin, V. B. (2001). Transfer and variation in cognitive reading strategies of Latino fourth-grade students in a late-exit bilingual program. *Bilingual Research Journal* 25 (4): 539–61.

Harrison, C. (1996). *Interchange 39. Methods of teaching reading: Key issues in research and implications for practice.* Glasgow: The Scottish Office Education and Industry Department.

Haviland, S. E. and H. H. Clark (1974). What's new? Acquiring new information as a process in comprehension. *Journal of Verbal Learning and Verbal Behaviour* 13: 512–21.

Hinds, J. (1987). Reader versus writer responsibility: A new typology. In: U. Connor and R. Kaplan (eds.). *Writing across Languages: Analysis of L2 Text.* Reading, MA: Addison-Wesley. 141–52.

Hirai, A. (1999). The Relationship between Listening and Reading Rates of Japanese EFL Learners. *The Modern Language Journal* 83: 367–84.

Hoey, M. (1983). *On the Surface of Discourse.* London: George Allen and Unwin.

Hoover, W. A. and P. B. Gough (1990). The simple view of reading. *Reading and Writing: An Interdisciplinary Journal* 2: 127–60.

Horiba, Y. (1996). Comprehension processes in L2 reading: Language competence, textual coherence, and inferences. *Studies in Second Language Acquisition* 18: 433–73.

Horiba, Y. (2000). Reader control in reading: Effects of language competence, text type, and task. *Discourse Processes* 29: 223–67.

Horiba, Y., P. W. van den Broek and C. R. Fletcher (1993). Second language readers' memory for narrative texts: Evidence for structure-preserving top-down processing. *Language Learning* 43: 345–72.

Hosenfeld, C. (1977). A preliminary investigation of the reading strategies of successful and nonsuccessful second-language learners. *System* 5: 110–23.

Hosenfeld, C. (1979). Cindy: A learner in today's foreign language classroom. In: W. C. Born (ed.). *The Foreign Language Learner in Today's Classroom Environment.* Montpelier, Vermont, Northeast Conference on the Teaching of Foreign Languages. 53–75.

Hosenfeld, C. (1984). Case studies of ninth graders. In: J. C. Alderson and A. H. Urquhart (eds.). *Reading in a Foreign Language.* London: Longman. 231–49.

Hu, M. and I. S. P. Nation (2000). Unknown vocabulary density and reading comprehension. *Reading in a Foreign Language* 13: 403–30.

Hu, Z., D. F. Brown and L. B. Brown (1982). Some linguistic differences in the written English of Chinese and Australian students. *Language Learning and Communication* 1 (1): 39–49.

Hudson, T. (1982). The effects of induced schemata on the 'short circuit' in L2 reading: non-decoding factors in L2 reading performance. *Language Learning* 32 (1): 1–32.

Huey, E. (1908). *The Psychology and Pedagogy of Reading.* Cambridge, MA: MIT Press.

Irwin, J. W. and C. J. Pulver (1984). Effects of explicitness, clause order and reversibility on children's comprehension of causal relationships. *Journal of Educational Psychology* 76: 399–407.

James, W. (1890). *The Principles of Psychology.* New York: Holt.

Jenkin, H., S. Prior, R. Richard, A. Wainwright-Sharp and E. Bialystok (1993). Understanding text in a second language: A psychological approach to an SLA problem. *Second Language Research* 9: 118–39.

Jiménez, R. T. (1997). The strategic reading abilities and potential of five low-literacy Latina/o readers in middle school. *Reading Research Quarterly* 32 (3): 224–43.

Jiménez, R. T., G. E. Garcia and P. D. Pearson (1996). The reading strategies of bilingual Latina/o students who are successful English readers: Opportunities and obstacles. *Reading Research Quarterly* 31 (1): 90–112.

Johnson, P. (1981). Effects on reading comprehension of language complexity and cultural background of a text. *TESOL Quarterly* 15: 169–81.

Johnson-Laird, P. N. (1983). *Mental Models.* Cambridge, MA: Harvard University Press.

Judson, H. F. (1980). *The Search for Solutions.* New York: Holt, Rinehart and Winston.
Just, M. A. and P. A. Carpenter (1980). A theory of reading: From eye fixations to comprehension. *Psychological Review* 87: 329–54.
Just, M. A. and P. A. Carpenter (1987). *The Psychology of Reading and Language Comprehension.* Boston: Allyn & Bacon.
Kang, H. W. (1992). Cultural inference in second language reading. *International Journal of Applied Linguistics* 2: 95–119.
Kaplan, R. (1966). Cultural thought patterns in intercultural education. Language Learning 16 (1, 2): 1–20.
Kaplan, R. (1987). *Fact and Counterfact: An Exploration of Chinese Writing.* TESOL Conference, Miami.
Kaplan, R. (1997). Contrastive rhetoric. In: T. Miller (ed.). *Functional Approaches to Written Text: Classroom*
Applications. English Language Programs United States Information Agency, Washington, D.C. 18–32.
Katz, L., R. Frost (1992). Reading in different orthographies: The orthographic depth hypothesis. In: R. Frost and L. Katz (eds.). *Orthography, phonology, morphology, and meaning.* Amsterdam: Elsevier.
Keenan, J., J. Golding, G. Potts, T. Jennings and C. Aman (1990). Methodological issues in evaluating the occurrence of inferences. In: A. C. Graesser and G. H. Bower (eds.). *The Psychology of Learning and Motivation*, Vol. 25. Orlando, Florida: Academic Press.
Kellerman, E. (1983). Now you see it, now you don't. In: S. M. Gass and L. Selinker (eds.). *Language Transfer in Language Learning.* Rowley, MA: Newbury House. 112–34.
Kern, R. (1988). *The Role of Comprehension Strategies in Foreign Language Reading.* Dissertation, University of California, Berkley.
Keshavarz, M. H., M. R. Atai and H. Ahmadi (2007). Content schemata, linguistic simplification, and EFL readers' comprehension and recall. *Reading in a Foreign Language* 19: 19–33.
Kilborn, K. and T. Ito (1989). Sentence processing strategies in adult bilinguals. In: B. MacWhinney and E. Bates (eds.). *The Cross-linguistic Study of Sentence Processing.* New York: Cambridge University Press. 256–91.
Kintsch, W. (1974). *The Representation of Meaning in Memory.* New York: Erlbaum.
Kintsch, W. (1988). The role of knowledge in discourse comprehension: a construction-integration model. *Psychological Review* 95: 163–82.
Kintsch, W. (1998). *Comprehension: A Paradigm for Cognition.* New York: Cambridge University Press.
Kintsch, W. (2004). The construction-integration model of text comprehension and its implications for instruction. In: R. B. Ruddell and N. J. Unrau (eds.). *Theoretical Models and Processes of Reading,* 5th edition . Newark, DE: International Reading Association. 1270–328.
Kintsch, W. and J. M. Keenan (1973). Reading rate and retention as a function of the number of propositions in the base structure of sentences. *Cognitive Psychology* 5: 257–79.
Kintsch, W. and T. A. van Dijk (1975). Comment on sa rapelle et on resume des histories. *Languages* 40: 98–116.
Kintsch, W. and T. A. van Dijk (1978). Towards a model of text comprehension and production. *Psychological Review* 85: 363–94.
Kleiman, G. M. (1975). Speech recoding in reading. *Journal of Verbal Learning and Verbal Behavior* 14: 323–39.
Koda, K. (1988). Cognitive process in second language reading: transfer of L1 reading skills and strategies, *Second Language Research* 4 (2): 133–56.
Koda, K. (1989). The effects of transferred vocabulary knowledge on the development of L2 reading proficiency. *Foreign Language Annals* 22: 529–42.

Koda, K. (2005). *Insights into Second Language Reading. A Cross-Linguistic Approach*. Cambridge: Cambridge University Press.

Koda, K. (2007). Reading and language learning: Crosslinguistic constraints on second language reading development. *Language Learning* 57 (1): 1–44.

Köckeis-Stangl, E. (1980). Methoden der Sozialisationsforschung. In: K. Hurrel-Mann and D. Ulich (eds.). *Handbuch der Sozialisationsforschung.* Weinheim and Basel: Beltz. 321–70.

Krasowicz-Kupis, G. (1999). *Rozwój Metajęzykowy a Osiągnięcia w Czytaniu u Dzieci 6–9 letnich.* Lublin: Wydawnictwo Uniwersytetu Marii Curie-Skłodowskiej.

Kroll, J. F. and J. Curley (1988). Lexical memory in novice bilinguals: The role of concepts in retrieving second language words. In: M. Gruneberg, P. Morris and R. Sykes (eds.). *Practical Aspects of Memory*, Vol. 2. London: John Wiley and Sons. 389–95.

Kroll, J. F. and A. Sholl (1992). Lexical and conceptual memory in fluent and nonfluent bilinguals. In: R. J. Harris (ed.). *Cognitive Processing in Bilinguals*. Amsterdam: Elsevier. 191–204.

Kroll, J. F. and E. Stewart (1994). Category inference in translation and picture naming: Evidence for asymmetric connections between bilingual memory representations. *Journal of Memory and Language* 33: 149–74.

Kubota, R. (1992). *Contrastive Rhetoric of Japanese and English: A Critical Approach*. Dissertation, University of Toronto.

Kucan, L. and I. L. Beck (1997). Thinking aloud and reading comprehension research: Inquiry, instruction and social interaction. *Review of Educational Research* 67 (3): 271–99.

Kurcz, I. and A. Polkowska (1990). *Interakcyjne i Autonomiczne Przetwarzanie Informacji Językowych*. Wrocław, Warszawa, Gdańsk and Łódź: Zakład Narodowy im. Ossolińskich.

Kusiak, M. (2000). *The Effect of Metacognitive Strategy Training on Reading Comprehension and Metacognitive Knowledge*. Dissertation, Jagiellonian University, Kraków.

Kusiak, M. (2001). The effect of metacognitive strategy training on reading comprehension and metacognitive knowledge. In: S. Foster-Cohen and A. Niżegorodcew (eds.). *EUROSLA Yearbook*, Vol. 1. Amsterdam: John Benjamins Publishing Company. 255–74.

Kusiak, M. (2003). Trening użycia strategii czytania w języku angielskim. *Neofilolog* 22: 19–25.

Kusiak, M. (2007). Badanie w działaniu jako narzędzie oceny nauczania. In: M. Jodłowiec and A. Niżegorodcew (eds.). *Dydaktyka Języków Obcych na Początku XXI Wieku*. Kraków: Wydawnictwo Uniwersytetu Jagiellońskiego. 349–58.

Kusiak, M. (2009). Rola języka polskiego w uczeniu się języków obcych. In: M. Pawlak, M. Derenowski and B. Wolski (eds.). *Problemy Współczesnej Dydaktyki Języków Obcych*. 55–66.

Kusiak, M. (2010a). Contrastive rhetoric – how does language influence its users? In: J. Aksman (red.) *Manipulacja: Pedagogiczno-społeczne Aspekty. Część I: Interdyscyplinarne Aspekty Manipulacji*. Kraków: Oficyna Wydawnicza Krakowskiej Akademii im. Andrzeja Frycza Modrzewskiego. 157–64.

Kusiak, M. (2010b). Interdyscyplinarność w badaniach procesu rozumienia tekstu. *Neofilolog* 35: 43–52.

Kusiak, M. (2011). The role of phonological awareness in beginning reading: A cross-linguistic perspective. In: J. Arabski and A. Wojtaszek (eds.). *The Acquisition of L2 Phonology*. Bristol: Multilingual Matters. 77–92.

Kusiak, M. (2012). How "educated" is educational talk in an academic FL classroom? In: M. Dąbrowska, J. Leśniewska and B. Piątek (eds.). *Languages, Literatures and Cultures in Contact: English and American Studies in the Age of Global Communication*, Vol. 2: *Language and Culture*. Kraków: Tertium. 333–51.

Kusiak, M. and E. Bandura (2007). Facilitating educated talk while working with written texts in an academic foreign language classroom. In: J. Arabski, D. Gabryś-Barker and A. Łyda (eds.). *PASE Papers 2007*, Vol. 1: *Studies in Language and Methodology of Teaching Foreign Languages*. Katowice: University of Silesia. 309–18.

Lardiere, D. (1998a). Case and tense in the 'fossilized' steady state. *Second Language Research* 14: 1–26.
Lardiere, D. (1998b). Dissociating syntax from morphology in a divergent L2 end-state grammar. *Second Language Research* 14: 359–75.
Lardiere, D. (2000). Mapping features to forms in second language acquisition. In: J. Archibald (ed.). *Second Language Acquisition and Linguistic Theory*. Oxford: Blackwell. 102–29.
Lasch, C. (1992). Is progress obsolete? *Time Special Issue* 15 October: 71.
Latkowska, J. (2001). The influence of the L2 on L1 competence: A study of crosslinguistic interaction in an L1 environment. In: J. Arabski (ed.). *Insights into Foreign Language Acqusition and Teaching.* Katowice: Wydawnictwo Uniwersytetu Śląskiego. 149–62.
Laufer, B. (1997). The lexical plight in second language reading; words you don't know, and words you can't guess. In: T. H. J. Coady (ed.). *Second Language Vocabulary Acquisition*. Cambridge: Cambridge University Press. 20–34.
Laufer, B. and D. Sim. (1985). Measuring and explaining the reading threshold needed for English for Academic Purposes Texts. *Foreign Language Annals* 18: 405–11.
Lee, G. A. (2006). Three factors in L2 reading ability: Using Rauding Theory to reanalyze a study by Nassaji and Geva. *Reading Psychology* 27 (5): 405–33.
Liu, O. L., M. Schedl, J. Malloy and N. Kong (2009). *Does Content Knowledge Affect TOEFL iBT Reading Performance? A Confirmatory Approach to Differential Item Functioning.* TOEFL iBT Research Report. Educational Testing Service: Princeton New Jersey.
Lorch, R. F. and E. J. O'Brien (1995). *Sources of Coherence in Reading.* Hillsdale, NJ.: Lawrence Erlbaum Associates. [online] www.questia.com [2.12.2009]
Louwerse, M. W. and A. C. Graesser (2006). Macrostructure. In: K. Brown (ed.). *Encyclopedia of Language and Linguistics.* Oxford: Elsevier Ltd. 426–9.
Lubelska, D. (1991). An approach to teaching cohesion to improve reading. *Reading in a Foreign Language* 7 (2): 567–98.
Lundeberg, M. A. (1987). Metacognitive aspects of reading comprehension: Studying understanding in legal case analysis. *Reading Research Quarterly* XXII (1): 407–32.
Lyons, J. (1968). *Introduction to Theoretical Linguistics.* Cambridge: Cambridge University Press.
MacWhinney, B. (2008). A Unified Model. In: N. Ellis and P. Robinson (eds.). *Handbook of Cognitive Linguistics and Second Language Acquisition*. Lawrence Erlbaum Press. 341–71.
Maier, N. R. F. (1931). Reasoning in humans: II. The solution of a problem and its appearance in consciousness. *Journal of Comparative Psychology* 12: 181–94.
Mandler, J. M. (1978). A code in a node: The use of a story schema in retrieval. *Discourse Processes* 1: 14–35.
Mandler, J. M. (1984). *Stories, Scripts, and Scenes: Aspects of Schema Theory.* Hillsdale, NJ: Erlbaum.
Mandler, J. M. (1987). On the psychological reality of story structure. *Discourse Processes* 10: 1–29.
Mandler, J. M. and M. DeForest (1979). Is there more than one way to recall a story? *Child Development* 50: 886–9.
Markkanen, R., M. S. Steffensen and A. Crismore (1993). Quantitative contrastive study of metadiscourse: problems in design and analysis of data. In: J. Fisiak (ed.). *Papers and Studies in Contrastive Linguistics*, Vol. 23. Poznań: Adam Mickiewicz University Press. 137–51.
Markman, E. M. (1975). *Realizing that you don't understand: Elementary school children's awareness of inconsistencies.* Unpublished manuscript, Stanford University.
Matalene, C. (1985). Contrastive rhetoric: An American Writing Teacher in China. *College English* 47 (8): 785–808.
Matsuyama, U. K. (1983). Can story grammar speak Japanese? *Reading Teacher* 36: 666–9.

McCallister, J. (1930). Reading difficulties in studying content subjects. *Elementary School Journal* 31: 191–201.

McCormick, K. (1994). *The Culture of Reading and the Teaching of English*. Manchester: Manchester University Press.

McCusker, L. X., M. L. Hillinger and R. G. Bias (1981). Phonological receding and reading. *Psychological Bulletin* (89): 217–45.

McDonald, J. (1987). Sentence interpretation in bilingual speakers of English and Dutch. *Applied Psycholinguistics* 8: 379–413.

McDonough, J. and S. McDonough (1997). *Research Methods for English Language Teachers*. London: Arnold.

McKoon, G. and R. Ratcliff (1981). The comprehension processes and memory structures involved in instrumental inference. *Journal of Verbal Learning and Verbal Behaviour* 20: 671–82.

McKoon,G. and R. Ratcliff (1986). Inferences about predictable events. *Journal of Experimental Psychology: Learning, Memory, and Cognition* 12: 82–91.

McKoon, G. and R. Ratcliff (1990). Textual inferences: models and measures. In: D. A. Balota, G. B. Flores D'Arcais and K. Rayner (eds.). *Comprehension Processes in Reading*. Hillsdale, NJ: Lawrence Erlbaum Associates. 515–36. [online] Questia.com [8.08.2012].

McLay, B. (2007). Reading Rate: Research versus Teaching. [online] http://www.learningassistance.com/2007/november/readingrate.html [10.08.2010].

McNamara, D. S., E. Kintsch, N. B. Songer and W. Kintsch (1996). Are good texts always better? Interactions of text coherence, background knowledge and levels of understanding in learning from text. *Cognition and Instruction* 14 (1). [online] www.questia.com [5.07.2010].

McNamara, D. S. and J. P. Magliano (2009). Self-explanation and metacognition: The dynamics of reading. In: D. J. Hacker (ed.). *Handbook of Metacognition in Education*. New York, NY: Taylor and Francis. 60–82.

McNamara, T. P., D. L. Miller and J. D. Bransford (1991). Mental models and reading comprehension. In: R. Barr, M. Kamil, P. Mosenthal and P. Pearson (eds.). *Handbook of Reading Research*, Vol. 2. London: Longman. 490–511.

McNamara, D. S., T. O'Reilly, R. Best and Y. Ozuru (2006). Improving adolescent students' reading comprehension with iSTART. *Journal of Educational Computing Research* 34: 147–71.

Meyer, B. J. F. (1971). *Idea Units Recalled from Prose in Relation to their Position in the Logical Structure, Importance, Stability and Order in the Passage*. Dissertation, Cornell University.

Meyer, B. J. F. (1975). *The organization of Prose and its Effects on Memory*. Amsterdam: North-Holland.

Meyer, B. J. F. (1986). Organizational aspects of text: Effects on reading comprehension and applications for the classroom. In: J. Flood (ed.). *Promoting Reading Comprehension*. Newark, Delaware: International Reading Association.

Meyer, B. J. F., D. M Brandt and G. J. Bluth (1980). Use of the top-level structure in text: Key for reading comprehension of ninth-grade students. *Reading Research Quarterly* 16: 72–103.

Meyer, D. E., R. W. Schvaneveldt and M. G. Ruddy (1974). Functions of graphemic and phonemic codes in visual word recognition. *Memory and Cognition* (2): 309–21.

Minsky, M. (1977). Frame system theory. In: P. N. Johnson-Laird and P. C. Wason (eds.). *Thinking: Reading in Cognitive Science*. Cambridge: Cambridge University Press. 355–76.

Mora, J. K. (2001). Learning to spell in two languages: Orthographic transfer in a transitional Spanish/English bilingual program. In: P. Dreyer (ed.). *Raising Scores, Raising Questions: Claremont Reading Conference 65th Yearbook*. Claremont, CA: Claremont Graduate University. 64–84.

Mora, J. K. (2007). Metalinguistic transfer in biliteracy instruction: Theory, research and effective practice. Paper presented at the Two-Way CABE conference, Burlingame, CA, July 10–13, 2007. [online] http://coe.solsu.edu/people/jmora [2.09.2009].

Morgan, J. and M. Sellner (1980). Discourse and linguistic theory. In: R. Spiro, B. Bruce and W. Brewer (eds.). *Theoretical Issues in Reading Comprehension*. Hillsdale, N.J.: Lawrence Erlbaum.

Morris, L. (2003). Linguistic knowledge, metalinguistic knowledge and academic success in a language teacher education programme. *Language Awareness* 12 (2): 109–23.

Morrow, L. M. (1985). Reading and telling stories: Strategies for emergent readers. *The Reading Teacher* 38: 870–5.

Myers, M. and S. G. Paris (1978). Children's metacognitive knowledge about reading. *Journal of Educational Psychology* 70: 680–90.

Nation, I. S. P. (2001). *Learning Vocabulary in Another Language*. Cambridge: Cambridge University Press.

Neisser, U. (1967). *Cognitive Psychology*. Englewood Cliffs, N.J.: Prentice-Hall.

Newell, A. and H. Simon (1963). GPS, a program that simulates a human thought. In: E. Feingenbaum and J. Feldman (eds.). *Computers and Thought*. New York: McGraw Hill.

Newell, A. and H. Simon (1972). *Human Problem Solving*. Englewood Cliffs, N.J.: Prentice-Hall. 279–93.

Nevo, N. (1985). Strategies in taking a multiple-choice reading comprehension test. Seminar paper, School of Education, Hebrew University of Jerusalem.

Olshavsky, J. (1976/1977). Reading as problem solving: An investigation of strategies. *Reading Research Quarterly* 12: 654–74.

O'Malley, J. M. and A. U. Chamot (1990). *Learning Strategies in Second Language Acquisition*. Cambridge: Cambridge University Press.

Otwinowska-Kasztelanic, A. (2001). Latent bilingualism and language learning. In: J. Arabski (ed.). *Insights into Foreign Language Acqusition and Teaching*. Katowice: Wydawnictwo Uniwersytetu Śląskiego. 106–20.

Otwinowska-Kasztelanic, A. (2007). Na drodze ku różnojęzyczności: Podnoszenie świadomości językowej przy nauczaniu słownictwa na przykładzie języka angielskiego. In: M. Jodłowiec and A. Niżegorodcew (eds.). *Dydaktyka Języków Obcych na Początku XXI wieku*. Kraków: Wydawnictwo Uniwersytetu Jagiellońskiego. 99–110.

Paradis, M. (2004). *A Neurological Theory of Bilingualism*. Amsterdam/Philadelphia: John Benjamins.

Pawlak, M. (2003). Teaching formal aspects of language through conscious reflection. In: H. Miatliuk, K. Bogacki and H. Komorowska (eds.). *Problemy Lingwistyki i Nauczania Jęzków Obcych*. Białystok: Wydawnictwo Uniwersytetu w Białymstoku. 371–8.

Pearson, P. D. (1975). The effects of grammatical complexity on children's comprehension, recall, and conception of certain semantic relations. *Reading Research Quarterly* 10: 155–92.

Pearson, D. and L. Fielding (1991). Comprehension Instruction. In: R. Barr, M. Kamil, P. Mosenthal and D. Pearson (eds.). *Handbook of Reading Research*, Vol. II. Mahwah, NJ: Lawrence Erlbaum. 815–60.

Pearson, P. D., J. Hansen and J. Gordon (1979). The effect of background knowledge on young children's comprehension of explicit and implicit information. *Journal of Reading Behavior* 11: 201–9.

Pearson, P. D. and D. D. Johnson (1978). *Teaching Reading Comprehension*. New York: Holt, Rinehart and Winston.

Perfetti, C. A. and S. Zhang (1995). Very early phonological activation in Chinese reading. *Journal of Experimental Psychology: Learning, Memory and Cognition* 21: 24–33.

Piasecka, L. (2001). Role of world knowledge in text comprehension. In: J. Arabski (ed.). *Research on Foreign Language Acquisition*. Katowice: Wydawnictwo Uniwersytetu Śląskiego. 123–32.

Piekarz, J. (1954). *Individual Responses in Interpretive Responses in Reading*. Dissertation, University of Chicago.

Pinker, S. (2004). Materia ducha. *Newsweek Poland* 42: 87.
Polanyi, M. (1958). *Personal Knowledge.* London: Routledge and Kegan Paul.
Polya, G. (1954). *Mathematics and Plausible Reasoning,* Vol. 1: *Induction and Analogy in Mathematics.* Princeton, NJ: Princeton University Press.
Pressley, M. and P. Afflerbach (1995). *Verbal Protocols of Reading: The Nature of Constructively Responsive Reading.* Hillsdale, NJ: Lawrence Erlbaum Associates.
Pritchard, R. and S. O'Hara (2008). Reading in Spanish and English: A comparative study of processing strategies. *Journal of Adolescent and Adult Literacy* 51 (8): 630–8.
Rayner, K. and A. Pollatsek (1989). *The Psychology of Reading.* Englewood Cliffs, NJ: Prentice-Hall.
Reid, J. (1988). *Quantitative Differences in English Prose Written by Arabic, Chinese, Spanish, and English Students.* Dissertation, Colorado State University.
Reppen, R. and W. Grabe (1993). Spanish transfer effects in the English writing of elementary school children. *Lenguas Modernas* 20: 113–28.
Ridgway, A. J. (2009). The inner voice. *IJES* 9 (2): 45–58.
Ridgway, T. (1995). Thresholds of the background knowledge effect in foreign language reading. *Reading in a Foreign Language* 11 (1): 151–68.
Robertson, D. A., M. A. Gernsbacher, S. J. Guidotti, R. R. W. Robertson, W. Irwin, B. J. Mock and M. E. Campana (2000). Functional neuroanatomy of the cognitive process of mapping during discourse comprehension. *Psychological Science* 11: 255–60.
Roller, C. M. (1990). The interaction of knowledge and structure variables in the processing of expository prose. *Reading Research Quarterly* 25: 79–89.
Rosenblatt, L. (1938). *Literature as Exploration,* 4th edition. New York: MLA.
Rosenblatt, L. (1978). *The Reader, the Text, the Poem: The Transactional Theory of the Literary Work.* Carbondale, IL: Southern Illinois University Press.
Rosenblatt, L. (2004). The transactional theory of reading and writing. In: R. B. Ruddell and N. J. Unrau (eds.). *Theoretical Models and Processes of Reading,* 5th edition. Newark, DE: International Reading Association. 1363–98.
Rubenstein, H., S. S. Lewis and M. A. Rubenstein (1971). Evidence for phonemic receding in visual word recognition. *Journal of Verbal Learning and Verbal Behavior* (10): 645–57.
Rumelhart, D. E. (1977). Understanding and summarizing brief stories. In: D. LaBerge and J. Samuels (eds.). *Basic Processes in Reading: Perception and Comprehension.* Hillsdale, N.J.: Lawrence Erlbaum Associates. 265-303.
Rupley, W. H. (1996). Exploration of the components of children's reading comprehension using rauding theory. Paper presented at the Annual Meeting of the Society for the Scientific Study of Reading. [online] http://eric.ed.gov/ERICWebPortal/search/detailmini.jsp?_nfpb=true&_&ERICExtSearch_SearchValue_0=ED409549&ERICExtSearch_SearchType_0=no&accno=ED409549 [08.08.2010].
Rusiecki, J. (1980). Latent bilingualism. *Papers and Studies in Contrastive Linguistics,* Vol. 12. 79–98.
Sadoski, M. and A. Paivio. (1994). A dual coding view of imagery and verbal processes in reading comprehension. In: R. B. Ruddell, M. R. Ruddell and H. Singer (eds.). *Theoretical Models and Processes of Reading,* 4th edition. Newark, DE: International Reading Association. 582–601.
Sadoski, M. and A. Paivio (2007). Toward a unified theory of reading. *Scientific Studies of Reading* 11 (4): 337–56.
Saffran, E. M. and O. S. M. Marin (1977). Reading without phonology: Evidence from aphasia. *Quarterly Journal of Experimental Psychology* 29: 515–25.
Salataci, R. and A. Akyel (2002). Possible effects of strategy instruction on L1 and L2 reading. *Reading in a Foreign Language* 14 (1): 1–17. [online] http://nflrc.hawaii.edu/rfl/April2002/salatci/salatci.html [3.03.2005].

Salski, Ł. (2005). Topical structure analysis in teaching EFL composition. Paper presented at 17th International Conference on Second/Foreign Language Acquisition, Uniwersytet Śląski.
Salski, Ł. (2012). *Contrastive Rhetoric and Teaching English Composition Skills*. Łódź: Wydawnictwo Uniwersytetu Łódzkiego.
Sanford, A. J. (1990). On the nature of text-driven inference. In: D. A. Balota, G. B. Flores D'Arcais and K. Rayner (eds.). *Comprehension Processes in Reading*. Hillsdale, NJ: Lawrence Erlbaum Associates. 515–36. [online] Questia.com [8.08.2012].
Sanford, A. (2006). Coherence: Psycholinguistic approach. In: K. Brown (ed.). *Encyclopaedia of Language and Linguistics*. Oxford: Elsevier Ltd. 585–91.
Sarig, G. (1987). High-level reading in the first and in the foreign language: Some comparative process data. In: J. Devine, P. Carrell and D. Eskey (eds.). *Research in Reading in English as a Second Language*. Washington, D.C.: TESOL. 105–23.
Sasaki, M. (1991). English and Japanese interlanguage comprehension strategies: An analysis based on the competition model. *Applied Psycholinguistics* 12: 47–73.
Sasaki, M. (2000). Effects of cultural schemata on students' test-taking processes for cloze tests: A multiple data source approach. *Language Testing* 17: 85–114.
Sasaki, M. (2008). Concurrent think-aloud protocol as a socially situated construct. *IRAL* 46: 349–74.
Schank, R. C. and R. Abelson (1977). *Plans, Scripts, Goals and Understanding*. Hillsdale, NJ.: Erlbaum.
Schmidt, R. (1994). Deconstructing consciousness in search of useful definition for applied linguistics. *AILA Review* 11: 11–26.
Schmitt, N. and M. McCarthy (2000). *Vocabulary: Description, Acqusition and Pedagogy*. Cambridge: Cambridge University Press.
Schoonen, R., J. Hulstijn and B. Bossers (1998). Metacognitive and language-specific knowledge in native and foreign language reading comprehension: An empirical study among Dutch students in grades 6, 8 and 10. *Language Learning* 48: 71–106.
Scollon, R. and S. B. K. Scollon. (1981). *Narrative, Literacy and Face Interethnic Communication*. Norwood, N.J.: Ablex.
Share, D. and K. E. Stanovich (1995). Cognitive processes in early reading development: Accommodating individual differences into a model of acquisition. In: J. S. Carlson (ed.). *Issues in Education: Contributions from Psychology*, Vol. 1. Greenwich, CT: JAI Press. 1–57.
Sharp, A. (2002). Chinese L1 schoolchildren reading in English: The effects of rhetorical patterns. *Reading in a Foreign Language* 14 (2): 1–20.
Shiffrin, R. and W. Schneider (1977). Controlled and automatic human information processing: II. Perceptual learning, automatic attending and a general theory. *Psychological Review* 84: 127–89.
Shimizu, M. (2005). *Inference Generation Processes of Japanese EFL Learners: Effects of Questioning on their Reading Comprehension*. Dissertation, Tsukuba, University of Tsukuba.
Short, E. J. and E. B. Ryan (1984). Metacognitive differences between skilled and less skilled readers: Remediating deficits through story grammar and attribution training. *Journal of Educational Psychology* 76 (2): 225–35.
Singleton, D. (1999). *Exploring the Second Language Mental Lexicon*. Cambridge: Cambridge University Press.
Skopinskaja, L. (2009). The role of critical reading in promoting dialogic interaction. In: M. Kusiak (ed.). *Dialogue in Foreign Language Education*. Kraków: Wydawnictwo Uniwersytetu Jagiellońskiego. 75–82.
Smagorinsky, P. (1998). Thinking and speech and protocol analysis. *Mind, Culture and Activity* 5: 157–77.

Smagorinsky, P. (2001). If meaning is constructed, what is it made from? Toward a cultural theory of reading. *Review of Educational Research* 71 (1): 133–69.
Smith, F. (1994). *Understanding Reading: A Psycholinguistic Analysis of Reading and Learning to Read.* Hillsdale, NJ.: Lawrence Erlbaum Associates.
Smith, H. K. (1967). The responses of good and poor readers when asked to read for different purposes. *Reading Research Quarterly* 3: 53–84.
Sochacka, K. (2004). *Rozwój Umiejętności Czytania.* Białystok: Trans Humana.
Stanley, R. M. (1984). The recognition of macrostructure: A pilot study. *Reading in a Foreign Language* 2 (1): 156–68.
Stanovich, K. 1980. Toward an interactive-compensatory model of individual differences in the development of reading fluency. *Reading Research Quarterly* 16: 32–71.
Steffensen, M. S. (1986). Register, cohesion and cross-cultural reading comprehension. *Applied Linguistics* 7 (1): 71–85.
Steffensen, M. S. (1988). Changes in cohesion in the recall of native and foreign texts. In: P. L. Carrell, J. Devine and D. E. Eskey (eds.). *Interactive Approaches to Second Language Reading.* Cambridge: Cambridge University Press. 140–52.
Steffensen, M. S., E. T. Goetz and X. Cheng (1999). A cross-cultural perspective on reading comprehension. *Reading Research Quarterly* 15: 10–29.
Steffensen, M. S., C. Joag-dev and R. C. Anderson (1979). A cross-cultural perspective on reading comprehension. *Reading Research Quarterly* 15: 10–29.
Strang, R. and C. Rogers (1965). How do students read a short story? *English Journal* 54: 819–23, 829.
Suarez, A. and P. Meara (1989). The effects of irregular orthography on the processing of words in a foreign language. *Reading in a Foreign Language* 6 (1): 349–56.
Swanson, H. Lee (1984). Phonological recoding and suppression effects in children's sentence comprehension. *Reading Research Quarterly* 19 (4): 393–403.
Tardieu, H., M.-F. Ehrlich and V. Gyselinck (1992). Levels of representation and domain-specific knowledge in comprehension of scientific texts. *Language and Cognitive Processes* 7 (3/4): 335–51.
Thornbury, S. (1997). *About Language: Tasks for Teachers of English.* Cambridge: Cambridge University Press.
Thorndike, E. L. (1917). Reading as reasoning: A study of mistakes in paragraph reading. *Journal of Educational Psychology* 8: 323–32.
Thorndyke, P. W. (1977). Cognitive structures in comprehension and memory of narrative discourse. *Cognitive Psychology* 9: 77–110.
Tobiasz, L. (2009). Język angielski w procesie uczenia się języka niemieckiego – pomoc czy przeszkoda? Krytyczna analiza ankiet przeprowadzonych wśród studentów anglistyki Uniwersytetu Śląskiego w grupach tłumaczeniowych z językiem niemieckim. *Neofilolog* 33: 257–68.
Torgesen, J., D. Houston, L. Rissman and M. Kosanovich (2007). *Teaching All Students to Read in Elementary School. A Guide for Principals.* Florida: Florida State University.
Trabasso, T. and J. Magliano (1996). Conscious understanding during comprehension. *Discourse Processes* 21 (3): 255–87.
Trabasso, T. and P. W. van den Broek (1985). Causal thinking and the representation of narrative events. *Journal of Memory and Language* 24: 612–30.
Ulijn, J. M. and G. A. M. Kempen (1976). The role of the first language in second language reading comprehension. Some experimental evidence. In: G. Nickel (ed.). *Proceedings of the 4th International Congress of Applied Linguistics*, Vol.1. Stuttgart: Hochschulverlag. 495–507.
van Dijk, T. and W. Kintsch (1983). *Strategies of Discourse Comprehension.* New York: Academic Press.

van Gelderen, A., R. Schoonen, K. De Glopper, J. Hulstijn, A. Simis, P. Snellings and M. Stevenson (2004). Linguistic knowledge, processing speed and metacognitive knowledge in first- and second-language reading comprehension: A componential analysis. *Journal of Educational Psychology* 96: 19–30.

van Gelderen, A., R. Schoonen, R. D. Stoel, K. de Glopper and J. Hulstijn (2007). Development of adolescent reading comprehension in L1 and L2: A longitudinal analysis of constituent components. *Journal of Educational Psychology* 99: 477–91.

van Lier, L. (1994). *The Classroom and the Language Learner. Ethnography and Second-language Classroom Research.* London: Longman.

van Lier, L. (1999). *Interaction in the Language Curriculum. Awareness, Autonomy and Authenticity.* Edinburgh: Longman.

Verhoeven, L. T. (1994). Transfer in bilingual development: The linguistic interdependence hypothesis revisited. *Language Learning* 44: 381–415.

Voss, J. F. and G. L. Bisanz (1985). Knowledge and the processing of narrative and expository texts. In: B. K. Britton and J. B. Black (eds.). *Understanding Expository Text. A Theoretical and Practical Handbook for Analysing Explanatory Text.* London, Hillsdale: Lawrence Erlbaum Associates. 173–98.

Vygotsky, L. S. (1962). *Thought and Language.* Cambrigde: MA: MIT Press.

Wallace, C. (2005). *Critical Reading in Language Education.* London: Palgrave Macmillan Ltd.

Walter, C. (2004). Transfer of reading comprehension skills to L2 is linked to mental representations of text and to L2 working memory. *Applied Linguistics* 25 (3): 315–39.

Walter, C. (2007). First- to second-language reading comprehension; not transfer, but access. *International Journal of Applied Linguistics* 17 (1): 14–37.

Whitney, P. and G. Kellas (1984). Processing category terms in context: Instantiation and the structure of semantic categories. *Journal of Experimental Psychology: Learning, Memory and Cognition* 10: 95–103.

Whyatt, B. (2007). The use of metalinguistic knowledge in the process of translation. A study of metalinguistic comments in students self-reports. Paper presented at Poznań Linguistic Meeting.

Wierzbicka, A. (1995). Emotion and facial expression: A semantic perspective. *Culture and Psychology* 1: 227–58.

Wierzbicka, A. (2001). A culturally salient Polish emotion: *Przykro* (pron. *pshickro*). In: J. Harkins, J. and A. Wierzbicka (eds.). *Emotions in Crosslinguistic Perspective.* New York: Mouton de Gruyter. 337–58.

Wilczyńska, W. and A. Michońska-Stadnik (2010). *Metodologia Badań w Dydaktyce. Wprowadzenie.* Kraków: Avalon.

Williams, R. C. (1983). Teaching the recognition of cohesive ties in reading a foreign language. *Reading in a Foreign Language* 1 (1): 35–54.

Yakhontova, T. (2002). "Selling" or "telling"? The issue of cultural variation in research genres. In: J. Flowerdew (ed.). *Academic Discourse.* London: Longman. 216–32.

Yamashita, J. (2004). Reading attitudes in L1 and L2, and their influence on L2 extensive reading. *Reading in a Foreign Language* 16 (1): 1–19.

Yang, Y. F. (2002). Reassessing readers' comprehension monitoring. *Reading in a Foreign Language* 14 (1). [online] http://nflrc.hawaii.edu/rfl/April2002/yang/yang.html [3.05.2008].

Yorio, C. A. (1971). Some sources of reading problems in foreign language learners. *Language Learning* 21: 159–77.

Young, K. and G. Leinhardt (1998). Writing from primary documents: A way of knowing history. *Written Communication* 15: 25–68.

Young, L. W. (1982). Inscrutability revisited. In: J. J. Gumperz (ed.). *Language and Social Identity.* Cambridge, Cambridge University Press.

Zhang, G. and H. A. Simon (1985). STM capacity for Chinese words and idioms: Chunking and acoustical loop hypothesis. *Memory and Cognition* 13: 193–201.
Zhang, L. J. (2001). Awareness in reading; EFL students' metacognitive knowledge of reading strategies in an acquisition-poor environment. *Language Awareness* 10b (4): 268–88.
Zhang, X. (2008). The effects of formal schema on reading comprehension – An experiment with Chinese EFL readers. *Computational Linguistics and Chinese Language Processing* 13 (2): 197–214.
Zimmermann, R. and K. P. Schneider (1987). Dialogical aspects of individual lexical search. *Multilingua. Journal of Cross-Cultural and Interlanguage Communication* 6b (2): 113–30.
Zupnik, Y. (1985). A comparison of cognitive processes in foreign-language and first-language responses. Seminar paper, School of Education, Hebrew University of Jerusalem.
Zwann, R. and C. Brown (1996). The influence of language proficiency and comprehension skill on situation model processing. *Discourse Processes* 21 (3): 289–327.

INDEX

TECHNICAL EDITOR
Anna Poinc-Chrabąszcz

PROOFREADER
Monika Zapała

TYPESETTER
Tomasz Pasteczka

Jagiellonian University Press
Michałowskiego 9/2, 31-126 Kraków
Phone: +48 12-631-18-81, +48 12-631-18-82, fax +48 12-631-18-83